IS THIS TOMORROW?

Visions of the Future by Architects and Artists

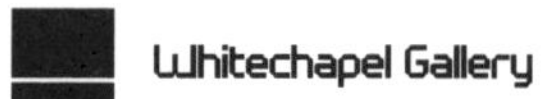

INTRODUCTION
Iwona Blazwick

When the architect Theo Crosby and curator Bryan Robertson presented twelve 'antagonistic co-operative groups' of artists and architects in *This Is Tomorrow* at the Whitechapel Gallery in 1956, it was against the backdrop of a city recovering from ruin. Throughout 1940 and 1941, the East End of London – an industrial area of docks, warehouses and factories – had been relentlessly bombed by the Luftwaffe. Miles of workers' houses and docklands were destroyed. The urban fabric of the Whitechapel Gallery's environs was punctuated by bombsites and abandoned buildings, its local communities traumatised by displacement and loss. The 1950s began as a desultory and impoverished era, described by artist Richard Hamilton as a world 'where everything was in black and white'. *This Is Tomorrow* offered visions of a future shaped by new ways of seeing, thinking and communicating. Twelve groups of artists and architects created environments that ranged from sensory experiments with Op and kinetic art to the spatial and geometric legacies of Constructivism to a passionate embrace of American popular culture. 'We hate good taste', declared Group Two (Richard Hamilton, John McHale and John Voelcker).

In the six decades that have passed, London has become technicoloured. The city has risen from its ruin to boast a skyline bristling with glass and steel towers. The 1956 Clean Air Act banished the 'pea-soup' yellow fog that made London's air toxic and its buildings grimy. New arrivals from post-independent West Indies and South Asia contributed to the growth of the National Health Service, London Transport, the city's culture and its cuisine. *This Is Tomorrow* exhibitors like Hamilton, Nigel Henderson, Eduardo Paolozzi, Victor Pasmore and Alison and Peter Smithson were to revolutionise the art schools, transfusing arts education with their excursions into science, nature and popular culture (as trialled in their legendary ICA show *Parallel of Life and Art* of 1953). The decade of *This Is Tomorrow* laid the groundwork for the cosmopolitan, entrepreneurial and dynamic London that became a mecca for the young and the creative in the late twentieth century.

Yet the sparse mosaic of lights illuminating London's new high-rises at night reveals them to be only partially occupied, many acquired as offshore investments. At their base lives an ever-growing population of homeless people. The air looks clean, yet there are rising levels of invisible pollution. STEM (Science, Technology, English and Maths), the notorious acronym that defines government policy towards education, simply pushes the arts to the margins. The impending departure of the UK from the European Union threatens London's ebullient growth, its multiculturalism and its creativity. On the world stage, populist right-wing movements are rising in response to a new post-industrial era where the financial and cultural certainties of employment are disappearing. The global economic growth that has made London a financial capital is taking an irreversible toll on the environment.

If *This Is Tomorrow* marked the beginning of an era, might *Is This Tomorrow?* herald its end? Our hope is that it will mark a turning point. This exhibition asks the questions and proposes the strategies that are as vital and generative as those of its predecessor. It more accurately reflects our global reality by involving artists and architects not only from the UK but also from Argentina, Bangladesh, Canada, China, France, Germany, Iran, Mexico, Spain, Tanzania and USA. *This Is Tomorrow* was originally conceived by a woman, the artist Paule Vézelay. Yet in 1956, of the thirty-seven exhibitors, only four were women. This exhibition addresses this imbalance.

The original exhibitors were given £40 each to realise their installations; today they have also been given a modest amount, and they can deploy new technologies spanning the digital to the bio-molecular that were only science fiction in the 1950s. These affect every aspect of design, from enabling multi-perspectival research and instant communication, to facilitating the evolution of new material structures and generating sources of energy. At the same time, our exhibitors draw on traditional artisanal skills to fuse ancient and modern, deep local knowledge with transnational data. They do not claim to work with a tabula rasa, instead shining a spotlight on the extraction of natural resources, surveillance as commerce and control, spectacle as capital, and the distortion of fact into fiction as features of our socio-political landscape. But they subject these forces to a symbolic *détournement*.

The participants in *Is This Tomorrow?* are not futurists nor utopians, but neither are they fatalistic. Unlike its historic counterpart, this exhibition does not make an assertion; rather, it asks a question. Notwithstanding a visceral comprehension of the issues we face, the artists and architects who are collaborating here bring pragmatism, spirituality, desire, optimism and humour to deliver evolving aesthetic responses to the twenty-first-century iteration of the future. Most significantly, the exhibition demonstrates the power of collaboration. If there are answers as to how we could or should live, they will come from such speculative exchanges between those practitioners who give form to everyday life.

IS THIS TOMORROW?

Lydia Yee

The role of the artist is to ask questions, not answer them.
– Anton Chekhov

Can architects and artists work together harmoniously? What does the art and design of the future look like? What sort of experiences will these new forms offer the viewer? These are questions that the organisers and participating architects and artists in the Whitechapel Gallery's exhibition *This Is Tomorrow* (1956) asked themselves more than sixty years ago. The resulting exhibition featured twelve propositions from small groups composed of architects, artists, designers and writers working together. *Is This Tomorrow?* takes this landmark exhibition as its model and reimagines it for the twenty-first century. The key questions remain relevant today, but artists and architects no longer see themselves working in autonomous disciplines and are engaged with broader social concerns. And rather than emphatically proclaiming 'This is tomorrow', they are raising timely, critical questions about our shared future.

This Is Tomorrow

Communications theory, New Brutalism, machine aesthetics, science fiction, popular culture and the vernacular were just a few of the areas of interest for architects and artists participating in *This Is Tomorrow*. These forward-looking preoccupations reflected a sense of post-war optimism in Britain, signalled by the end of food rationing, the establishment of a free National Health Service and large-scale rebuilding projects. They also reflected the concerns of the Independent Group (IG) members in the exhibition, who had been discussing these topics during their meetings held at the Institute of Contemporary Arts (ICA) between 1951 and 1955. Other exhibition protagonists looked to reconnect with earlier artistic figures and movements – including Constructivism, Le Corbusier and Marcel Duchamp – whose legacies were interrupted by the Second World War.

The participants' interests and affiliations split into two main factions – the Independent Group and the Constructivists – and this was reflected by the way in which the exhibition came together. The initial idea for architects, painters and sculptors to work together on an exhibition was suggested by Paule Vezelay

(1892–1984), the English representative of the French Constructivist association Le Groupe Espace, whose 1951 manifesto called for 'an effective collaboration between architects, painters, sculptors and plasticians, and to organise, through plasticity, the harmonious development of human activities'.[1] Following bitter debates, the architect and writer Theo Crosby (1925–1994) took plans forward for an exhibition based on collaborations between architects and artists without the involvement of Groupe Espace, whose ideas about integration of the arts were seen as dogmatic.

Presented at the Whitechapel Gallery from 9 August to 9 September 1955, the resulting exhibition featured thirty-seven UK-based architects, painters, sculptors, designers and writers – mostly men in their thirties, plus four women – who worked together in twelve small groups. In the catalogue, Lawrence Alloway (1926–1990), art critic, member of the IG and at the time Assistant Director of the ICA, introduced the exhibits as 'devoted to the possibilities of collaboration', the results of which, 'appear to be setting up a programme for the future'.[2] Architectural critic Reyner Banham (1922–1988) also contributed an introduction in the catalogue, titled 'Marriage of Two Minds', written in free verse and in lowercase except for the headers: 'HIS' mind is analogous to gesamtkunstwerk, godlike, groupe espace, leonardo da vinci; 'HERS' to collaborators, guild, worpswede, bauhaus, gothic cathedral. Their union ultimately makes 'you' the cult object, culture hero, end product.[3] The third introduction, written by architect and writer David Lewis (b. 1922), reaffirmed the Constructivist principle of the integration of art and architecture 'in co-operative unity and in the social interest'.[4]

Possibilities of Collaboration

Architects and artists have worked together, or at least alongside each other, for more than two millennia, with the latter making sculpture, reliefs, paintings, mosaics and murals for churches, funerary architecture, mosques and temples designed by the former. Giotto, El Greco, Michelangelo, Rafael, Bernini and, more recently, Le Corbusier, El Lissitzky and Theo van Doesburg were renowned as artists as well as architects. But in the 1950s,

1 Le Groupe Espace Manifesto was published in *Art d'Aujourd'hui*. no. 8 (October 1951).

2 Lawrence Alloway, in Theo Crosby (ed.), *This Is Tomorrow* (London: Whitechapel Gallery, 1956), n.p. Reprinted 2010.

3 Reyner Banham, in Theo Crosby (ed.), *This Is Tomorrow*, n.p.

4 David Lewis, in Theo Crosby (ed.), *This Is Tomorrow*, n.p.

it was rare for proponents of the two disciplines to work together in a truly non-hierarchical manner. The organisers of *This Is Tomorrow* envisioned collaboration as a way of integrating the arts, citing the examples of cathedral builders, the Bauhaus and the *Gesamtkunstwerk*. The approach to collaboration among the participants varied; in some projects a particular architect or artist appears to have taken the lead, while others were more integrated and individual contributions not easily discernible.

Today, architecture and art are increasingly intertwined. Practitioners from both disciplines collaborate on cultural buildings, private houses and even sports stadiums, while artists design their own buildings and architects exhibit their works in museums and galleries. Research and collaboration are integral to both practices. Yet each discipline has its own specificity, institutional framework and boundaries, which are in many ways less porous. Having abandoned their early twentieth-century unifying, utopian aim, architects and artists continue to share an interest in form and content, but often diverge over questions of function and intention. Collaboration affords each the opportunity to draw on different approaches, different types of experience, and different points of view, and to embrace a level of unpredictability.

Unlike the artists and architects in *This Is Tomorrow* – who were closely connected through teaching, professional organisations and informal groups such as the Central School of Arts and Crafts, CIAM (International Congresses of Modern Architecture), Modern Architectural Research (MARS) Group and the IG – those participating in *Is This Tomorrow?* hail from five continents and most met through the invitation to participate in this project. We approached architects and artists whom we admired and suggested possible collaborators, often based on shared interests or culture, setting up what were in effect blind dates. Although geographical proximity has been important to some of the teams, others have collaborated while based in different countries and even different continents.

A Programme for the Future

If the future from the standpoint of 1956 was generally positive, it was tempered by the threat of a growing nuclear arms race. There was, however, little direct evidence of this concern in *This Is Tomorrow* other than an image of a nuclear explosion included in a collage of visual material on a tackboard, which was part of the presentation by Group Twelve, including Alloway and fellow IG members Geoffrey Holroyd and Toni del Renzio. Among the twelve projects in *This Is Tomorrow*, roughly half made reference to the future through imagery and ideas from the mass media and the use of plastics, other new materials and prefabricated elements.

From the standpoint of 2019, the future appears less bright than it did sixty-three years ago. Although nuclear war does not seem to be the imminent threat it once was, we face an environmental catastrophe in the coming decades given that our current targets for curbing greenhouse gas emissions are unlikely to prevent warming by another three degrees. Moreover, scientific and technological developments – including artificial intelligence, big data and biotechnology – are moving at such a fast and unpredictable pace that we cannot imagine how they will change the nature of human society.[5] In *New Dark Age: Technology and the End of the Future*, James Bridle warns that the technological overload of information is clouding our ability to comprehend the unprecedented challenges confronting humanity today. 'Computers are not here to give us answers', he writes, 'but tools for asking questions'.[6]

The ten projects in *Is This Tomorrow?* raise questions about some of the most urgent issues in the twenty-first century, including climate change, challenges posed by technology and the problem of rising inequality. While architecture by its nature must both address the present and look to the future, artists are more likely to look to the past to learn about our present. Working together, architects and artists are able to mix seemingly disparate approaches and concerns, pragmatic and fantastic, real and fictional. Some projects connect past and future, for example, through the wisdom and traditions of indigenous cultures to offer us new ways to think about the issues we face today. Others make links between seemingly disparate phenomena, such as fracking and queer activism, microbes and new possibilities for housing, the internet and our emotional needs.

A Lesson in Spectatorship

If collaboration and the future were important organising principles for *This Is Tomorrow*, the role of the viewer was paramount to its public reception. The exhibition not only heralded Pop art and New Brutalism, but also anticipated Minimalist, Conceptual and installation art through a recognition of the phenomenological,

5 See Yuval Noah Harari, *Homo Deus: A Brief History of Tomorrow* (London: Vintage, 2017).

6 James Bridle, *New Dark Age: Technology and the End of the Future* (London: Verso, 2018), p. 6.

informational and spatial dimensions of art. Although these were not direct outcomes of the exhibition, the organisers acknowledged the importance of the audience to their project, often by directly addressing them with the pronoun 'you', as Banham did in his introduction. In the press release and catalogue, Alloway affirms that the exhibition is 'a lesson in spectatorship' in which 'the visitor is exposed to space effects, play with signs, a wide range of materials and structures, which, taken together, make of art and architecture a many channeled activity'. He concludes: 'This is a reminder of the responsibility of the spectator in the reception and interpretation of the many messages in the communications network of the whole exhibition.'[7] The collaborations between architects and artists in *Is This Tomorrow?* help us to visualise the interconnections we cannot see in a network that is infinitely more complex and contradictory than the imagined future of the 1950s.

7 Alloway, in Theo Crosby (ed.), *This Is Tomorrow*, n.p.

REENACTING THE RADIANT FUTURE: NOTES FROM THE BORDERS OF ART AND ARCHITECTURE

Pedro Gadanho

Yesterday's Tomorrows

There was a group of friends who always toasted to the radiant future. They considered themselves witty. Lost in translation, they were referencing a depressing Atom Egoyan film in which all the children from a small town are killed in a bus crash. Had Egoyan's film been called *The Radiant Future*, instead of *The Sweet Herafter*, it could have been quoting an obscure novel by Russian philosopher Aleksandr Zinoviev. In Zinoviev's *The Radiant Future*, a permanent slogan is erected at the fictional intersection of the Avenue of Marxism-Leninism and Cosmonaut Square, proclaiming a future that never came to fruition. The giant slogan – 'Long Live Communism – The Radiant Future of All Mankind!' – was shoddily but expensively installed. It was then successively torn, stolen, repaired, and at some point reinstated in titanium, finally becoming a meeting point for junkies and drunks. For Zinoviev, the promise of a fully radioactive, pulsating future offered a juicy metaphor for the decline of communist ideals.

Magnetic Future

As Ross Wolfe's art and architecture blog *The Charnel House* is kind enough to remind us, there are many meteoric and metaphorical futures still begging for appraisal. Reviewing Franco 'Bifo' Berardi's book *After the Future* (2011) Wolfe reminds us that the future is a powerful magnet that generates attraction and hubris, and yet simultaneously produces rejection and abjection. In the case of the profusely revisited Whitechapel show *This Is Tomorrow* of 1956, the magnetism of the future meant the uncharted potential of transdisciplinary collaboration between artists and architects. Yet, here, one must face the elephant in the room. *This Is Tomorrow* enjoys a well-deserved cult status as a precursor of British Pop art, as a pioneer in creating 'environments' that went against the art establishment's status quo, and, ultimately, as a persistent media phenomenon. Beyond this vast impact, however, the actual contents of the show are mostly forgotten, apart from the contributions of two groups. The first of these was Group Two, in which future Pop art stars, Independent Group members Richard Hamilton and John

McHale, convoked architect John Voelcker to help with a stage set. Here, any hint of architectural thinking was subsumed by the arrangement of popular culture references in what we would now call an installation. The other memorable contribution balanced the contrasting disciplinary strategies of art and architecture more successfully. Group Six comprised two architects and two artists, also of the Independent Group. While Nigel Henderson was an art insider and Eduardo Paolozzi brought in the aesthetics of *art brut*, architects Peter and Alison Smithson contributed with their provocative thinking on post-war housing. The complex, unexpected result was unlike any other architectural pavilion built over the next decades. As unfulfilled as the promise of collaboration finally was, there was a glimmer of how such cooperative undertakings could yield a 'third discourse', a shared language to be deployed in the hinterland between the increasingly distant practices of art and architecture.

Reenacting the Unfulfilled

Reenactment is the new remix. More than remembering, revisiting, reediting or referencing, reenacting revives the spirit of the precedent beyond sampling. Unlike a memorial, reenactment celebrates the eternal sunshine of the spotless, original essence. On its journey to curatorial legend, *This Is Tomorrow* has been quoted and studied, had several of its fragments reassembled, has been an object of archival revision and has been feted as an institutional landmark. Confirming the pressing need to reaffirm our favourite histories, Hollywood-style or otherwise, the time has come for the ultimate reenactment: the remake. As its clever title discloses, *Is This Tomorrow?* arrives with three fundamental trials. One, it tests Lawrence Alloway's premise that 'yesterday's tomorrow is not today'.[1] Second, after the former show's aspirations, it engages in the major task of redefining the issues that distinguish today's 'way of life'. And, third, it reenacts from scratch the unfulfilled promise of collaboration between artists and architects vis-à-vis such crucial issues. The latter is a particularly arduous challenge. In the sixty years that have passed since the original endeavour, complexity has demanded increased levels of collaboration, but not of the non-hierarchical kind that *This Is Tomorrow* sought to recapture at its time.

1 Lawrence Alloway, in Theo Crosby (ed.), *This Is Tomorrow*, London: Whitechapel Gallery, 1956.

Theo Crosby, the architect, writer and urban thinker who developed the idea of collaboration for the 1956 exhibition, was right to sense that the future of rapidly evolving cities demanded interdisciplinary endeavours. But he failed to anticipate that such collaborations would be imminently technical, rather than pertaining to the creative and humanist spheres.[2] Today, architects certainly collaborate, but with engineers, researchers, archaeologists, economists, or whatever specialist a project may require. 'Collaboration' is the gentle name for technical cooperation under well-defined leadership. As for artists, the most successful of them may run large studios with numerous contributors attending to design, development, production or communication, but they certainly have their own authorship at heart. In both cases, 'collaboration' becomes a euphemism for the need for a major team effort to realise increasingly ambitious projects – including the occasional artist to provide out-of-the box inspiration for architects, and the odd designer to draw schemes for artist's more complicated displays. The idea of two authors co-labouring for a joint purpose, while it occurs in a new age of art or architecture collectives, seems to belong in the laboratorial world of scientific papers. As such, the purposeful reenactment of art and architecture collaborations is most welcome, but not without its difficulties. For collaboration to be more than co-working, a rare chemistry is required. For instance, my one curatorial experience in which different architectural authors came together for joint proposals was indeed a rugged path. As magnetic a topic as the unequal future of cities was, productive conflicts echoed the show's title *Uneven Growth*.[3] Nonetheless, after much psychological management, the belief emerged that the end-result of those six collaborations could not have been reached individually by each of the participating teams. If genuine creative collaborations are improbable in real contexts, the cultural sphere is probably the one arena in which they can still be tested. To quote Beckett, if only for the sake of failing better, we must cling to the hope that the insights resulting from one disciplinary

2 He did realise it, however, a few years later, at the time of his 1973 Hayward exhibition *How to Play the Environment Game*. While he came up with a notion of 'pessimist utopia', he also pointed to urban planning having become a 'game' for technical specialists. See the entry for Theo Crosby at https://en.wikipedia.org/wiki/Theo_Crosby, accessed December 2018.

3 *Uneven Growth, Tactical Urbanisms for Expanding Megacities*, organised by Pedro Gadanho with Phoebe Springstubb, Museum of Modern Art, New York, 22 November 2014 – 25 May 2015. For the full presentation of the six collaborations in the exhibition, see Pedro Gadanho (ed.), *Uneven Growth, Tactical Urbanisms for Expanding Megacities* (New York: Museum of Modern Art, 2015).

accumulation of knowledge can still illuminate and help answer the questions raised by another. And cultural institutions may well be the last places in which we can give it another try.

Yesterday and Today

At the time of *This Is Tomorrow*, the technology-enthralled birth of British Pop was a forewarning of the commodification and fetishism of a booming consumer society. On the other hand, the Independent Group's utopian motivation already revealed an awareness of the failures of modernism. Yet we must acknowledge that, by today's standards, in 1956 the future was sparkling with optimism. Even if its tomorrows were not exactly what its antecedents had predicted, today's tomorrows look considerably bleaker. To be sure, ten years after World War II had ended, the 'rough poetry' of Group Six's *Patio and Pavilion* still carried traces of the precariousness of a no-future epoch.[4] But prospects of a global nuclear conflict, the 1973 oil crisis, or even the vague pessimism of Crosby's book *Architecture: City Sense*, were still years away. Fast forward to today, and we are still riding the ripple effect of a different type of conflict: the financial crisis of 2008. While we continue to discuss rising economic inequality and when exactly the next recession will hit,[5] we are also busy anticipating the catastrophic, yet largely unheeded effects of climate change, ecological depletion and frantic urbanisation. And while it is not difficult to demonstrate that the unconscious pressure of such trends translates into new forms of populism and fascism, we are now less sure about the absolute benignity of irresistible and accelerating technological development. While scientists are speaking of a sixth mass extinction already underway, we can only find a cathartic comfort in the idea that the Anthropocene will become a mere blip in the long course of geological time.[6]

4 For an in-depth analysis of Group Six's project in *This Is Tomorrow*, see Ben Highmore, 'Rough Poetry: "Patio and Pavilion" Revisited', in *Oxford Art Journal* 29, no. 2 (June 2006), pp. 269–90.

5 See 'The Next Recession: How Bad will it Be', *The Economist*, 13 October 2018.

6 This was for me the conclusion of a curatorial research project that started with an optimistic outlook on our technological capacity to mitigate the effects of the climate crisis, and finally had to schizophrenically balance optimism and pessimism. See Pedro Gadanho (ed.), *Eco-Visionaries, Art, Architecture and New Media After the Anthropocene* (Berlin: Hatje Cantz, Berlin, 2018). For an online account of the project see Pedro Gadanho, 'Take a Dive in the Deep Side', in *DAMN°* 68, Gent, 2018, http://www.damnmagazine.net/2018/06/04/take-dive-deep-side/ accessed December 2018.

Singing Tomorrows

In 1956, expressing fascination with popular culture and a nascent consumer technology sounded as sane and rational as investigating the formal languages that would solve the housing needs of a continent torn by war. In those singing tomorrows, it was not perhaps predicted that consumer society could become a toxic trap, nor was it dreamed that modernist suburbs would soon house social riots. Neither was it conceived that artists and architects would end up having so little impact on any kind of societal transformation – even when they meet in the same think-tanks. With artists ensnared by the art market, and architects made prisoners of an on-demand industry, it is hard to envisage them as the activists for whom Crosby called. This, however, only makes the reenactments of *Is This Tomorrow?* all the more urgent.

Future Postponed

Over the past twenty-five years, I've intermittently written about the incestuous relationship of art and architecture. Like the galaxies in the universe, the different fields of knowledge expand, and so they deepen their histories, their accumulated information, their disciplinary tracts and their professional idiosyncrasies. With the hinterland between them similarly expanding, it becomes understandably difficult to bridge the gap between two idioms that have steadily grown apart. With their borders rigidifying along the lines of what Ortega y Gasset called the 'barbarism of specialism',[7] it also becomes increasingly impossible to perform the task of translating one language into the other. As I revisited the topic over the years, I eventually moved from the lyricism of youth, when I hailed Baudelaire's *Correspondances*,[8] to the mix of scepticism and stubborn pragmatism typical of a later age. Along the way, around 2000, Wittgenstein, Barthes, Eco, Crimp, Krauss and Serra prompted me to theorise about the museum as a stage for conflict between two discourses, and to stress the need for a third language that could span the gap between detaching world views.[9] Fifteen years later, looking at Isa Genzken's urban sculptures, I was impelled to reflect on 'the mélange of repulsion and attraction,

7 José Ortega y Gasset, 'La barbarie del "especialismo"', in Martín Gardner (ed.), *Los grandes ensayos de la ciencia*, (Mexico: Nueva Imagen, 1998) pp. 91–96.

8 See Pedro Gadanho, 'Correspondências', in Miguel von Haffe and Luís Palma (ed.), *Confidências Para o Exílio #2*, Porto, 1994.

9 See Pedro Gadanho, 'Posologia para um Breve Encontro,17 Ensaios Mínimos sobre Arte, Arquitectura e Contaminação', in Paulo Mendes and Sara Andrade (eds.) *Contaminantes / Comunicantes* (Lisbon: Ordem dos Arquitectos / Sociedade Nacional de Belas Artes, 2000).

distance and proximity, envy and detachment, which seems to characterize the love and hate relationship between practices of art and architecture today'.[10] As time went by, I evoked conversations, affinities, comparisons, equivocations, endearments, exchanges, disturbances, intersections, permeabilities and even romance. But curiously, I've rarely discussed collaboration – as if that were the last outpost, the magnetic force that stood firmly out of reach of either artists or architects; as if this were the ever-postponed, radiant future of art and architecture coming together.

Divergent Yesterdays

If we want to draw on the language of astronomers, the birth of the art museum triggered a quantum divergence in the practices of art and architecture. With the gradual moving apart of these once joint creative universes, the time of *This Is Tomorrow* corresponds with the last historical moments in which hierarchical collaborations between artists and architects were still the rule of law. As some may vaguely remember, under the guise of such alliances, artists were commonly invited to intervene in public spaces and atriums of public buildings, thus entering a necessary, often technical dialogue with architects. When prospects of these decorative interventions became untenable to an art field that had jumped to new conceptual leaps, such collaborations came to their inevitable end. Hence, the appealing logic of Crosby's lucid, yet desperate call for an authentic collaboration between artists and architects.

Tentative Todays

The plea for art and architecture's collaboration in *This Is Tomorrow* implied a future that never quite succeeded. Now, however, there are new factors that offer prospects for hypothetical conciliation. Perhaps the moment is ripe for new attempts. For one, a 'third language' has indeed emerged out of art's involvement with new understandings of space after the late 1960s with Lefebvre and others, when space was 'socialised' and no longer the formal domain of architects and planners – not to mention the even earlier, abstract realm of mathematicians.[11] Thus artists eagerly

10 See Pedro Gadanho, 'Other Encounters: More Micro-Essays on Art and Architecture', in Gregory Lang and Didier Gourvennec Ogor (eds.), *Dimensions Variables, Artistes et Architecture* (Paris: Pavilion de l'Arsenale, 2015).

11 The different visions of space by artists and architects was one of the themes in an exhibition triggered by Frederick Kiesler's *Endless House* project, as well as by his ideas on the fusion of art and architecture. See *Endless House, Intersections of Art and*

appropriated and integrated the multiple languages of space as a part of their increasingly mixed use of several media. The emergence of site-specific practices, installation, experiential and 'interactive' environments, even the invention of relational aesthetics, allowed for art practices that can now enter an open dialogue with architects who share a similar post-formal sensibility. On the other hand, there is the recent evolution of the architectural field. As I have suggested elsewhere,[12] as architecture itself splits into two divergent sub-fields, one of its sectors of practice is entering an orbit that intersects with the logic of the art world. That is, while the larger professional field becomes an acritical technical service, a smaller subfield, akin to architecture's understanding as a cultural production, becomes closer to the mechanisms of production, dissemination and legitimation that we see in the restricted subfield of art – as Pierre Bourdieu has classically described it. In the context of exhibitions, museums and biennials, there is again context for what we could ironically call 'equal opportunity' or 'common ground' collaborations. As the world of architecture breaks in two, there is again opportunity for its smaller fragment to enter a fruitful, critical dialogue with what remains of culture's avant-garde.

Fictional Tomorrows

It is weirdly reassuring to realise that novelist J.G. Ballard was directly inspired by the speculative nature of *This Is Tomorrow* to pursue his distorted portraits of post-war society. As he wrote, the show's effect on him was that of 'a vote of confidence' in his choice of science fiction.[13] One feels excited to imagine what potent literary oeuvre might spore from the show's remake during an age in which technology, catastrophe, turbo capitalism, celebrity culture and the suburbanisation of democracy have surpassed Ballard's wildest, sci-fi dreams.

Architecture, organised by Pedro Gadanho with Phoebe Springstubb, Museum of Modern Art, New York, 27 June 2015 – 6 March 2016. The exhibition was followed by an essay on the notion of a Kiesler-inspired *conceptual continuum* and its reunion of art and architecture in the realm of dwelling. See Pedro Gadanho, 'Open-Ended Matter', in Klaus Bollinger and Florian Medicus (eds.), *Endless Kiesler* (Basel: Birkhäuser, 2015).

12 Pedro Gadanho, 'Architecture, Networked Cultures and How to Make the Most of Them', in *MAJA* #70, Tallin, December 2011.

13 J.G. Ballard, *Miracles of Life* (2008), p.188, quoted in Theo Inglis, 'Yesterday's Tomorrow is Not Today: J.G. Ballard and This Is Tomorrow', https://medium.com/@theo_inglis/yesterdays-tomorrow-is-not-today-jg-ballard-and-this-is-tomorrow-5f11674be4e8, accessed December 2018.

Projects

1 6a architects
Amalia Pica

2 Adjaye Associates
Kapwani Kiwanga

3 APPARATA
Hardeep Pandhal

4 Cao Fei
mono office

5 Andrés Jaque /
Office for Political Innovation
Jacolby Satterwhite

6 Mariana Castillo Deball
Tatiana Bilbao Estudio

7 Rana Begum
Marina Tabassum Architects

8 David Kohn Architects
Simon Fujiwara

9 Farshid Moussavi Architecture
Zineb Sedira

10 Rachel Armstrong
Cécile B. Evans

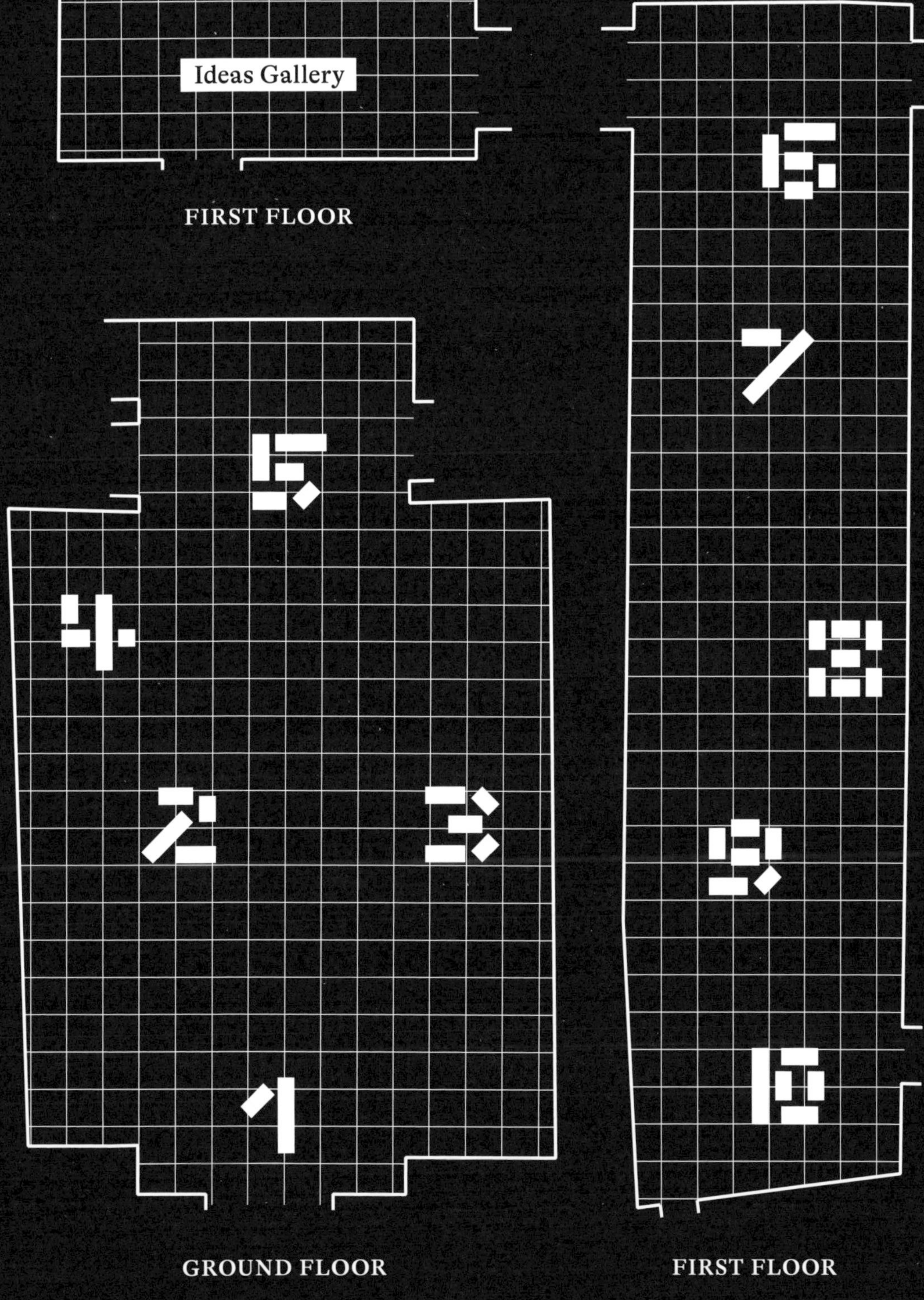
Ideas Gallery
FIRST FLOOR
GROUND FLOOR
FIRST FLOOR

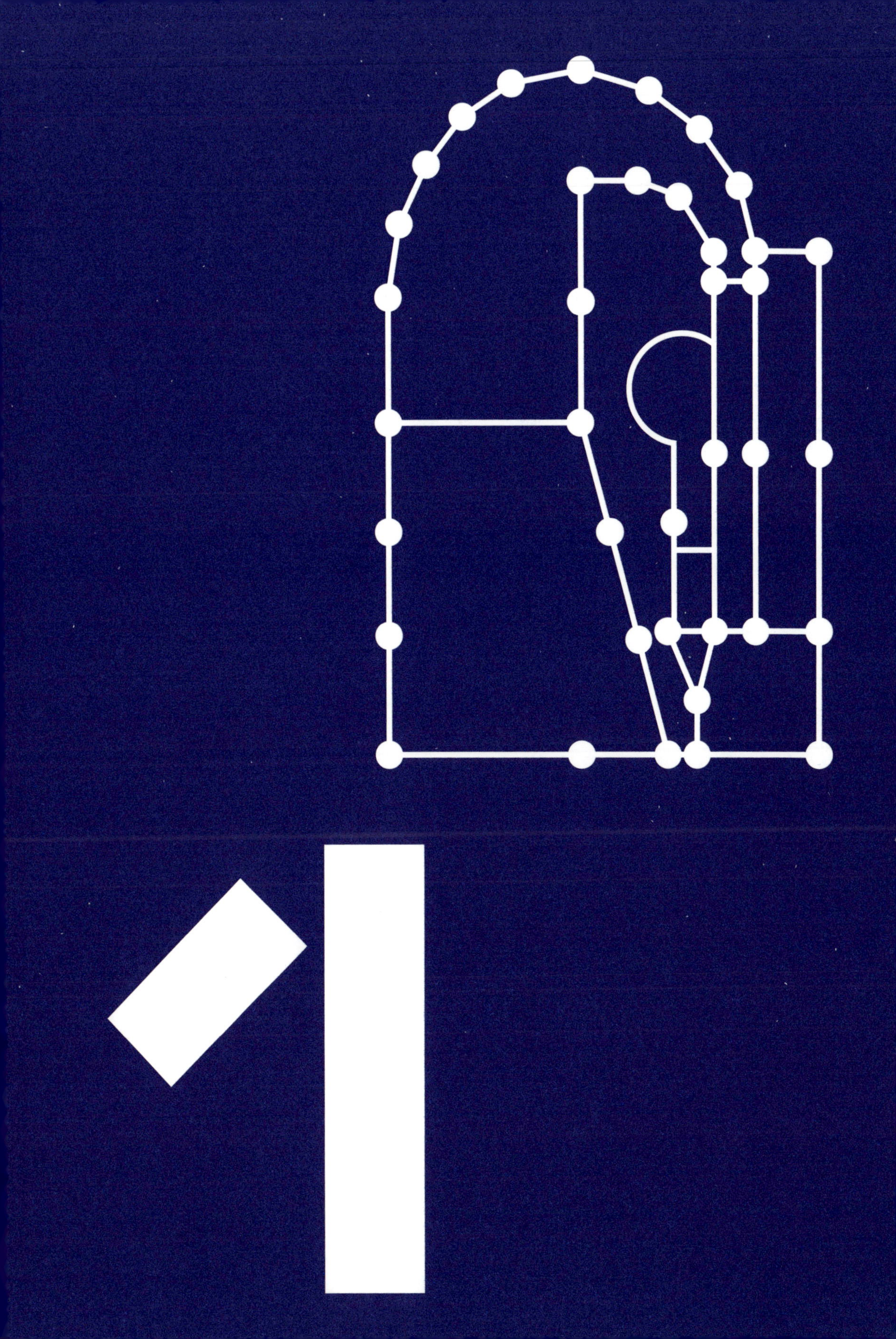

6a architects
Amalia Pica

PROJECT TEAM

Tom Emerson
Stephanie Macdonald
Amalia Pica
Owen Watson

Enclosure

Have your ducks in a row (English). There are 1,095,376,000 ducks on the planet.[1] There are 97,000 giraffes[2] and between one and ten quadrillion ants.[3] There are 7.6 billion humans alive today.[4] The human population increases by seventy-five million a year – the combined population of California and Canada. Wild animal populations have decreased by 60% over the last fifty years.[5] *Chickens come home to roost (English).* Of the nineteen billion chickens living in the world,[6] 2.5 billion are European. There are also 208 million sheep in the EU. Ewes consume between 2–3% of their live weight in dry matter daily.[7] Small Shetland ewes need 8–10 square metres of grazing per day to sustain themselves.[8] Their fleeces are available on eBay for £8.20 (Buy It Now).[9] On Tuesday evening in Shrewsbury, standard-weight lambs (32–39 kgs) averaged £1.60/kilo and sold to a top price of £1.71/kilo for 35 kg lambs.[10] *Peigner la girafe / Combing the giraffe (French).* A giraffe's neck is six feet long and weighs about 600 lbs.[11] The first giraffe seen in Europe arrived in 48 BC and was the property of Julius Caesar. Puzzled Romans called it a 'cameleopard' and fed it to the lions in the Colosseum.[12] In 1487, Lorenzo de Medici was gifted a giraffe. It was an immediate sensation and freely roamed the streets of Florence, fed by people from second-floor balconies. It died soon after its arrival, suffering a broken neck when it became trapped between the roof beams of its stable.[13] There was not another giraffe in Europe for 300 years. Gift certificates to shoot a giraffe currently cost $2,000, including caping (head removal) and delivery to a taxidermist.[14] *Never look a gift horse in the mouth (English).* Animals are often exchanged between countries and individuals as gifts. There are over forty pelicans in St James' Park in London. They are descendants of the gifts from the Russian Ambassador in 1640. Since the Tang Dynasty (625–705) China has gifted pandas to other countries, often upon securing a trade deal. In a process commonly referred to as 'Panda Diplomacy', since 1984, pandas have been offered to other nations exclusively as ten-year loans. As such, all pandas in zoos around the world are solely the property of the Chinese Government. The American-born panda Tai Shan (Butterstick) was repatriated to China a few days before President Obama met the Dalai Lama against China's wishes.[15] *Ants follow fat, an' bees follow honey (Jamaican).* The Argentine ant, ***Linepithema humilespecies***, has invaded six continents within the last century, colonising fifteen countries.[16] Laika, a stray dog from Moscow, became the first living creature to orbit the Earth in 1957 aboard *Sputnik 2*. While Soviet officials said at the time that she had died peacefully after a couple of weeks of leaving earth, it was recently revealed that in fact she died of overheating and panic only a few hours after the start of the mission.[17] Pavlov's dogs were of many different breeds and mongrels. One of them is preserved and displayed at the Pavlov Museum in St Petersburg. Pavlov increased his laboratory budgets by bottling the gastric juice he drew from lab dogs and selling it as a remedy for dyspepsia. Dog salivation was not what won the scientist his Nobel Prize, but rather his studies on digestive physiology.[18] It is possible for a human to have a successful blood transfusion from a chimpanzee.[19] Also from a pig.[20] It is unknown whether human blood is suitable for a pig or chimpanzee. *Put lipstick on a gorilla (English).* Copito de Nieve (Snowflake) was a white west-lowland gorilla who lived in the Barcelona Zoo. He attracted much attention and several requests were made to capture more of his kind. It was found, however, that he had non-syndromic oculocutaneous albinism. He is to date the only known albino gorilla.[21] The MGM film character Lassie was played by a male rough collie dog called Pal in six films. The subsequent nineteen-year long series starred several of his descendants as the famous female dog. Leo is the longest-used lion in the MGM cinematic logo, appearing in films since 1957. He was born in Dublin Zoo. *Malaen a zyly ei daith / The snail deserves the end of its journey (Welsh).*

1 Food and Agriculture Organization of the United Nations (FAOSTAT).
2 https://www.bbc.co.uk/news/science-environment-38240760
3 Lynn Margulis, Eduardo Punset, *Mind, Life and Universe: Conversations with Great Scientists of Our Tim* (Vermont: Chelsea Green Publishing Co., 2008), p. 44.
4 UN, World Population Prospects 2017, https://esa.un.org/unpd/wpp/
5 WWF, Living Planet Report 2018.
6 FAOSTAT.
7 http://www.pir.sa.gov.au/__data/assets/pdf_file/0007/272869/Calculating_dry_matter_intakes.pdf
8 https://smilingtreefarm.com/blog/how-much-grass-does-sheep-eat
9 https://www.ebay.co.uk/itm/Shetland-raw-unwashed-wool-sheep-fleece-knitting-weaving-spinning-felting-/264056653
10 https://www.hallsgb.com/auctions/news/207-shrewsbury-market-report-2nd-october-2018
11 https://www.livescience.com/27336-giraffes.html
12 http://content.time.com/time/specials/packages/article/0,28804,2049797_2049795_2049798,00.html
13 Marina Belozerskaya, *The Medici Giraffe and Other Tales of Exotic Animals and Power* (New York: Little, Brown, and Co. 2006), pp. 87–129.
14 http://www.africahuntlodge.com/giraffe_hunt_package.asp
15 https://www.vox.com/2014/5/23/5742002/panda-diplomacy-china-soft-power-kathleen-buckingham-malaysia-panda-loan
16 https://futurism.com/10-crazy-facts-about-ants
17 http://news.bbc.co.uk/1/hi/sci/tech/2367681.stm
18 https://www.smithsonianmag.com/smart-news/what-kind-of-dog-was-pavlovs-dog-22159544
19 https://geneticliteracyproject.org/2016/01/25/ape-human-pig-human-blood-donations-xenotransfusions-work/
20 Ibid.
21 https://en.wikipedia.org/wiki/Snowflake_(gorilla)

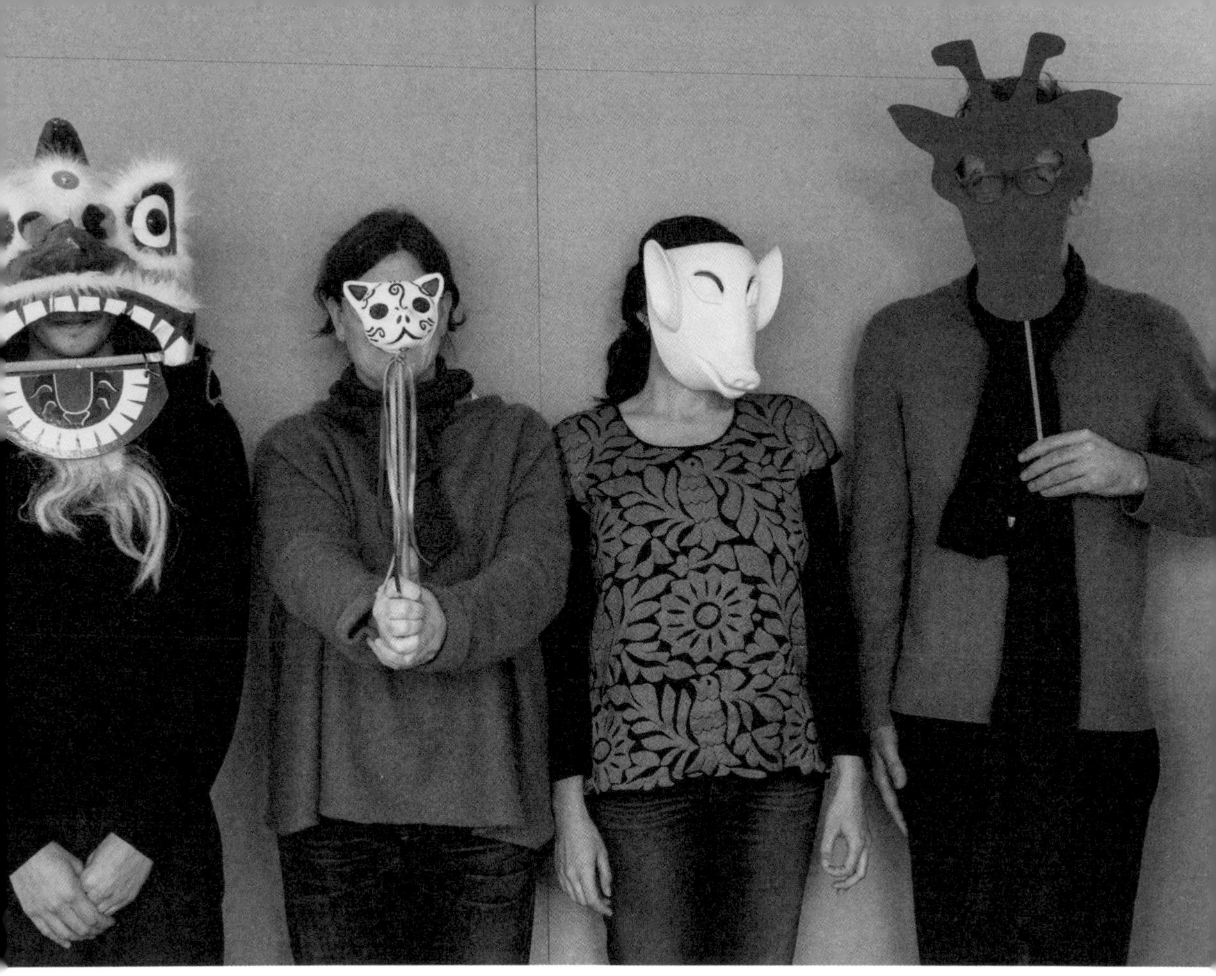

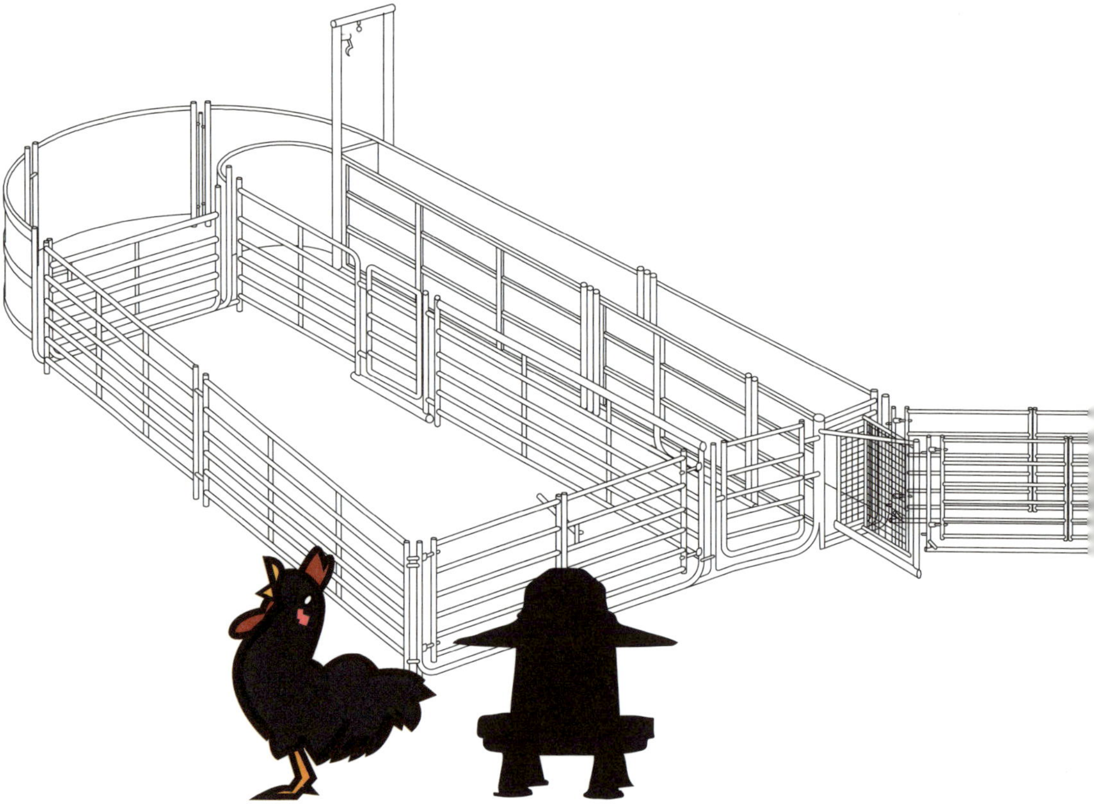

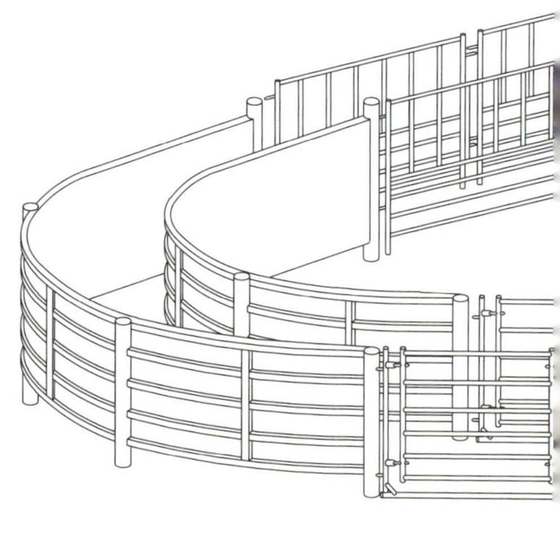

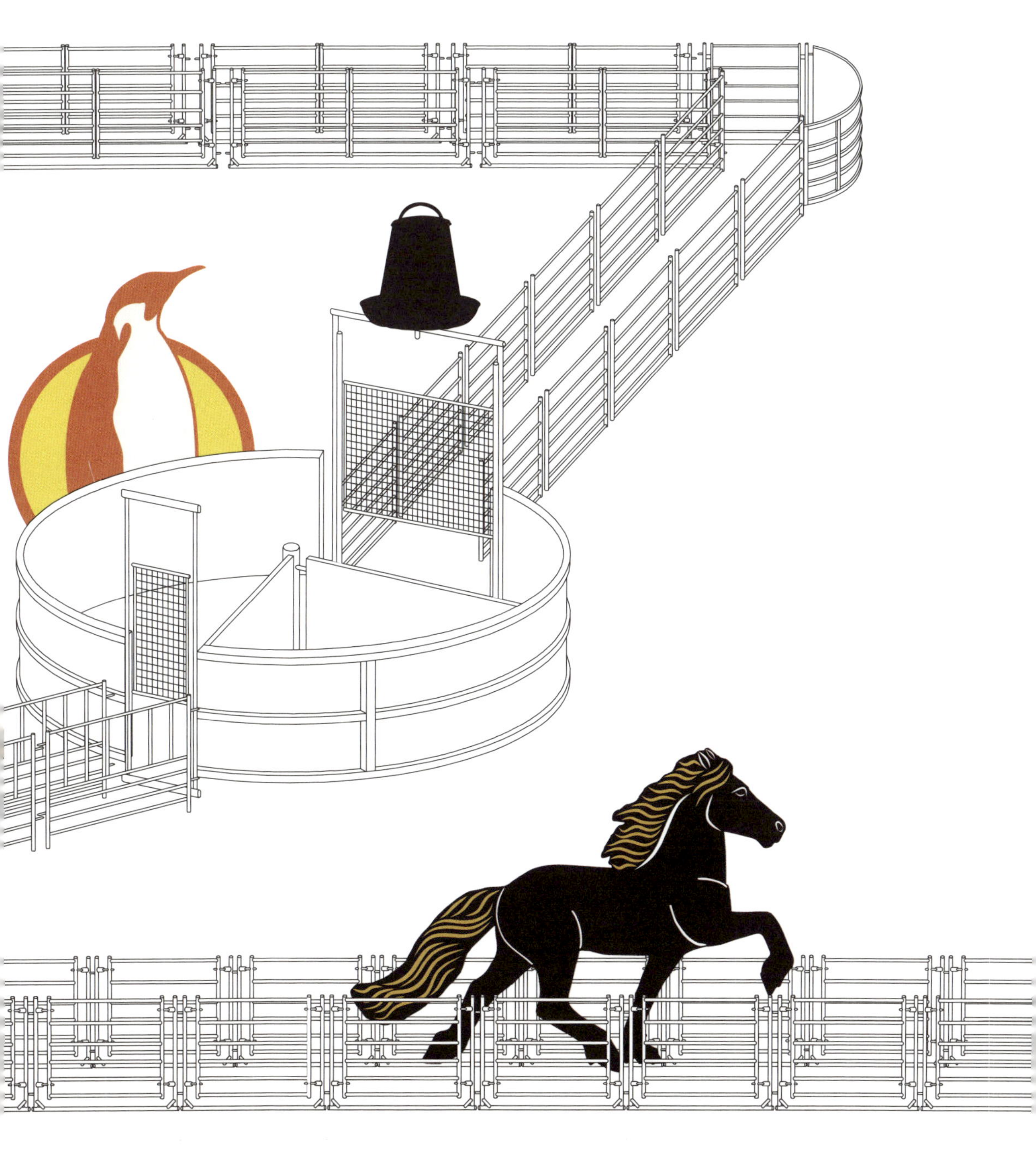

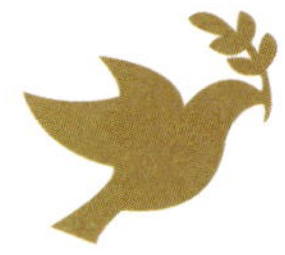

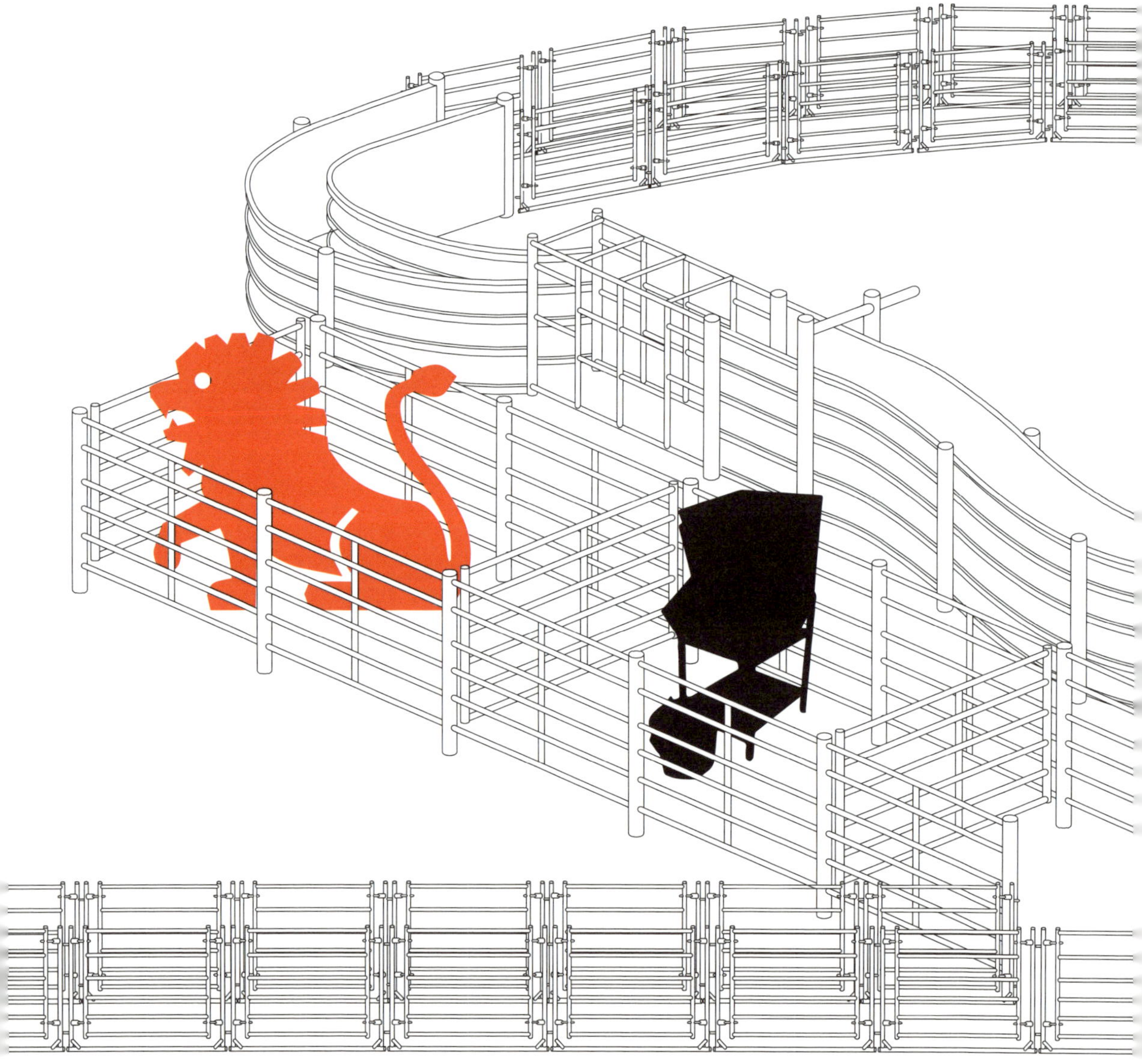

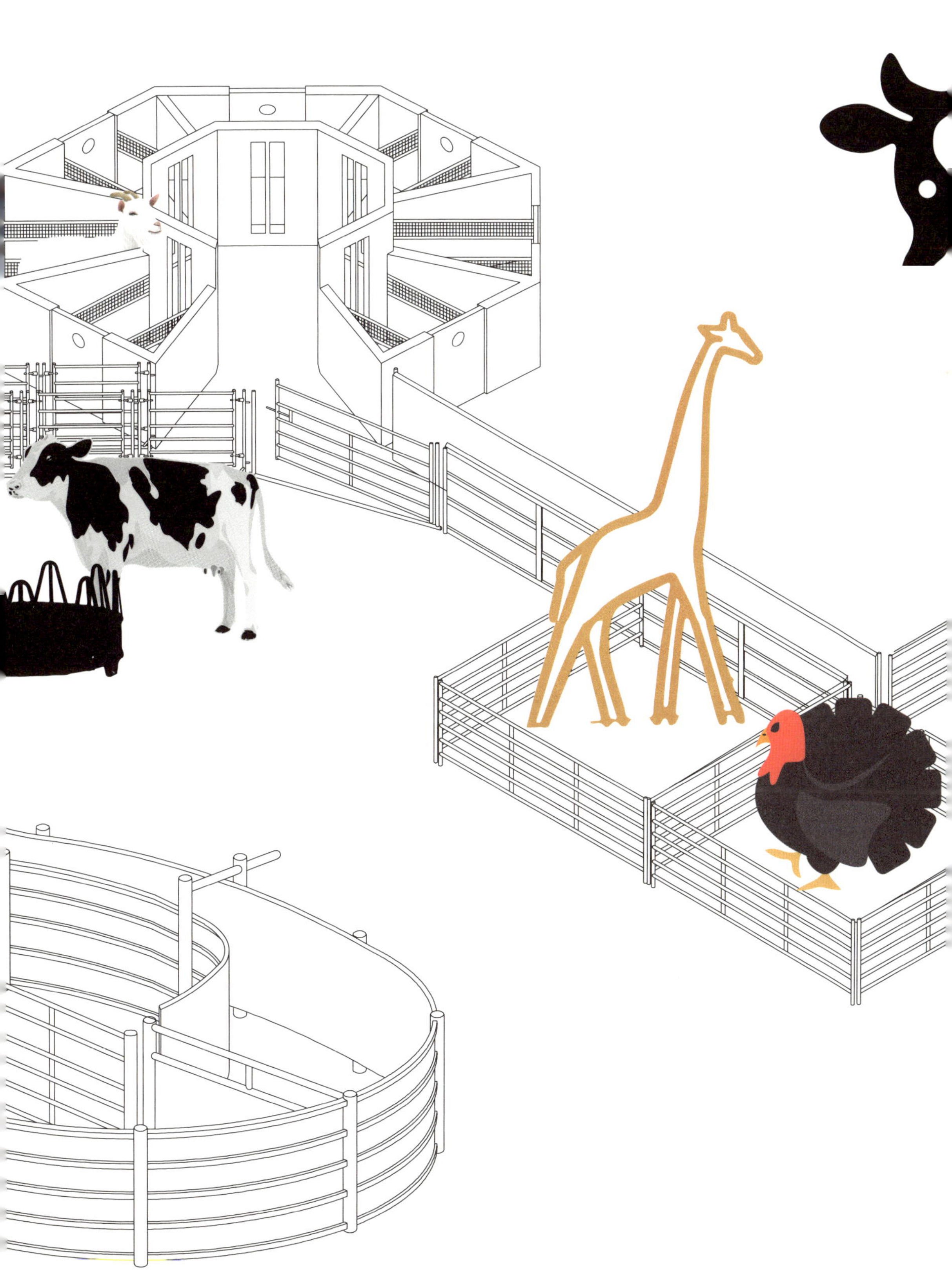

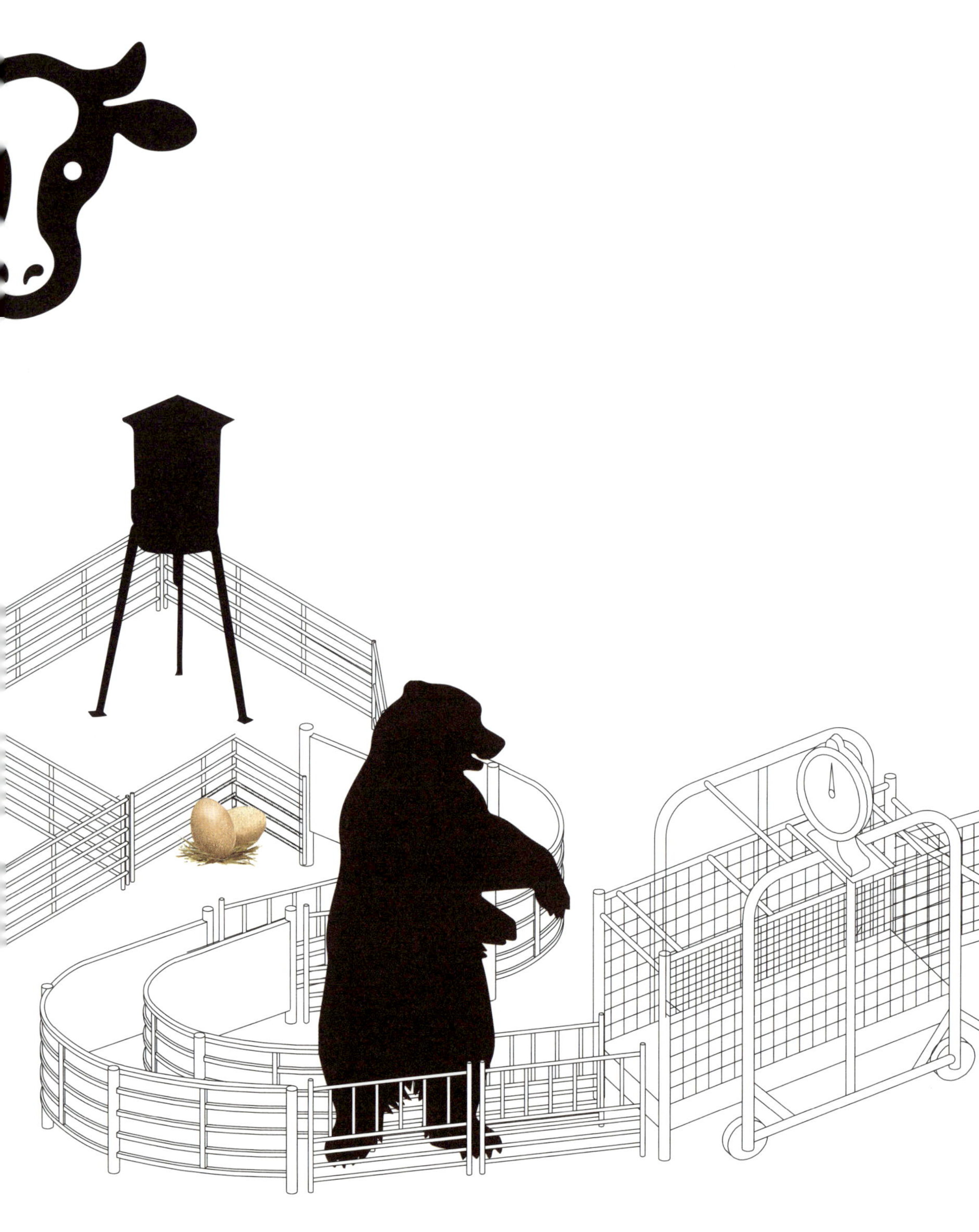

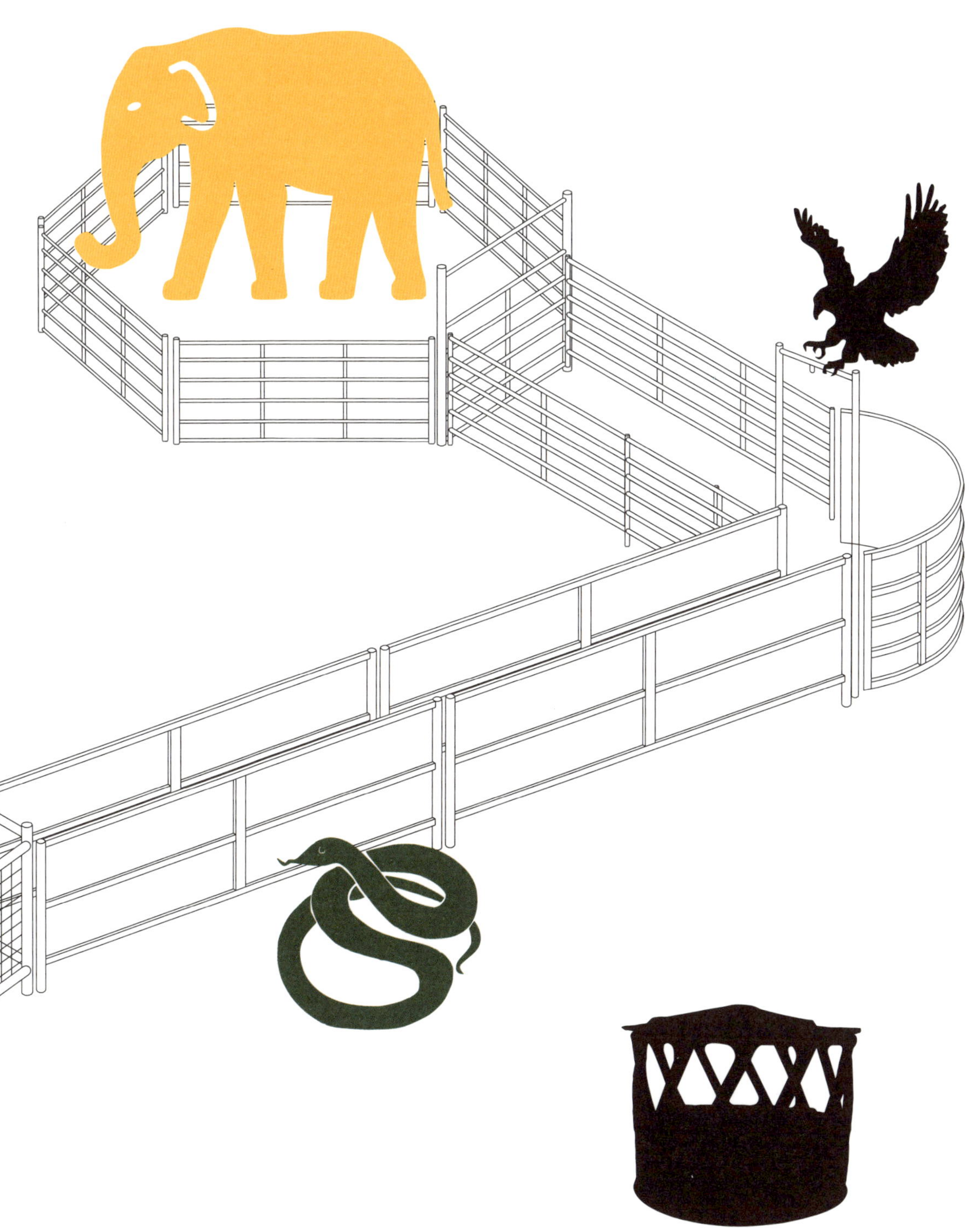

IMAGES

p. 25
Left to right: Owen Watson, Stephanie Macdonald (6a architects); Amalia Pica; Tom Emerson (6a architects). Photo: Rafael Ortega

pp. 26–31
6a architects and Amalia Pica, *Enclosure*, November 2018

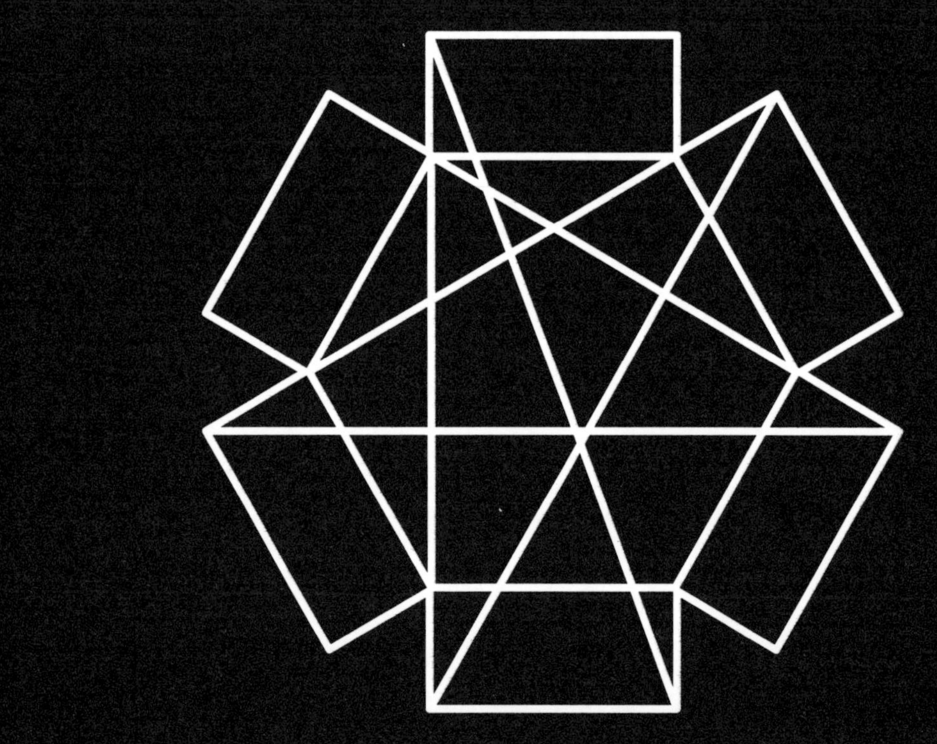

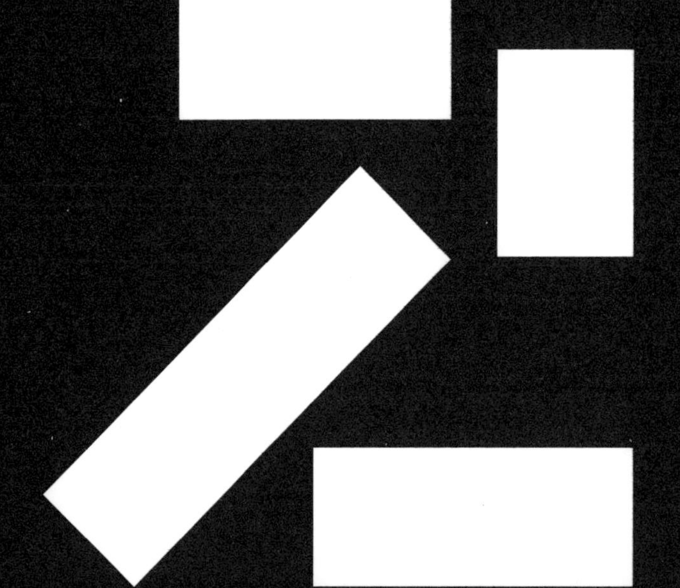

Adjaye Associates
Kapwani Kiwanga

PROJECT TEAM

Sir David Adjaye
Kapwani Kiwanga
Duncan Wilson

Sankofa Pavilion

David Adjaye

Let's start by talking about our initial ideas for the *Sankofa Pavilion*.

Kapwani Kiwanga

A proposition for the future is quite a complicated one to respond to. That's why we saw this as an opportunity to create spaces in which people could come together and have discussions. The title, which you proposed, speaks to both this and the brief for the exhibition.

DA

Yes. Sankofa is an Ashanti word for reaching into the past to guide you into your future.

KK

It links to an idea of the past informing the future, revealing the muddy divisions between time and the question of repercussions or resonances from one time to another.

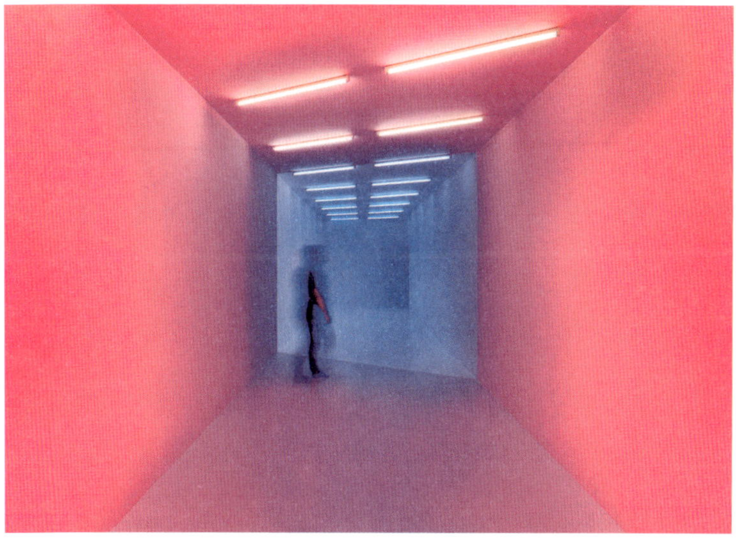

I saw the space that we were hoping to create as at once a place that would allow for exchange and one that could register as a recording device of sorts. The idea of recording is interesting because it's always fallible – a recording can never document a past moment precisely. Rather than exploring the literal technology of sound recording, it was more interesting to consider ways of marking and remembering an exchange without trying to hold onto a solid and immutable thing. This is why we have the fabric, which can absorb sound vibrations and voices into its woven texture. Glass, on the other hand, reflects sound more than it absorbs it.

DA

Glass is an important element as we move towards construction materials becoming embedded with future technologies that we can't even see. One of the primary constituents of glass is silicon, which is a fantastic conducting material for technology. So what looks like a crystalline object, a complex network of geometries that embeds possibilities within it, might actually become a reality. Perhaps what we're prototyping is actually a future form, a kind of maquette, without knowing what the future will hold. It's almost like Leonardo drawing his flying machine, without knowing what an aeroplane would eventually be like.

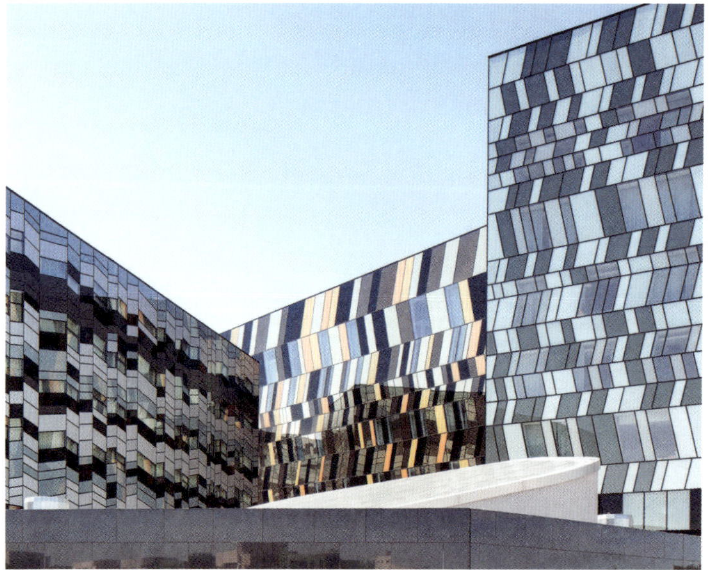

KK

It's also important that we embrace the fact that glass contains this element of fragility and imperfection. Archive recordings are all somehow tainted and imperfect. The fragility and the strength of both glass and fabric holds this tension in a nice way.

I also remember that we talked in our first conversation about a dialogue between isolation and transparency. People would feel that they were in a space that was quite contained but still part of a larger ecosystem. The division of individual and collective groups within a network was also part of the proposition.

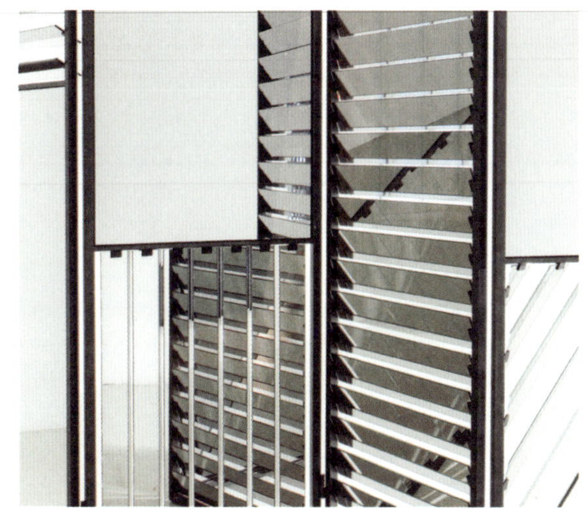

DA

Yes. When we first talked about collaborating, I was very excited about the way in which you create installations, more than sculptural objects. And for me, as an architect, I was interested to see if we could work within a human tradition of people coming together, using some configuration of space as a device to debate futures or to debate pasts. I began aggregating the sorts of forms associated with coming together in a dialogue. Within this typology, you might think of anything from an amphitheatre right down to a booth.

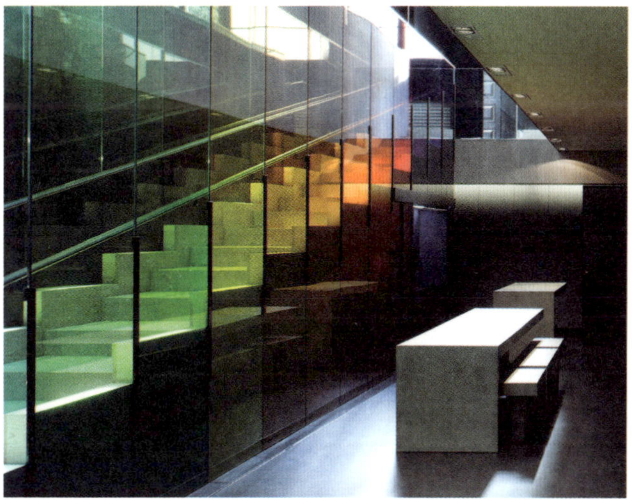

KK

The research I was doing in parallel, was trying to think about which materials would be used to in some way record the sound and presence of bodies coming together in space. I'd earlier come across the contested realm of archaeo-acoustics and the notion that ceramic or other ancient objects could have recorded languages or sounds from their times. Could we use clay or other materials to listen to past sonic events? The craft of pottery links to the question of sound being embedded in the material of the earth.

I think that's similar to what we're talking about here, and fabric could also be a material that records ideas. In my research, I came across fabrics, paints and other materials that absorb sound. At MIT and elsewhere research is being undertaken on fibres that will be able to both record and produce sound.[1]

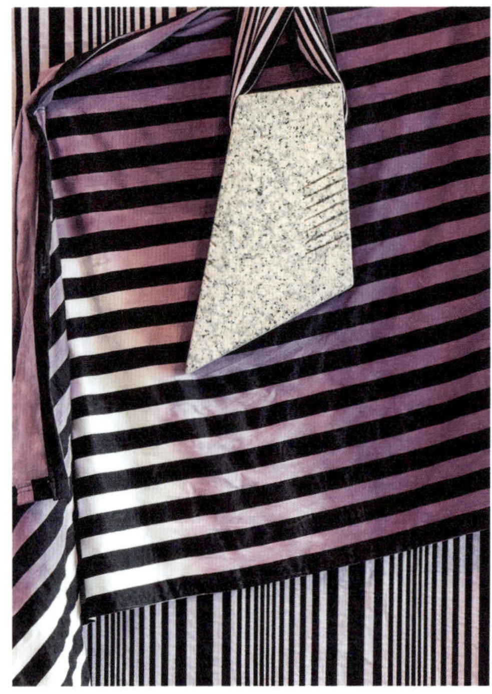

The fabric, formed of woven strands, is already somehow imbued with a past. In the installation, it acts as a kind of witness to the gathering of people inside the pavilion. It will be folded and secreted away. Once it's opened from its hermetic seal, it will be layered and muddied with the noise of a future present.

While we undertake routines that focus on trying to remember or mark a moment, accepting the fact that time is always running past us is important. I like the symbolic image of Sankofa as a bird. One can imagine it eventually taking

1 See Larry Hardesty, 'Fibers that can hear and sing', MIT News, 12 July 2010. http://news.mit.edu/2010/acoustic-fibers-0712, accessed 13 December 2018.

flight; escaping. For me, it evokes the character of the past's continual flight away from resolution, but the importance of reaching back nonetheless. Thank you for suggesting this title for the collaboration.

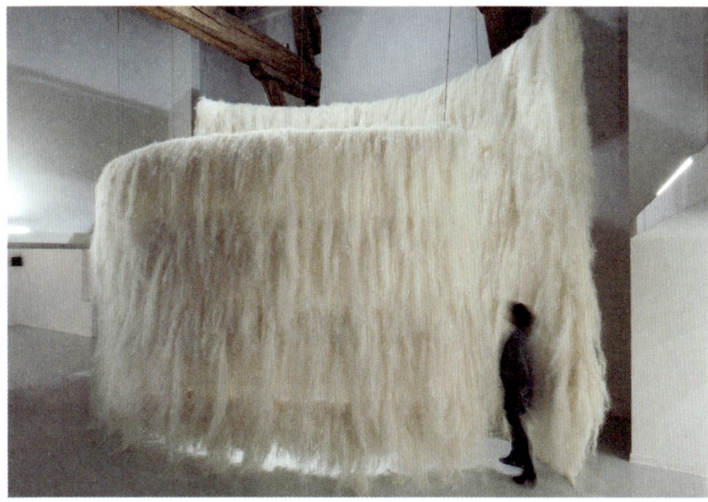

DA

It's a really wonderful experiment, and I love that you say that it is a collaboration, because that's exactly what it should be. What's been wonderful about this experience of working together, with your role as an artist, has been to move away from the constraints and conventions of architecture, and into the possibility of dreaming. The context of 'tomorrow' also gave us an opportunity not to be so literal about the idea of a spatial composition.

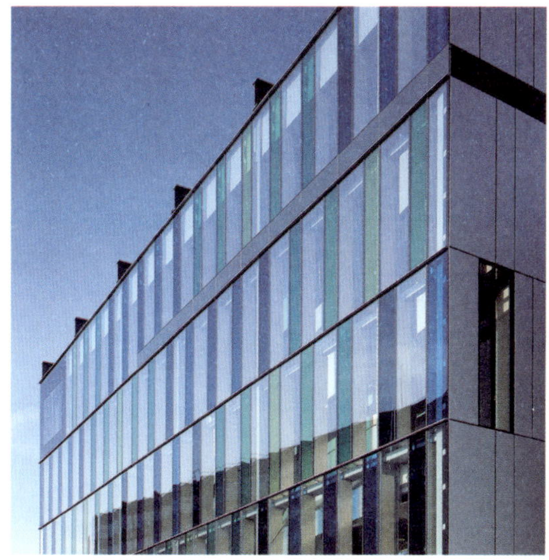

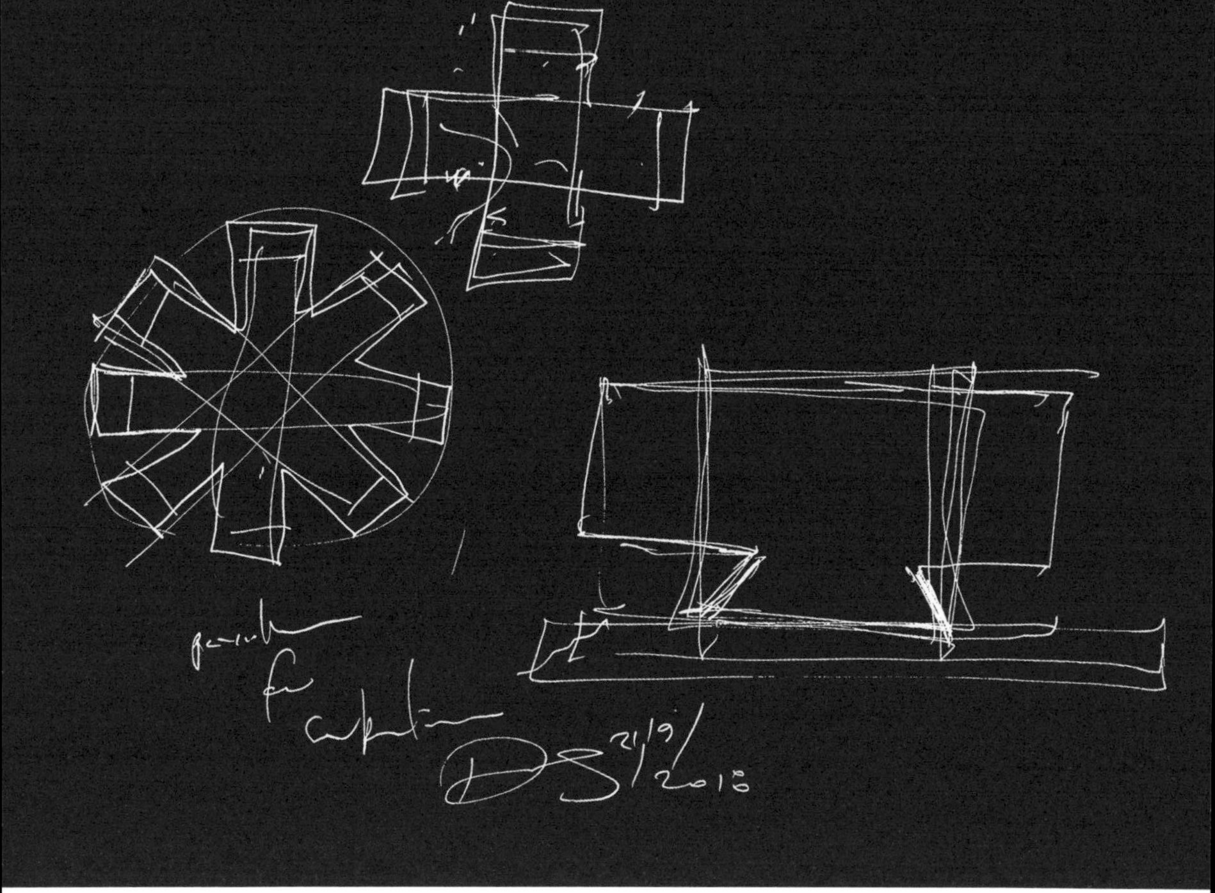

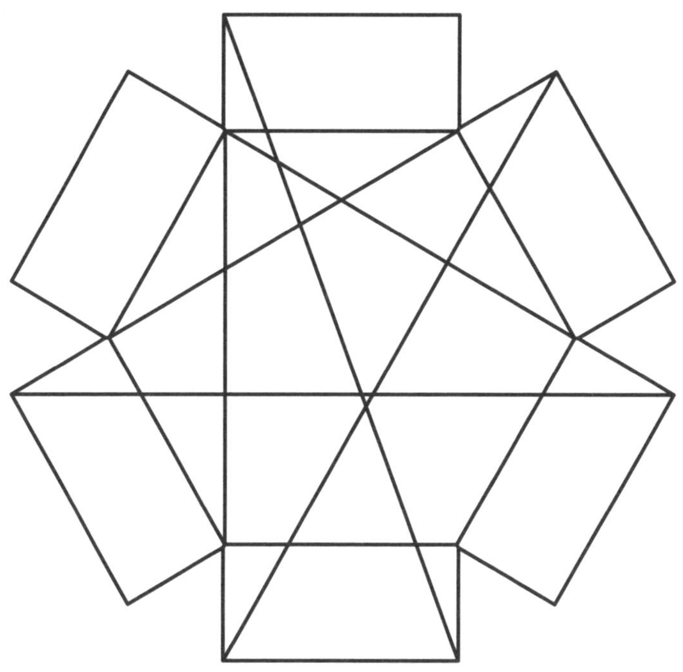

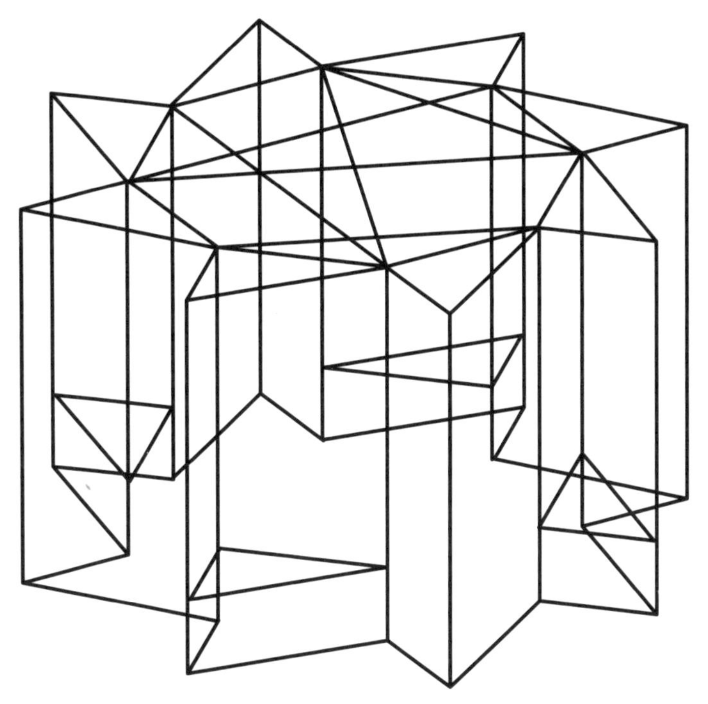

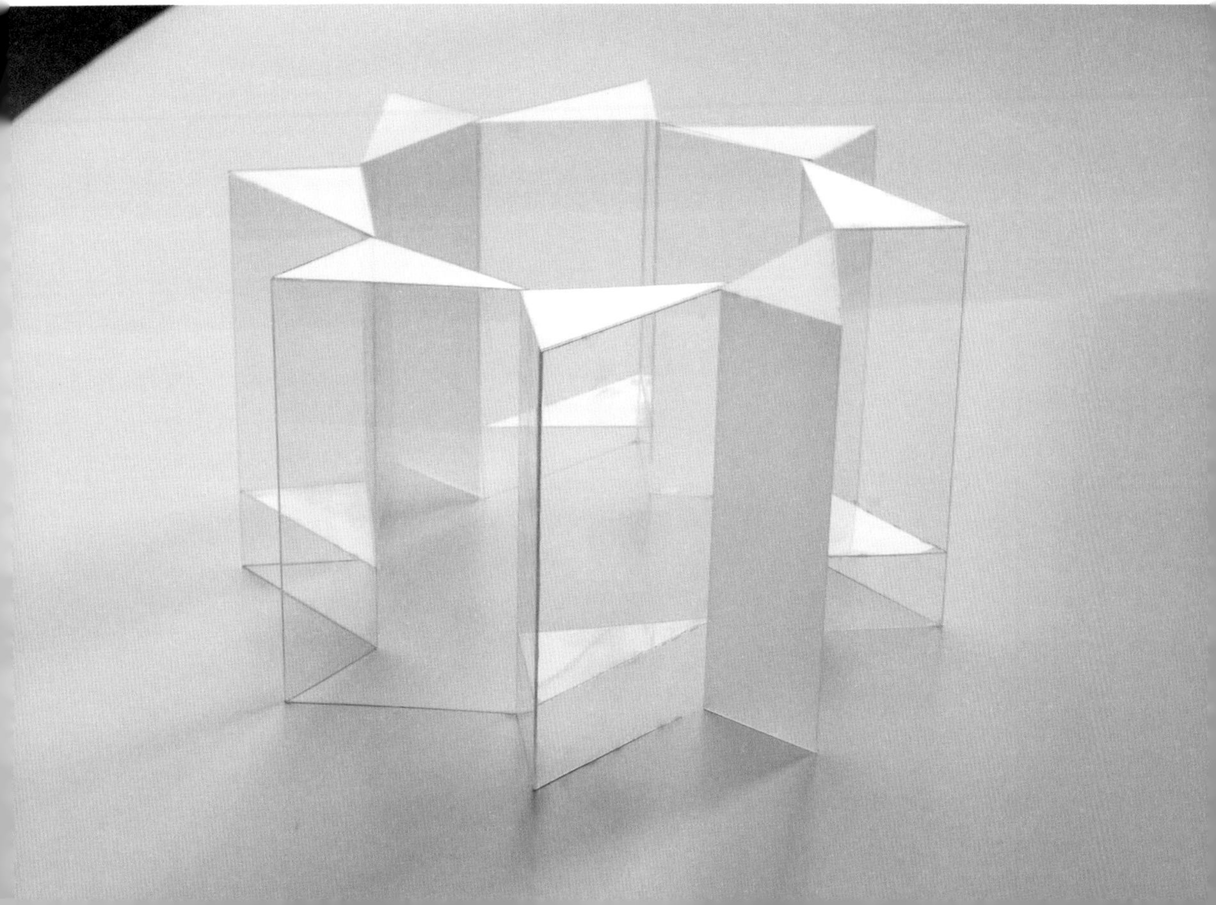

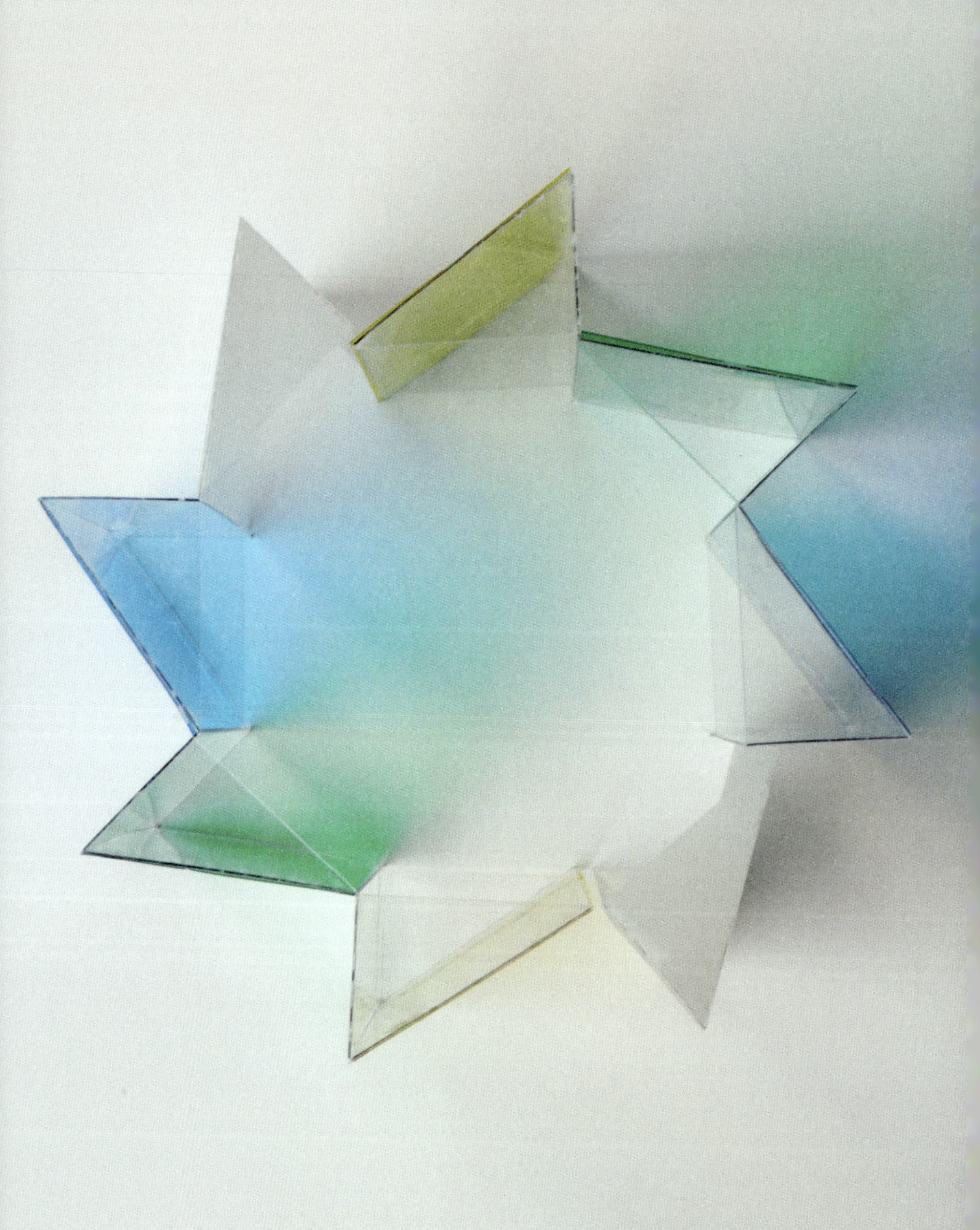

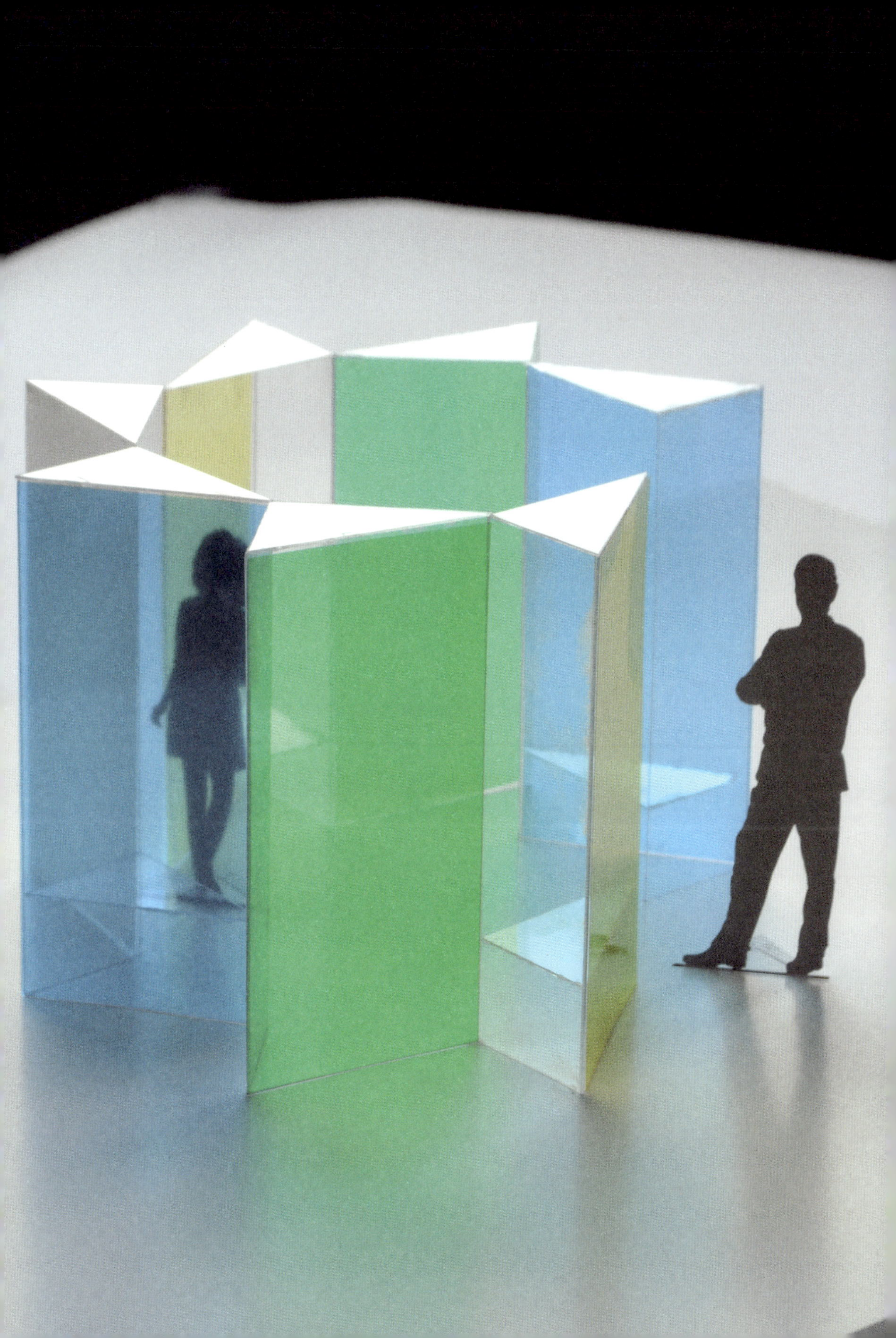

p. 35
Kapwani Kiwanga, *pink-blue*, 2017, Baker-Miller pink paint, white paint, white fluorescent lights, blue fluorescent lights, dimensions variable. Installation view, Yuz Museum, Shanghai, China, 2018. Photo: Toni Hafkenscheid

p. 36
Adjaye Associates, SKOLKOVO (Moscow School of Management), Moscow, 2010. Photo: Ed Reeve

p. 37
Above: Kapwani Kiwanga, *Jalousie*, 2018, steel, two-way mirror, silicone, 220 × 320 cm. Installation view, Galerie Jérôme Poggi, Paris

Below: Adjaye Associates, Kvadrat Showroom, London, 2009. Photo: Ed Reeve

p. 38
Kapwani Kiwanga, *Soft Measures: Evaporite*, 2018, carved granite, fabric, dye, 142 × 95 × 8 cm. Photo: Keith Hunter

p. 39
Above: Kapwani Kiwanga, *White Gold: Morogoro*, 2016, sisal fibres, metal bars, wire rope, 600 × 500 × 400 cm. Installation view, Ferme du Buisson, Noisiel, France, 2016. Photo: Emile Ouroumov

Below: Adjaye Associates, Whitechapel Idea Store, London, 2005. Photo: Edmund Sumner

p. 40
Above: David Adjaye, sketch for *Sankofa Pavilion*, 2018, ink on paper.

Below: Adjaye Associates, preparatory study for *Sankofa Pavilion*, 2018, digital rendering

p. 41
Above: Adjaye Associates, preparatory study for *Sankofa Pavilion*, 2018, digital rendering

Bottom: Adjaye Associates, preparatory model for *Sankofa Pavilion*, 2018, acrylic

pp. 43–44
Adjaye Associates, preparatory models for *Sankofa Pavilion*, 2018, acrylic

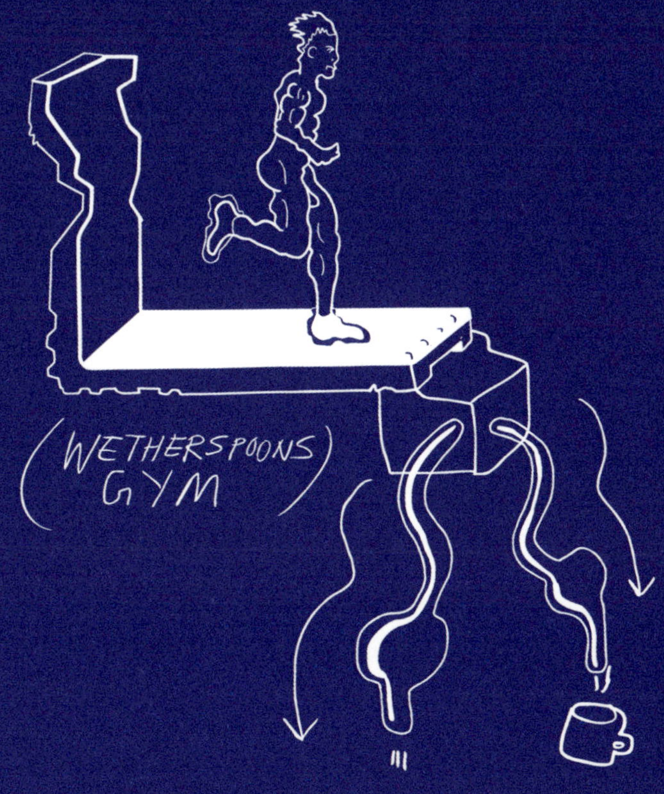
(WETHERSPOONS GYM)
WHAT ABOUT CURATOR?

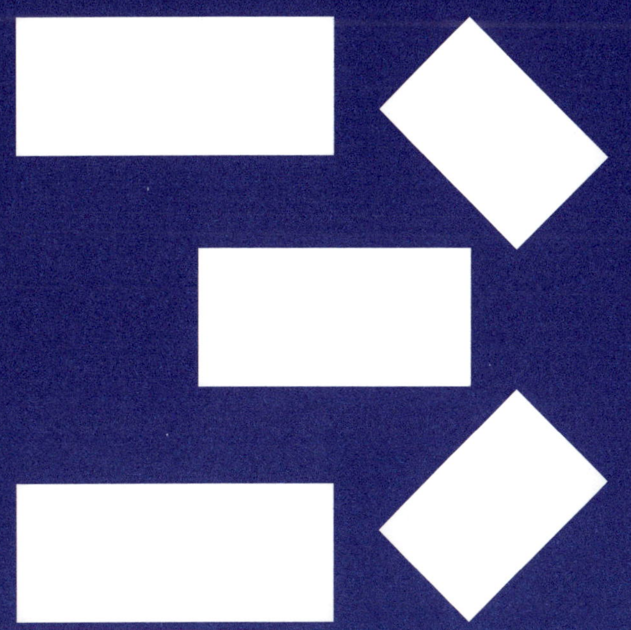

APPARATA
Hardeep Pandhal

PROJECT TEAM

Oliver Choyce
Nicholas Lobo Brennan
Hardeep Pandhal
Astrid Smitham

Thugz Mansion

Thugz Mansion is a dream, the refashioning and corruption of Imperial ruins, an invitation to interstitial embodiment. The stage is a weapon and you're its ammo!

We've been up for years. We made use of what's here, but suggest our own kind of livelihood.

A place barely pulled together, hanging, strapping, propping, against what was given.

A place to sit, to lie, to rest, with a roof over head, a stealth retreat.

It is a proposed code of conduct to deal with authoritative malfeasance, taking matters into one's own hands.

A spot where we belong, that's just for us. A chromed-out mansion in paradise.

I

wanked underneath my family tree
and made shit up that interests me
fluids leaking fluidly
over funding policies
put a box around me
and charge me tuition fees
cuz money grows on family trees
analogy from heraldry
bar sinister dividing me
from my own family tree
chopping trees freely
deforesting calmly
so properties a lottery
wood pecking dynasties
pecker wood die please
i'm on a chainsaw frenzy
with the grand theft auto cheats

II

with the benefit of hindsight – an arse on my face like
it's a pair of shades with the arse tight
asking what the past was like?
restorative dog bite, red brick termite,
back bite kick back horse might seduct like
frog legs bubble butt in gods face we must thrust
pic-a-nic scene beef layered trifle
pic-a-mix with a rifle – explode on impact with a bible
trees look like mushroom clouds rivals,
permanent state of explosion
marks the birth of a nation
a ministry of frowns
concealed by graduand gowns
graduate to what? a ministry of clowns

Hardeep Pandhal

BASTARDS

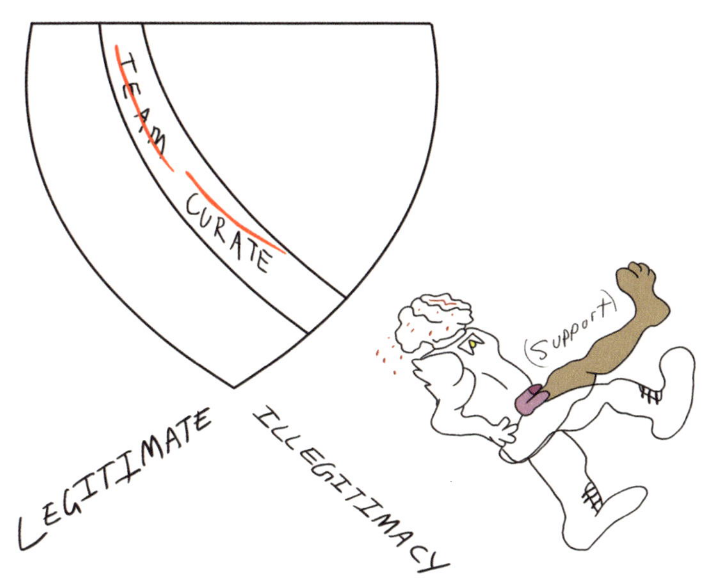

WHAT ABOUT THUGZ MANSION?

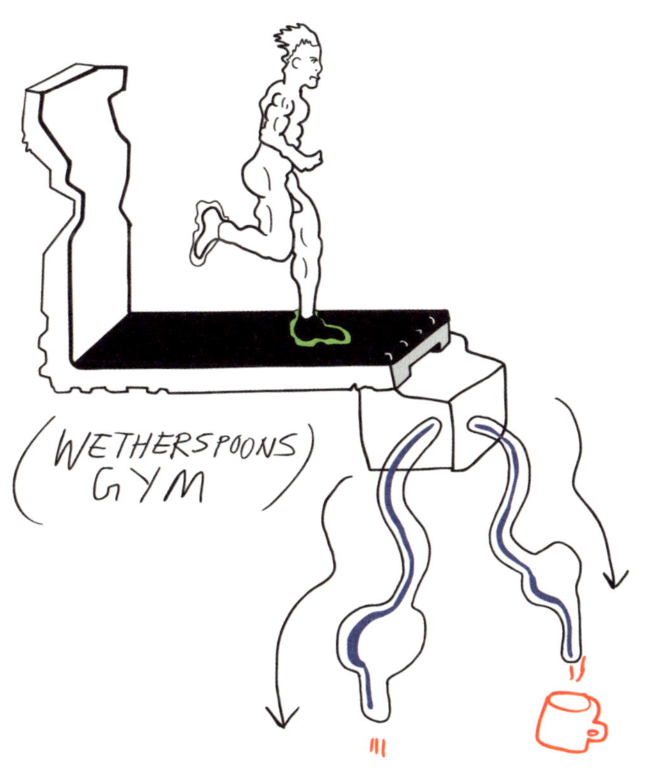

WHAT ABOUT CURATOR?

An optimistic exhibition, when each year was better than the last: house building, the foundation of the NHS, positive futures. Alison and Peter Smithson's *Patio and Pavilion* made in collaboration with Eduardo Paolozzi and Nigel Henderson already contained ideas realised in the Smithson's *Upper Lawn Pavilion* (1959–62) and later brutalist work.

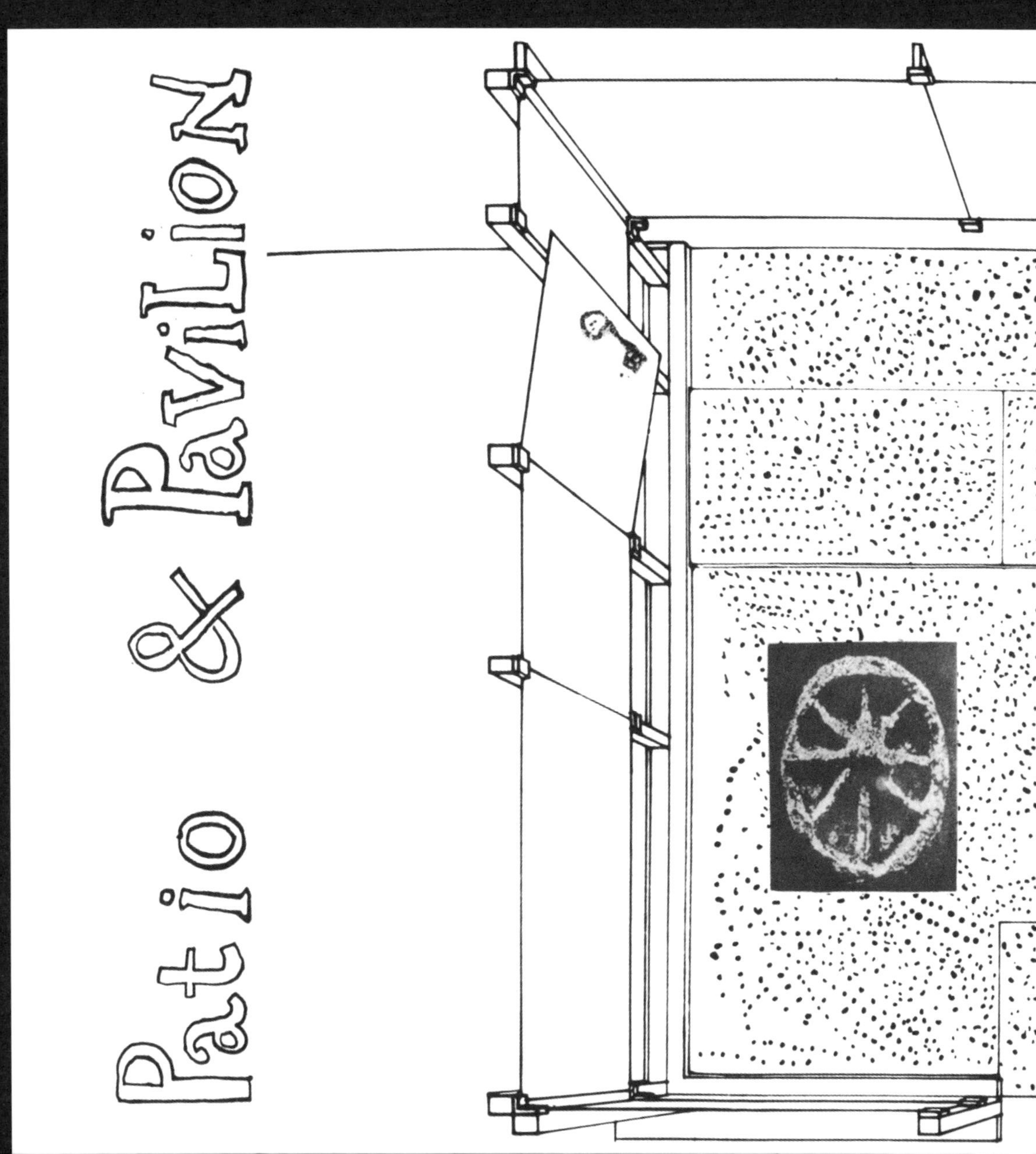

The catalogue had extensive advertisements for the building products of the future: Perspex, glass, concrete, steel work, gypsum, cork. These compete with works sketched in the catalogue, describing an almost shared view of the future.

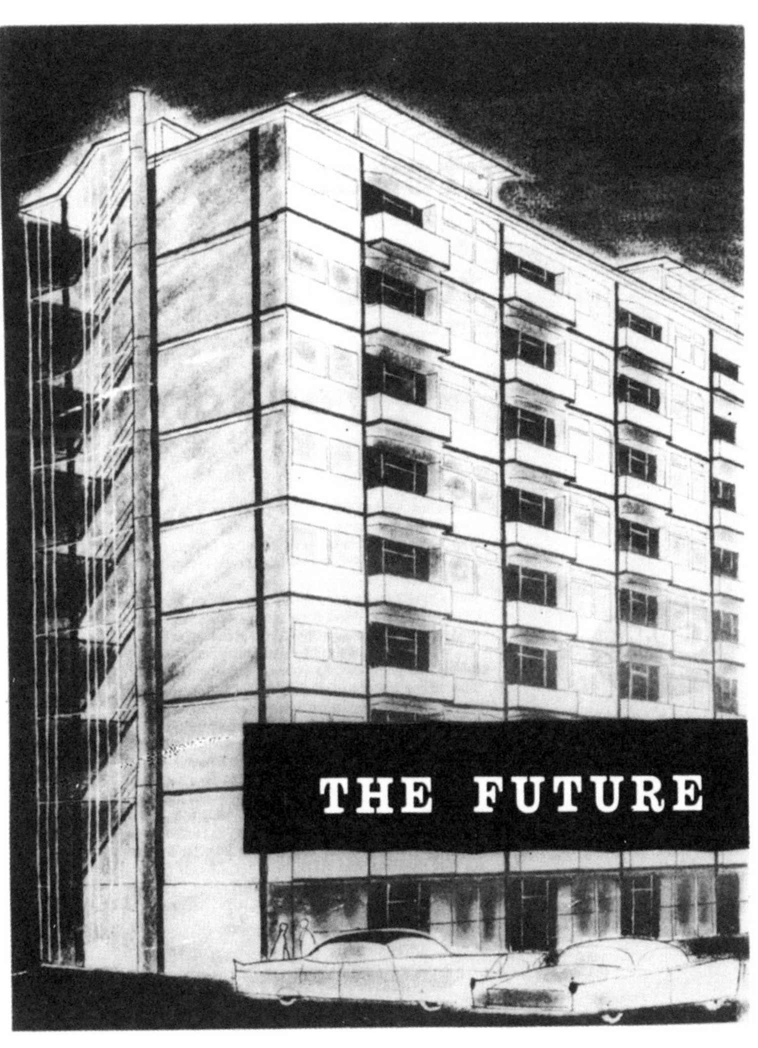

To the Reader: When we learn from Stendhal that he wrote one of his books for only a hundred readers, we are both astonished and disturbed. The world will be neither astonished nor, probably, disturbed if the present book has not one hundred readers like Stendhal's, nor fifty, nor twenty, nor even ten. Ten? Maybe five. It is, in truth, a diffuse work, in which I, Braz Cubas, if indeed I have adopted the free form of a Sterne or of a Xavier de Maistre, have possibly added a certain peevish pessimism of my own. Quite possibly. The work of a man already dead. I wrote it with the pen of Mirth and the ink of Melancholy, and one can readily foresee what may come of such a union. Moreover, solemn people will find in the book an aspect of pure romance, while frivolous folk will not find in it the sort of romance to which they have become accustomed; thus it is and will remain, disrespected by the solemn and unloved by the frivolous, the two great pillars of public opinion.

But I still entertain at least the hope of winning public favor, and the first step in that direction is to avoid a long and detailed prologue. The best prologue is the one that has the least matter or that presents it most briefly, even to the point of obscurity. Hence I shall not relate the extraordinary method that I used in the composition of these memoirs, written here in the world beyond. It is a most curious method, but its relation would require an excessive amount of space and, moreover, is unnecessary to an understanding of the work. The book must suffice in itself: if it please you, excellent reader, I shall be rewarded for my labor; if it please you not, I shall reward you with a snap of my fingers, and good riddance to you. 1

Braz Cubas

[8]

I was cleaning a room and, meandering about, approached the divan and couldn't remember whether or not I had dusted it. Since these movements are habitual and unconscious, I could not remember and felt that it was impossible to remember. . . . If some conscious person had been watching, then the fact could be established. If, however, no one was looking, or looking unconsciously, if the whole complex lives of many people go on unconsciously, then such lives are as if they had never been. (p. 12) 2

When the meaning of the temenos has been banalized or polluted, critical intent has had to search for alternative ways of expression outside the classical canon. Strangemaking has then had to take a path that is altogether different: to destroy the classical canon, now itself the embodiment of "the deadening effect of habitualization." A new passage has had to be opened up—disrupting symmetries, shifting axes, breaking corners, bursting through boundaries, abandoning hierarchization and tripartition, opting instead for deformed and irregualr patterns, ignoring elements, members, and their ranks. Catharsis has had to flee the classical schemata of taxis, genera, and symmetry and forge another formal anticlassical canon.

3

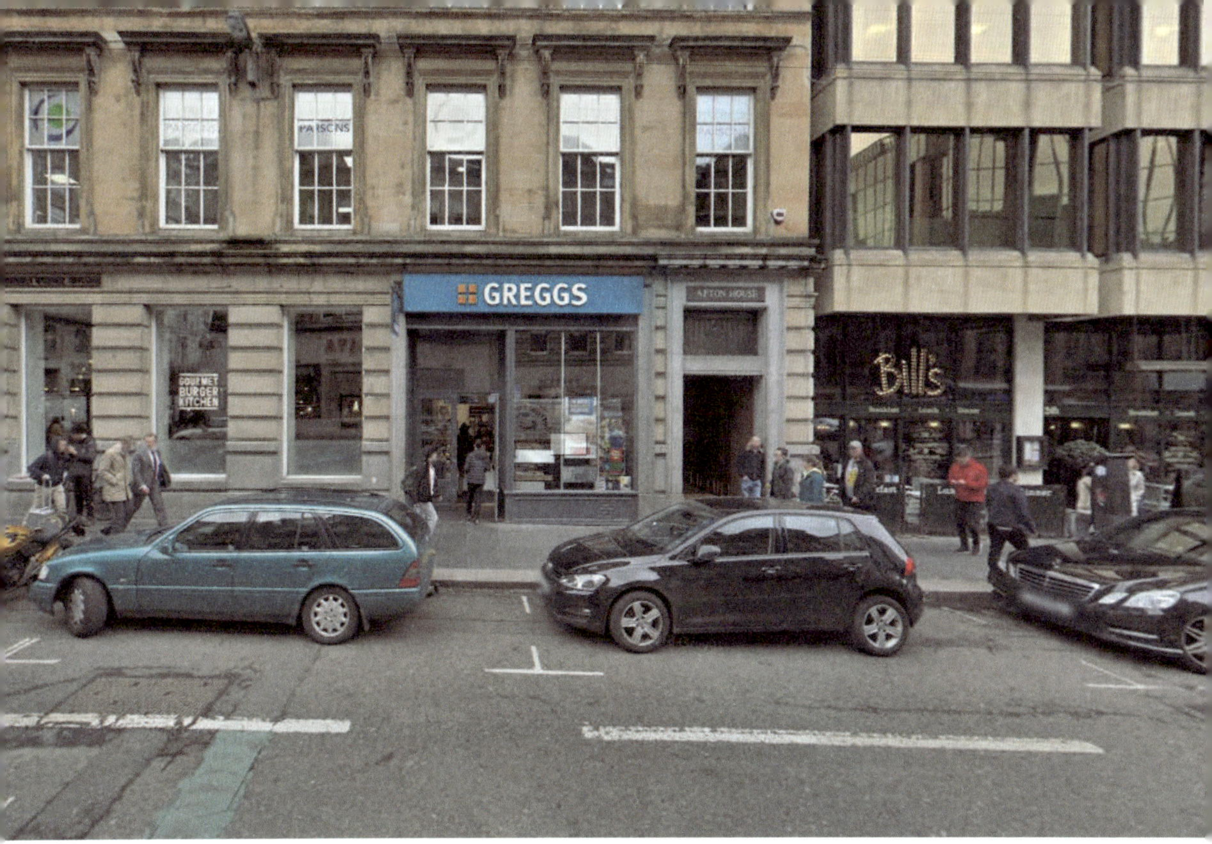
GREGGS
GOURMET BURGER KITCHEN
Bill's

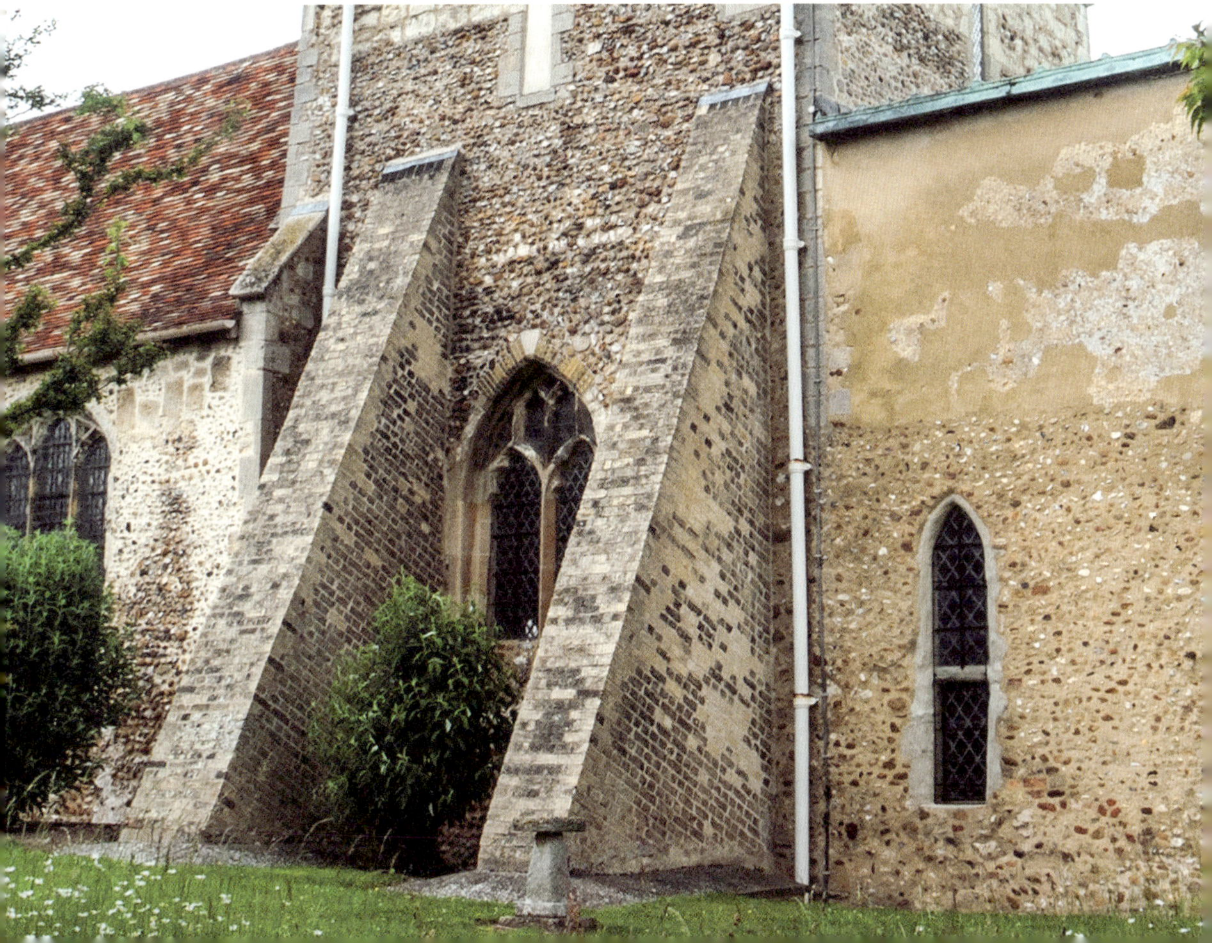

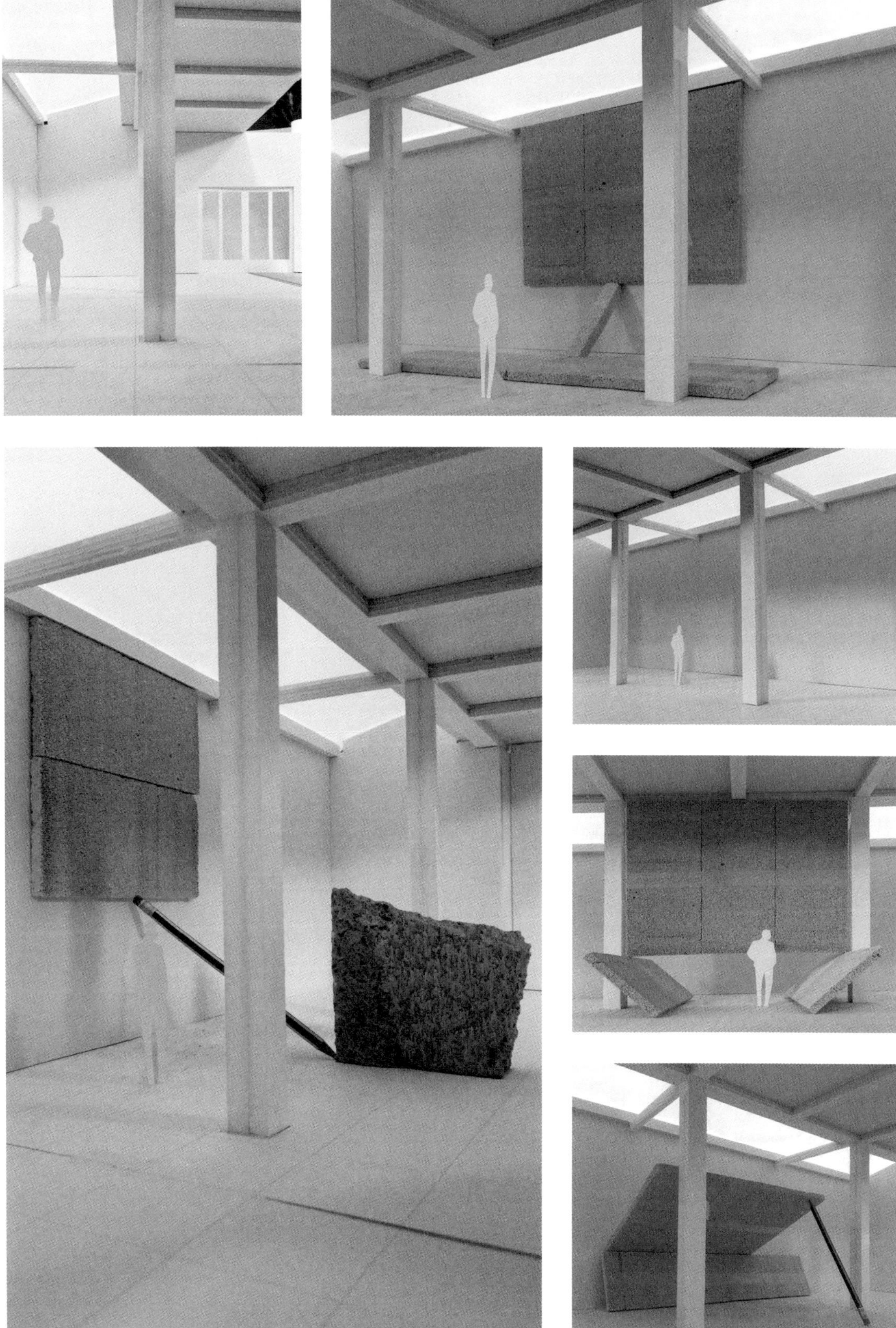

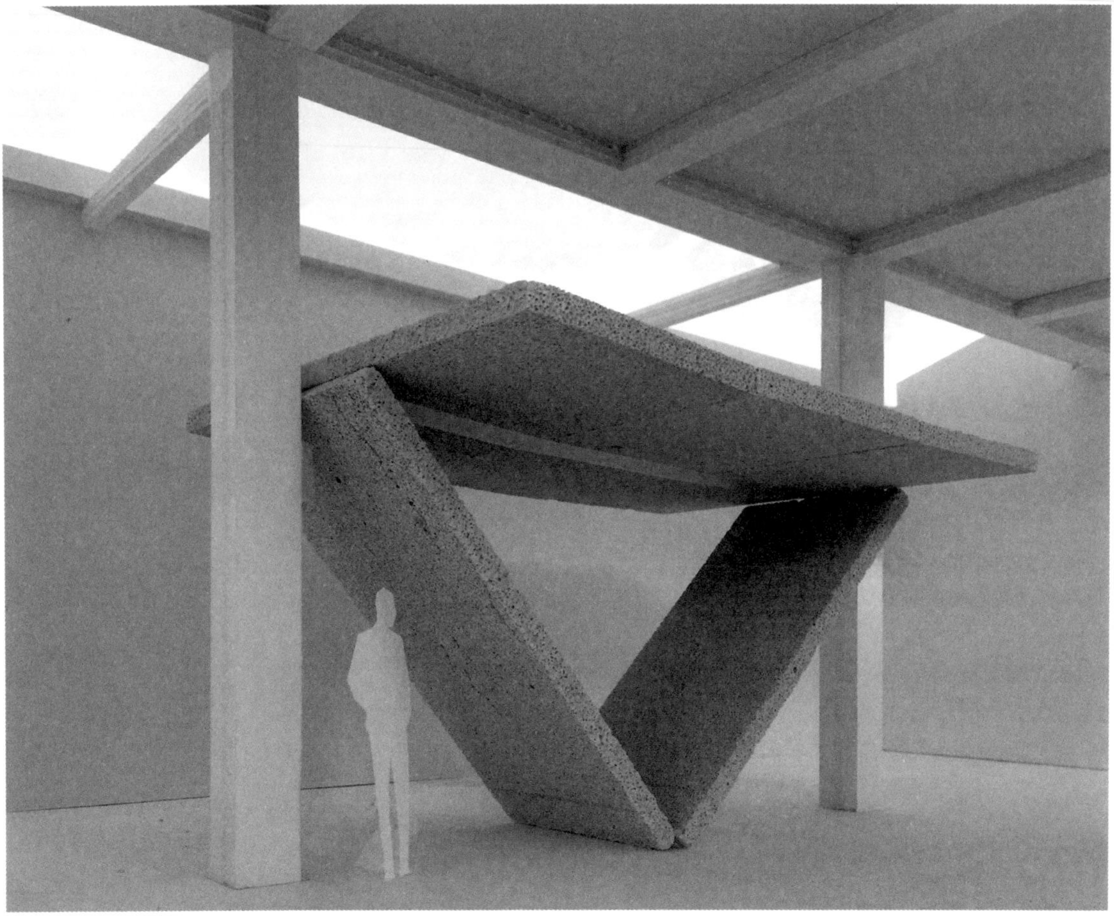

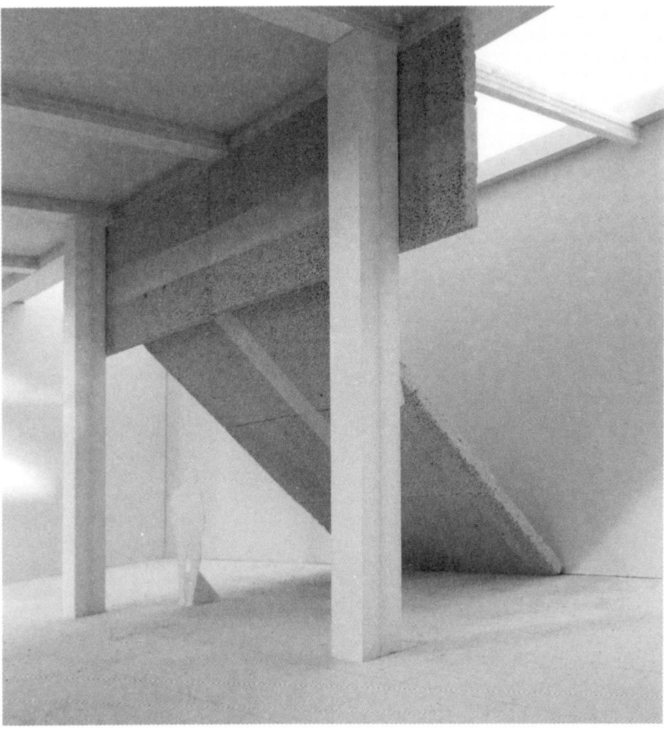

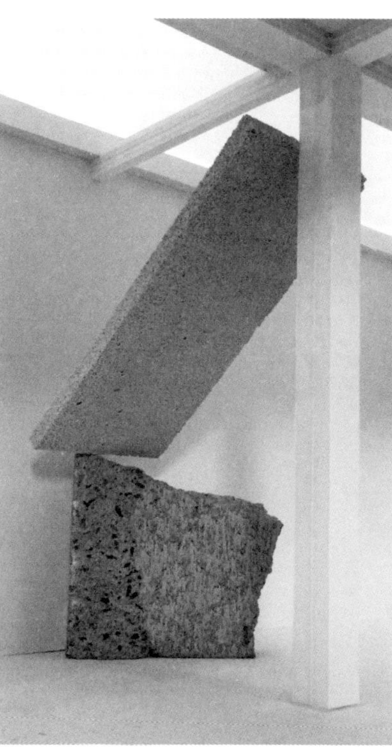

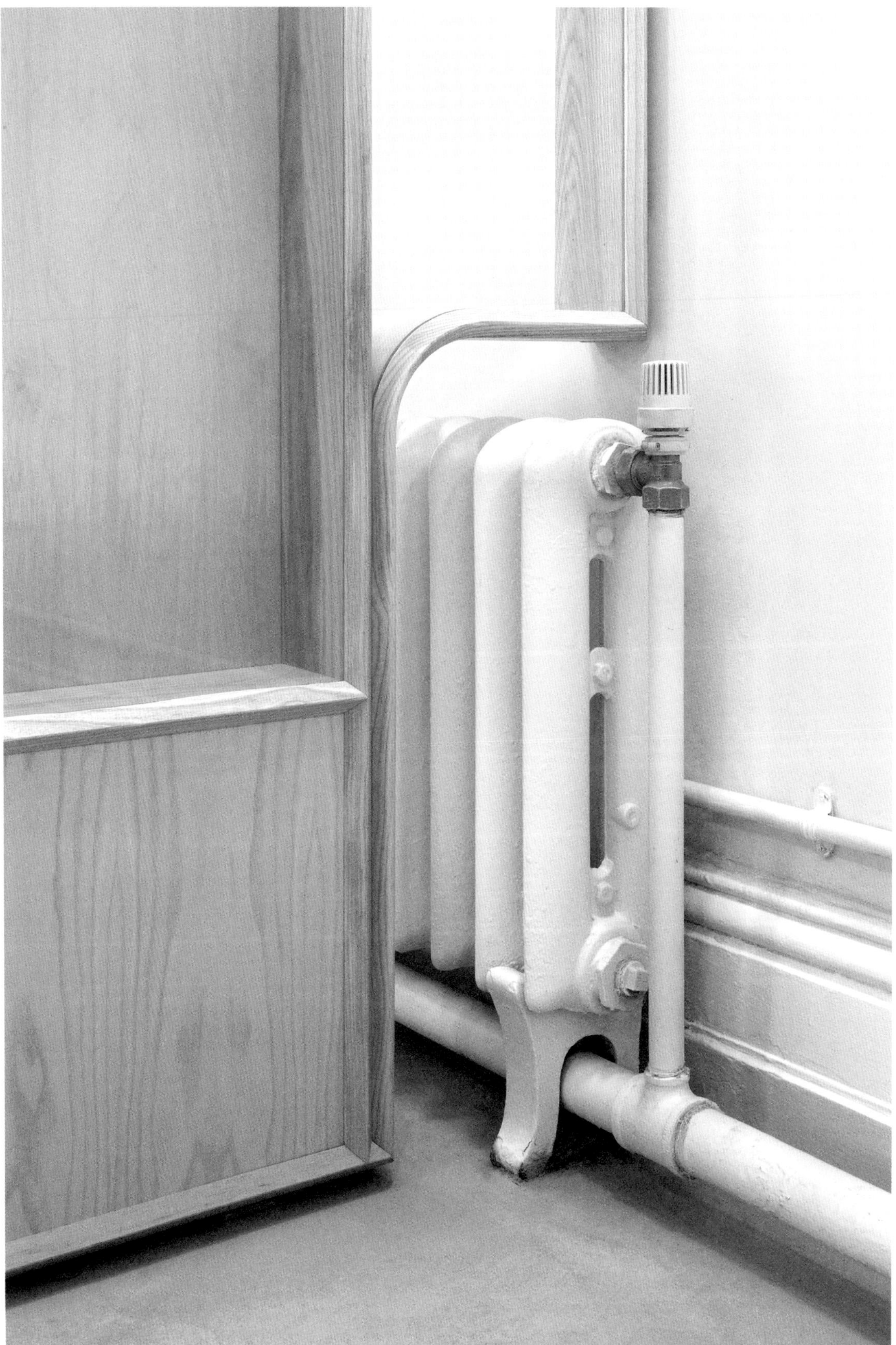

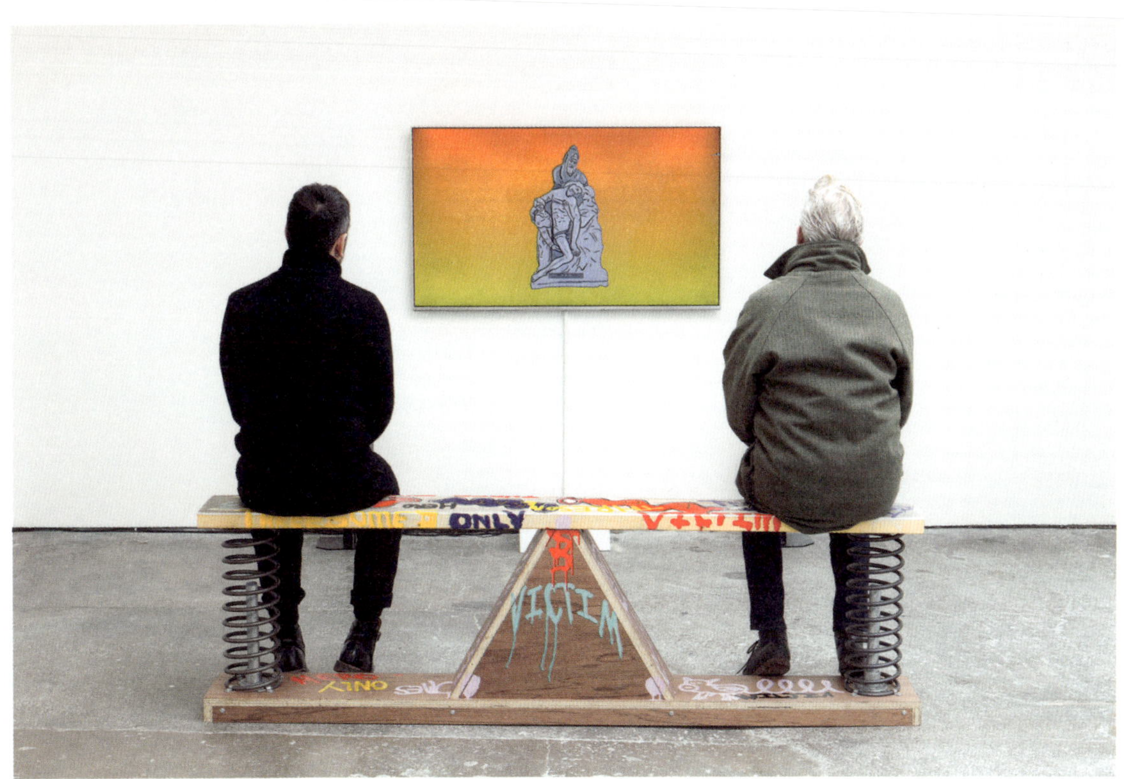
ONLY
VICTIM

p. 49
Hardeep Pandhal, *Thugz Mansion*, 2018, drawing

p. 50
Nigel Henderson, Eduardo Paolozzi, Alison Smithson and Peter Smithson, drawing for *Patio & Pavilion* (detail). Published in Theo Crosby (ed.), *This Is Tomorrow*, Whitechapel Gallery, London, 1956.

p. 51
'The future is wrapped in Fibreglass', advertisement for Fibreglass Ltd., Ravenhead, Lancashire, UK (detail). Published in Theo Crosby (ed.), *This Is Tomorrow*, Whitechapel Gallery, London, 1956.

p. 52
(1) Machado de Assis, *Epitaph of a Small Winner* (1888), William L. Grossman (trans.), Bloomsbury, London, 1998, p. 3.

(2) Leo Tolstoy, *Diary*, entry dated March 1, 1897, in Viktor Shklovsky *'Art as Technique'*, *Russian Formalist Criticism: Four Essays*, L. T. Lemon and M. J. Reis (trans.), University of Nebraska Press, Lincoln and London, 1965, p. 20.

(3) Alexander Tzonis and Liane Lefaivre, *Classical Architecture: The Poetics of Order*, MIT Press, Cambridge, Massachusetts, 1986, p. 279.

p. 53
Above: Greggs, 28 West Nile Street, Glasgow, Scotland. Street View image capture, May 2018, ©2019 Google

Below: Buttresses, St John's Church, Duxford. Photo: David Ross / Britain Express

pp. 54–55
APPARATA and Hardeep Panhal, studies for *Thugz Mansion*, December 2018

p. 56
APPARATA, Old Manor Park Library, 2015. Photo: Emil Charlaff

p. 57
Hardeep Pandhal, *Liar Hydrant*, installation view, Cubitt Gallery, London, 2018. Photo: Mark Blower

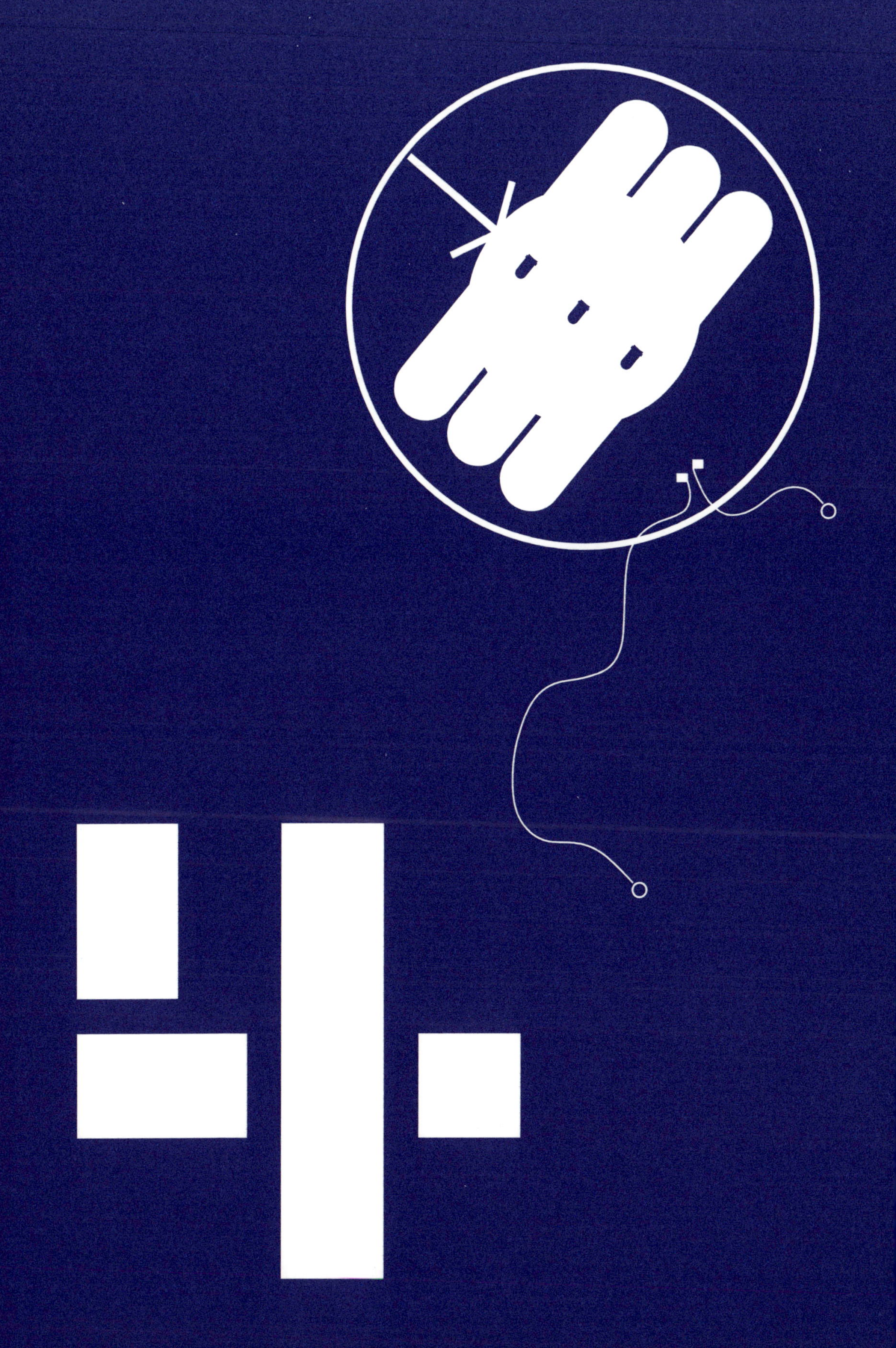

Cao Fei
mono office

PROJECT TEAM

Pablo Alfonso Resa Abad
Miguel Esteban Alonso
Cao Fei
Kit Huen
Zhao Liqun

I Want to be the Future: The Anatomy of Technological Seduction

We believe that the future is defined by the actions of individuals who together construct a collective understanding of tomorrow. Obsessed by becoming part of the digital world, consumers are adapting themselves and their environments to a technological society.

Due to the large-scale development of its low-tech industries, China is often held up as a synecdoche of the future, a country symbolising the relationship between technology and the common people, which is both seductive and uneasy. At best, such passion for technology drives the country's creativity and economy; at worst, it is symptomatic of a population withdrawing from the reality of modern China.

Our interest lies in the forms, spaces and personal fictions that people create every day from the objects they purchase online or the way in which they use their physical environment to perform new functions related to the technological world. This hyperreal vision of the near future reflects the impact of accelerating economic growth, technological development and globalisation on society. The emergent landscape of consumption is driven by a powerful internet economy whose future form is unknown. What kind of spatial environments could this economy create?

The 'device' acts as a dispenser for these fictions, where creativity and daring lead to fantastical but perfectly possible futures. Such future visions are based on the study of common human interactions with technology in wide and varied fields such as transportation, commerce, dating, mobility or housing. Our understanding of these realities gives rise to a new image of tomorrow, whose morphology is based on the self-adaptation of physical and sentimental spaces, creating a catalogue of objects and emotions.

We share an interest in an anthropological and behavioral perspective on society, the environment and the future, and in the relationship between people and technology. This has been constantly reflected in the architectonic, urban and artistic activity of mono office, while Cao Fei's international programme of exhibitions has continually explored the intersection of human behaviour and the conditions of late capitalism.

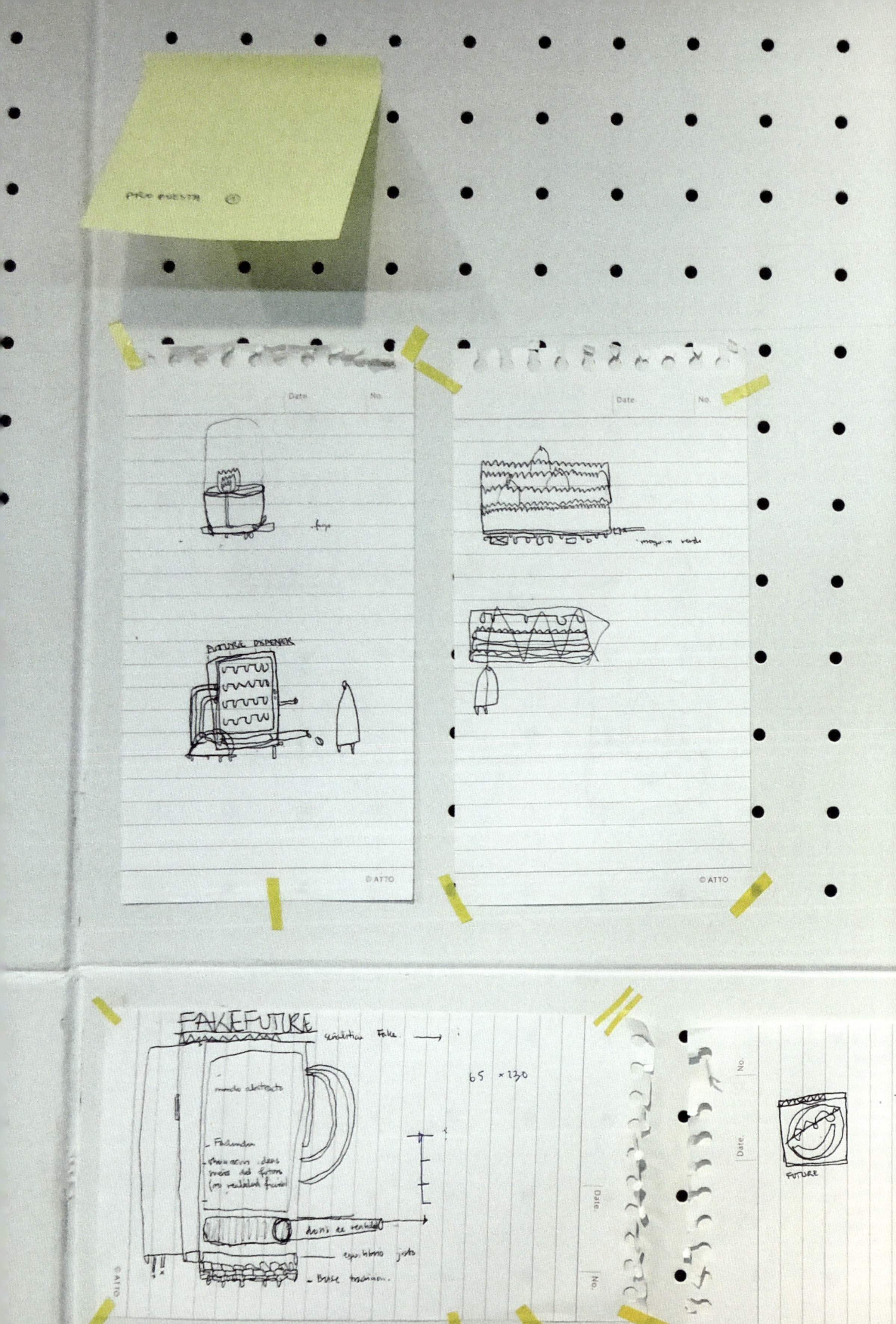
Date
No.
FUTURE DISPENSER
© ATTO
Date
No.
© ATTO
FAKEFUTURE
65 × 130
Date
No.
ATTO
No.
Date.
FUTURE

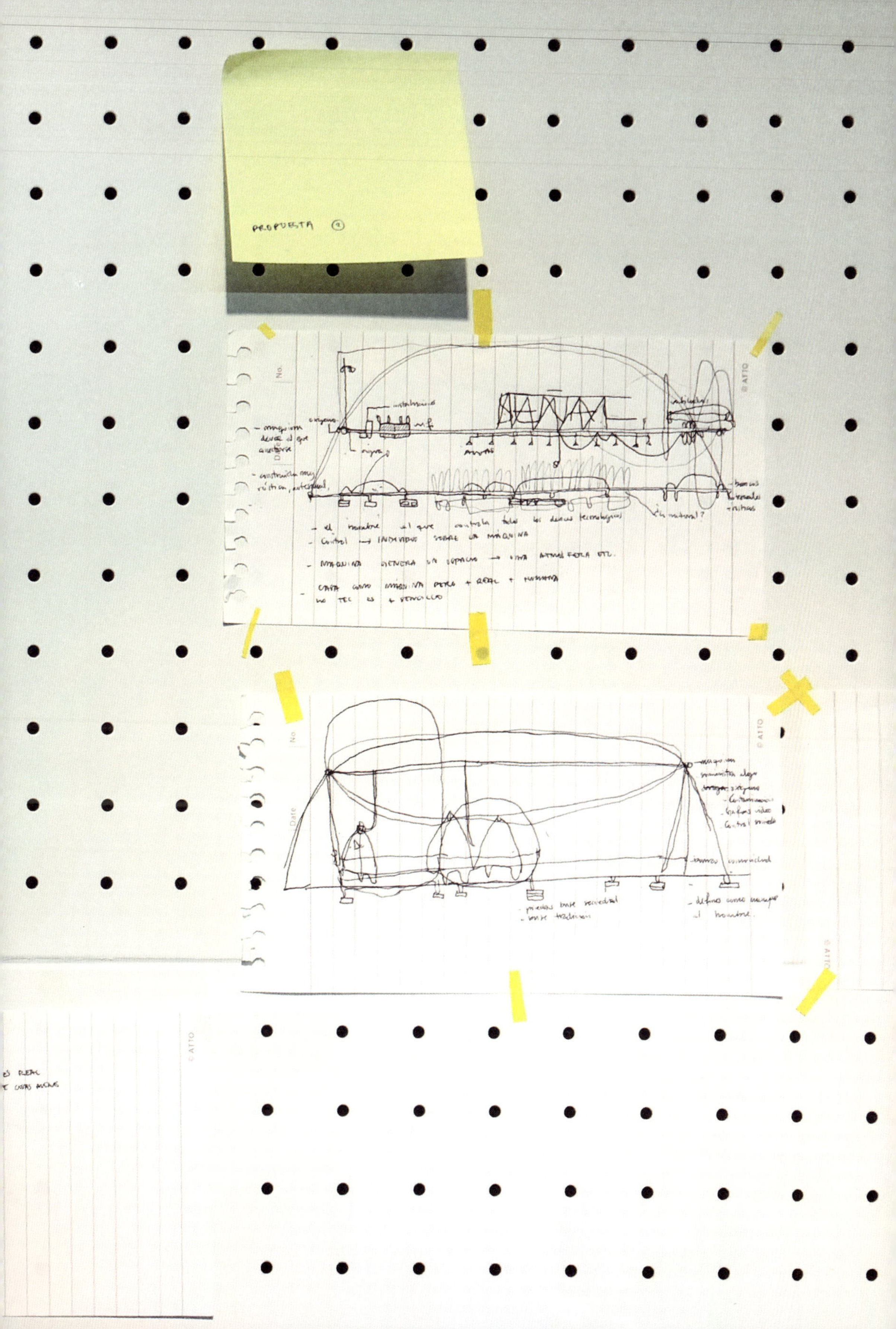
PROPUESTA
No.
Date
© ATTO

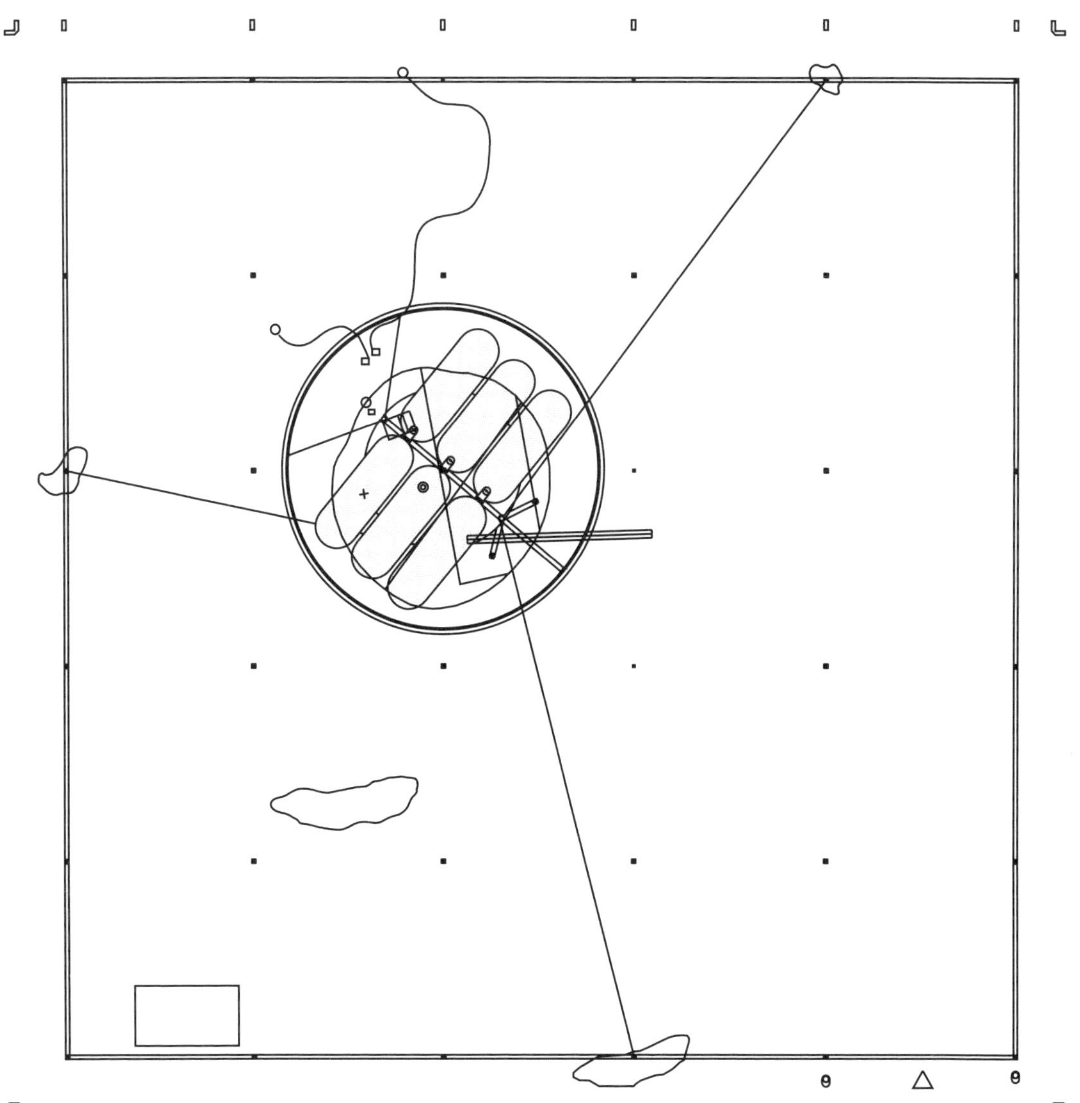

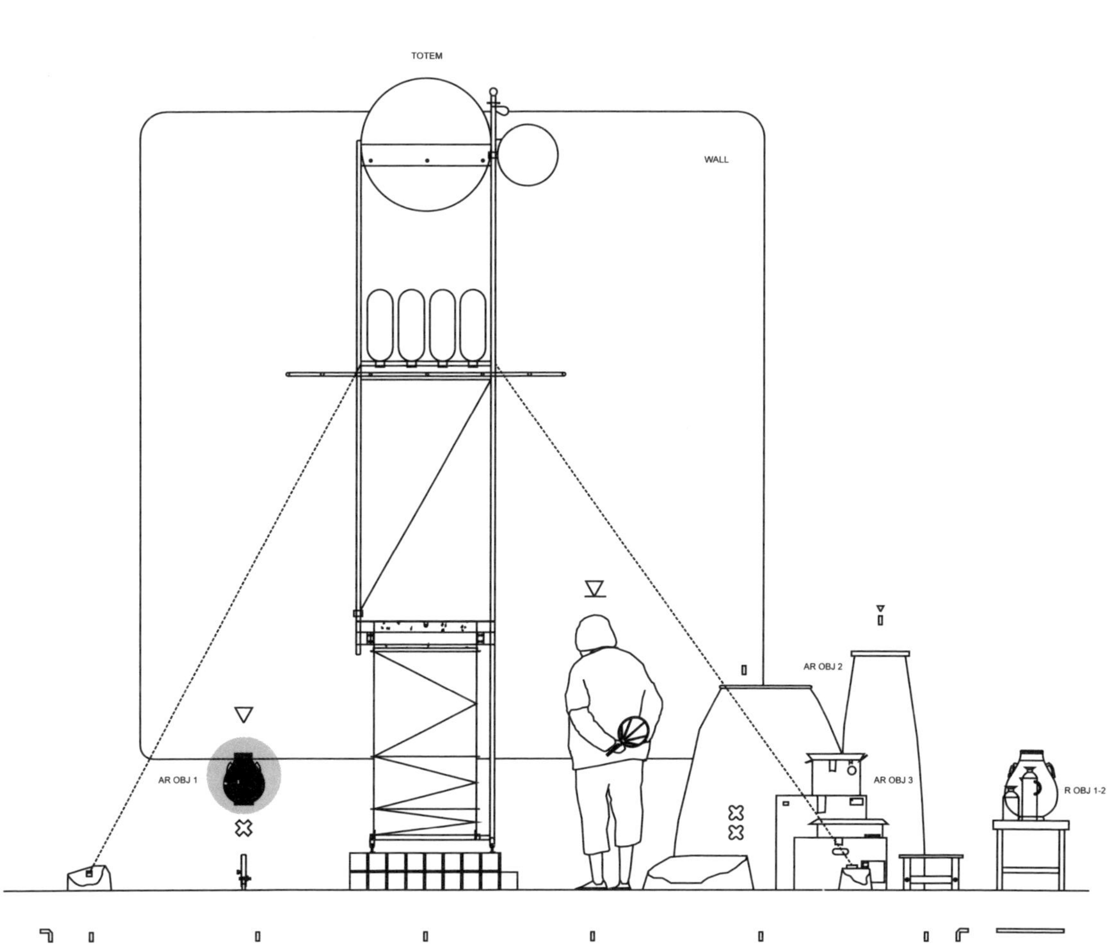
TOTEM
WALL
AR OBJ 2
AR OBJ 1
AR OBJ 3
R OBJ 1-2

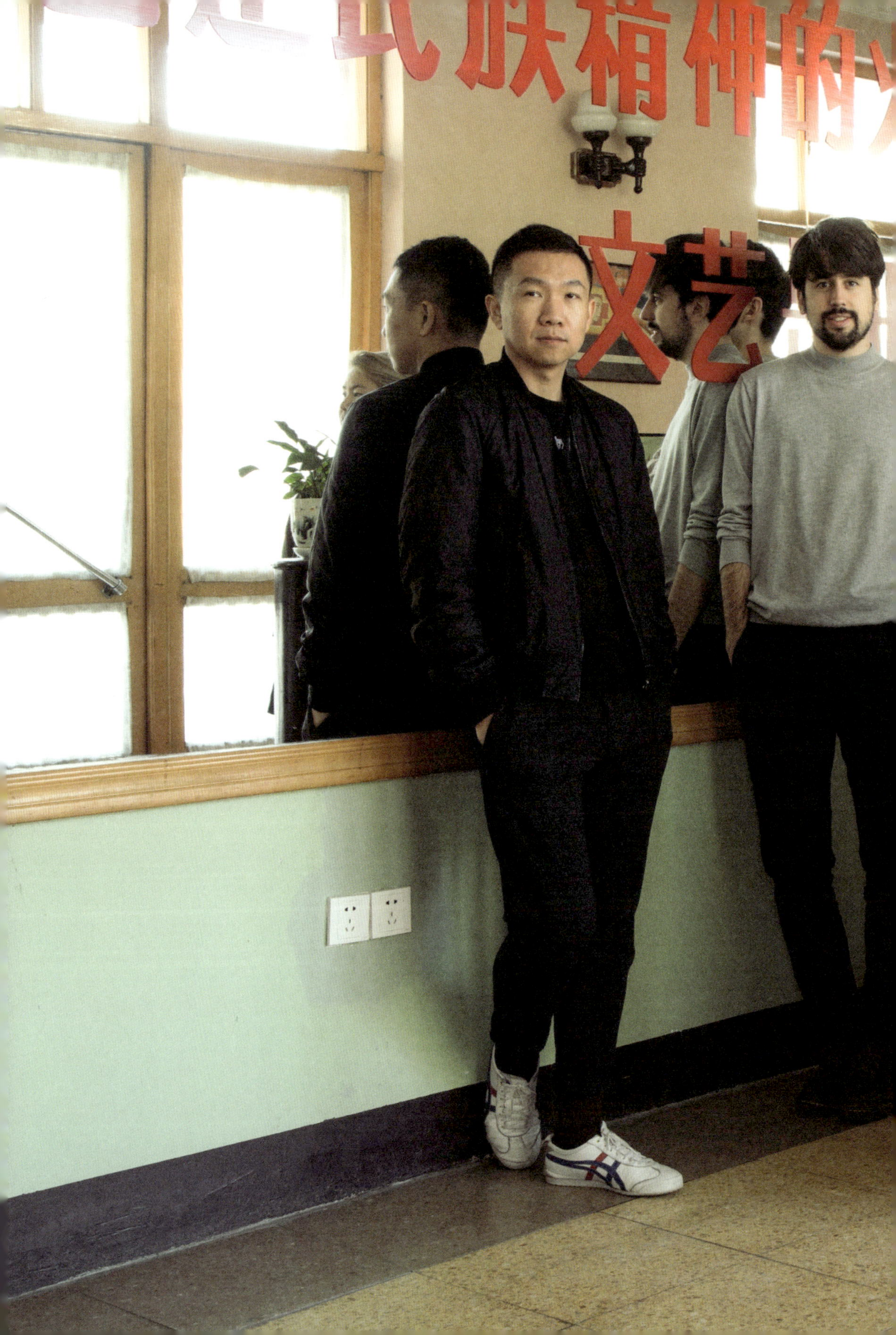
族精神的
文艺

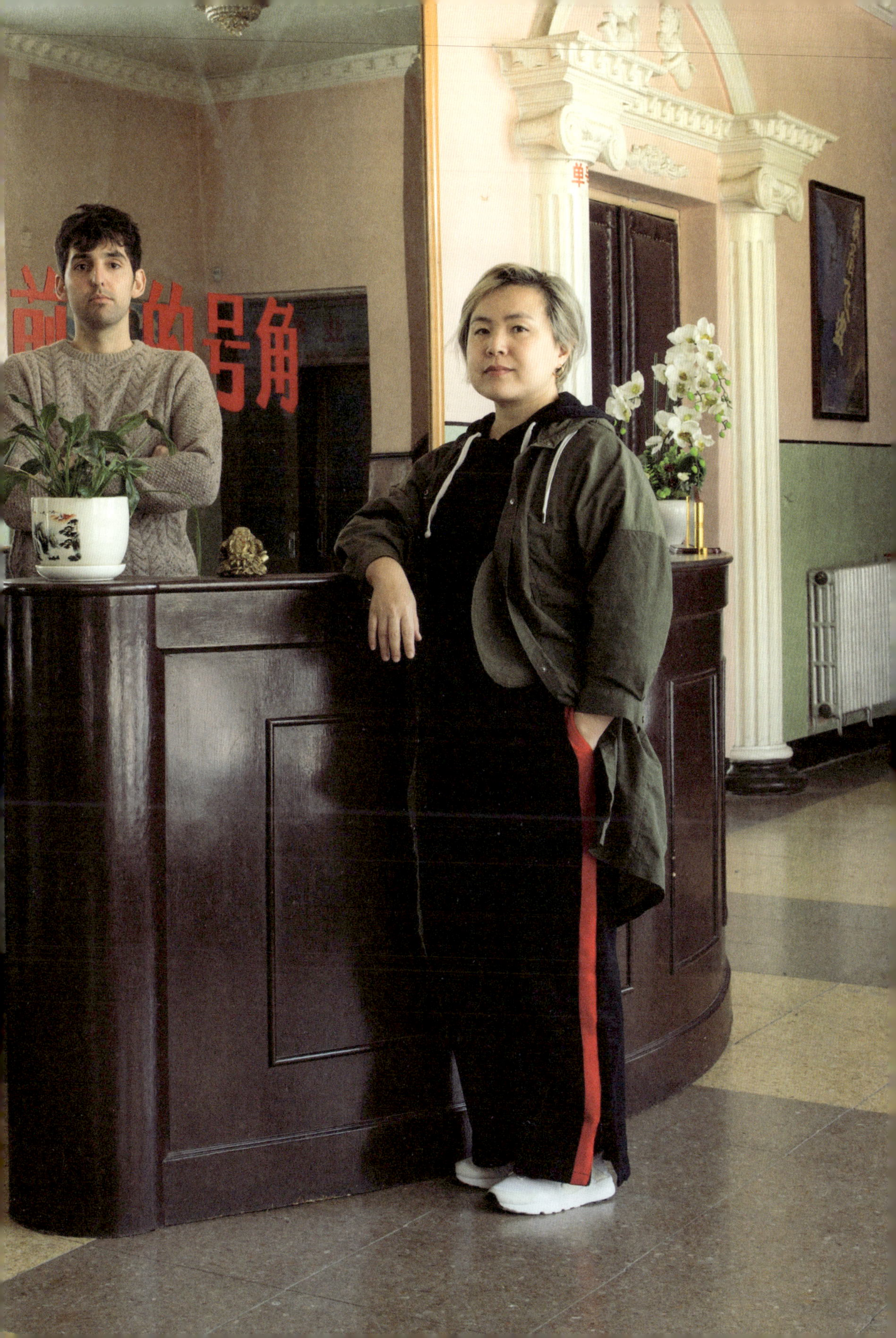
号角

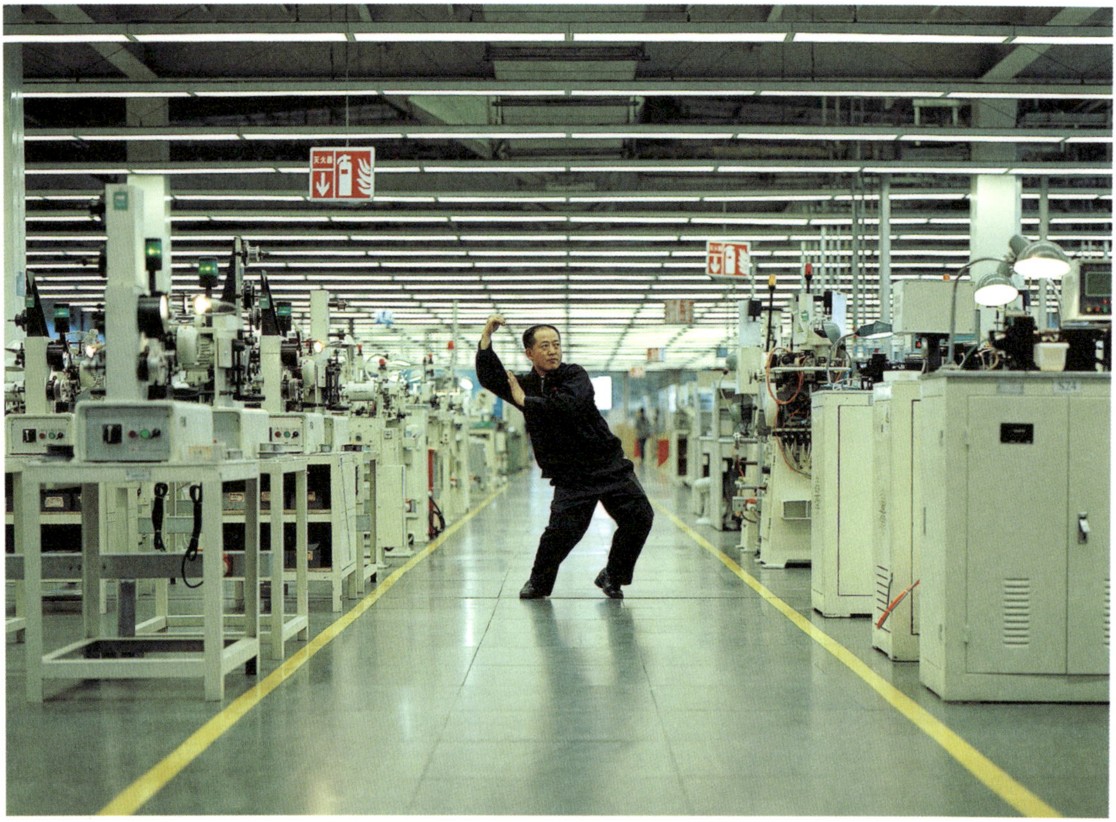

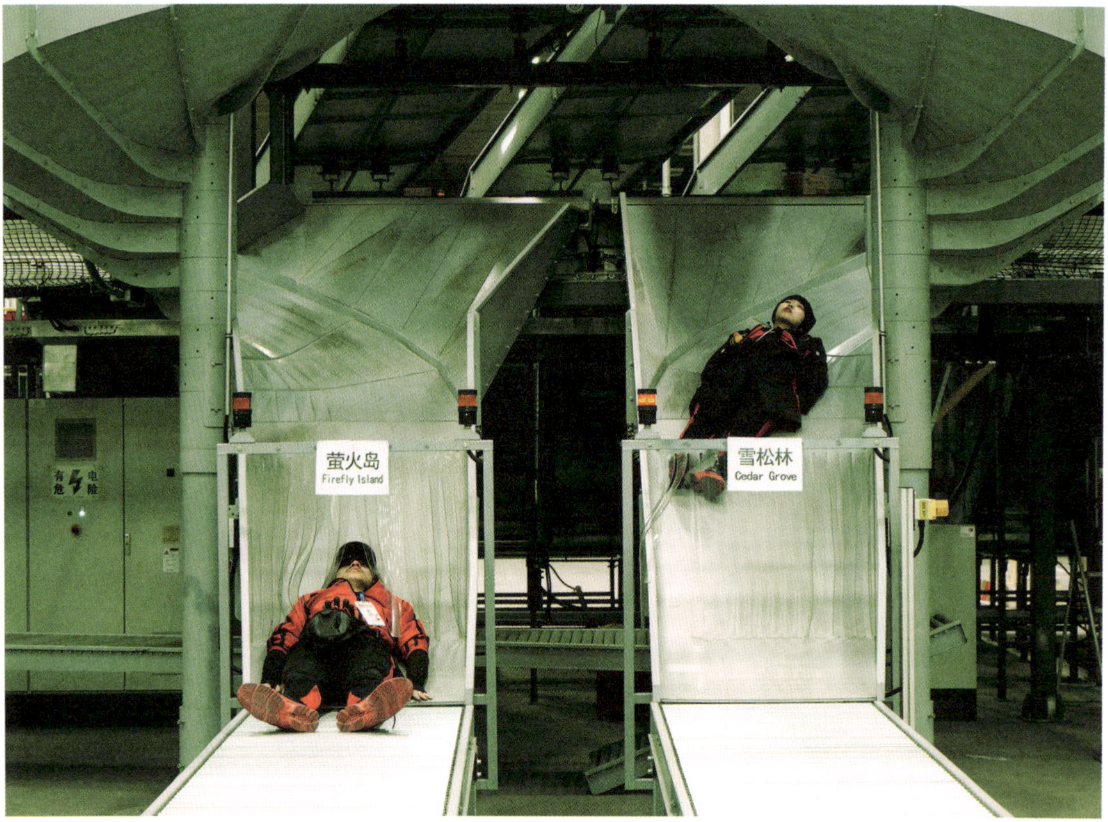

萤火岛
Firefly Island
雪松林
Cedar Grove
有电危险

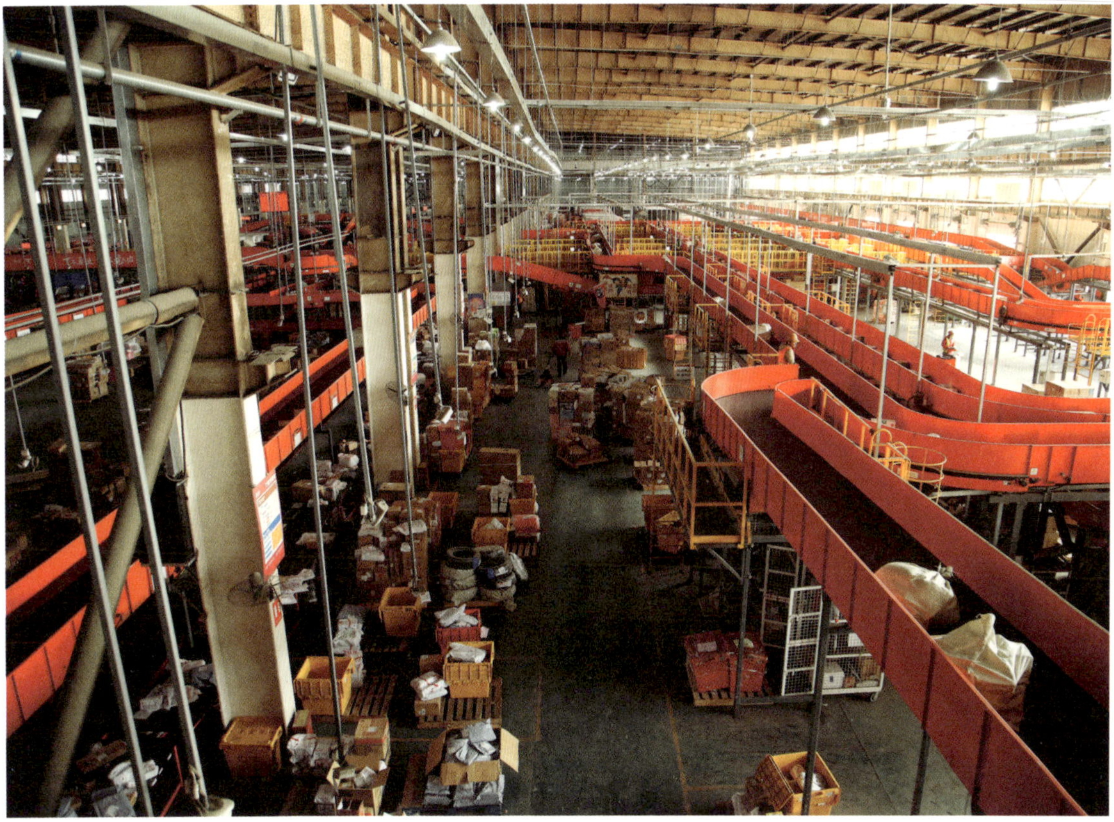

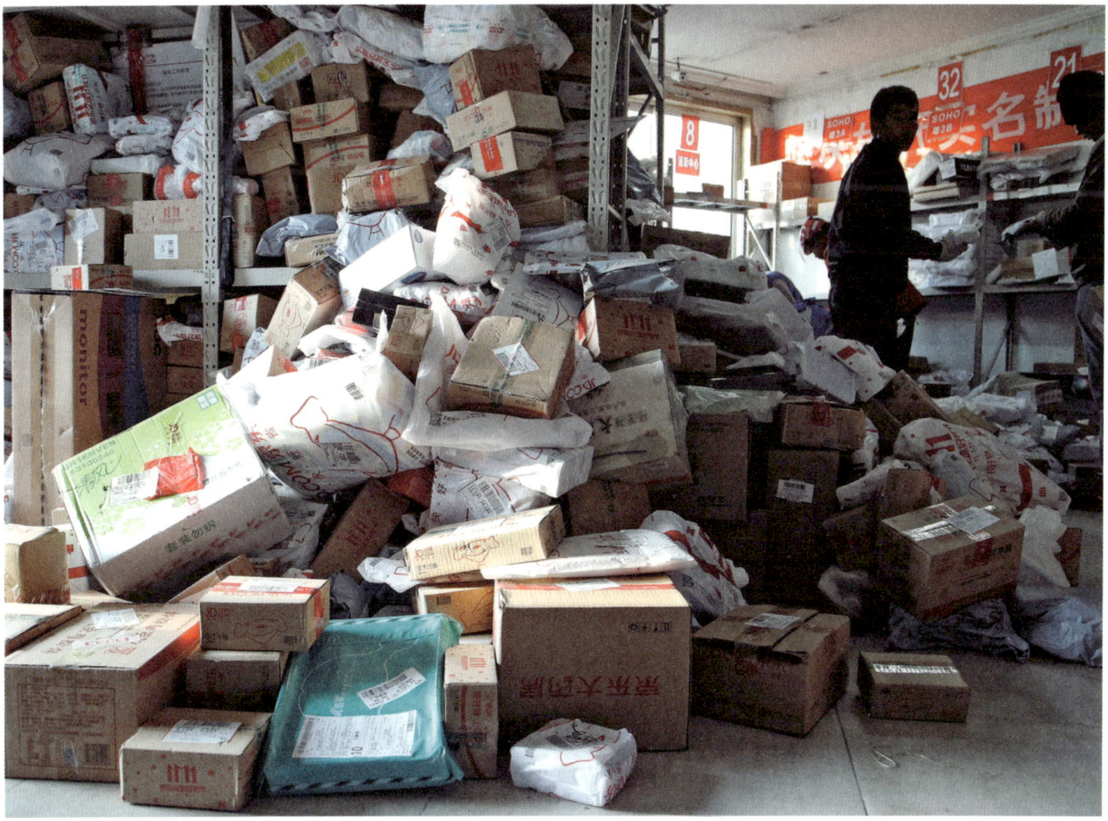

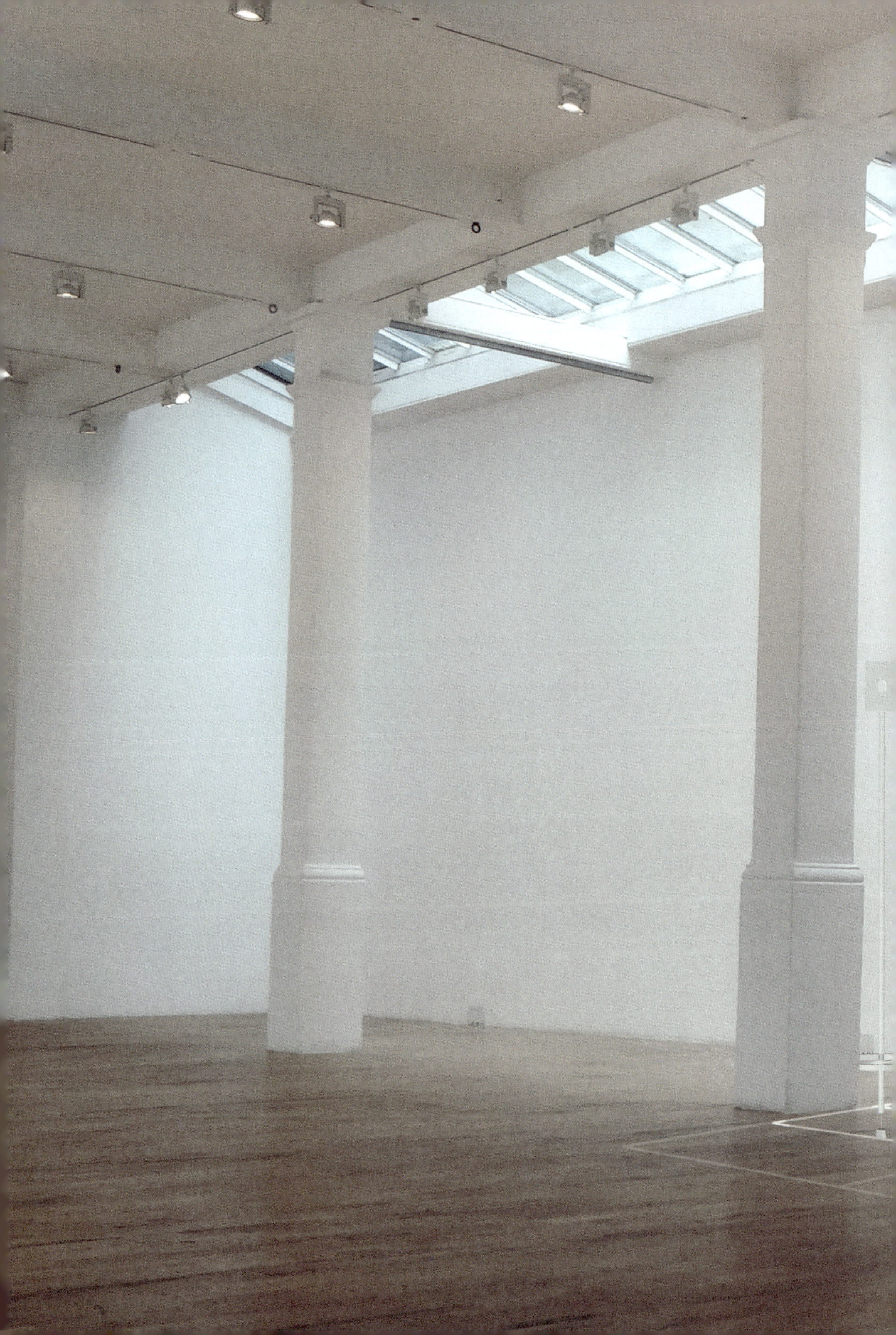

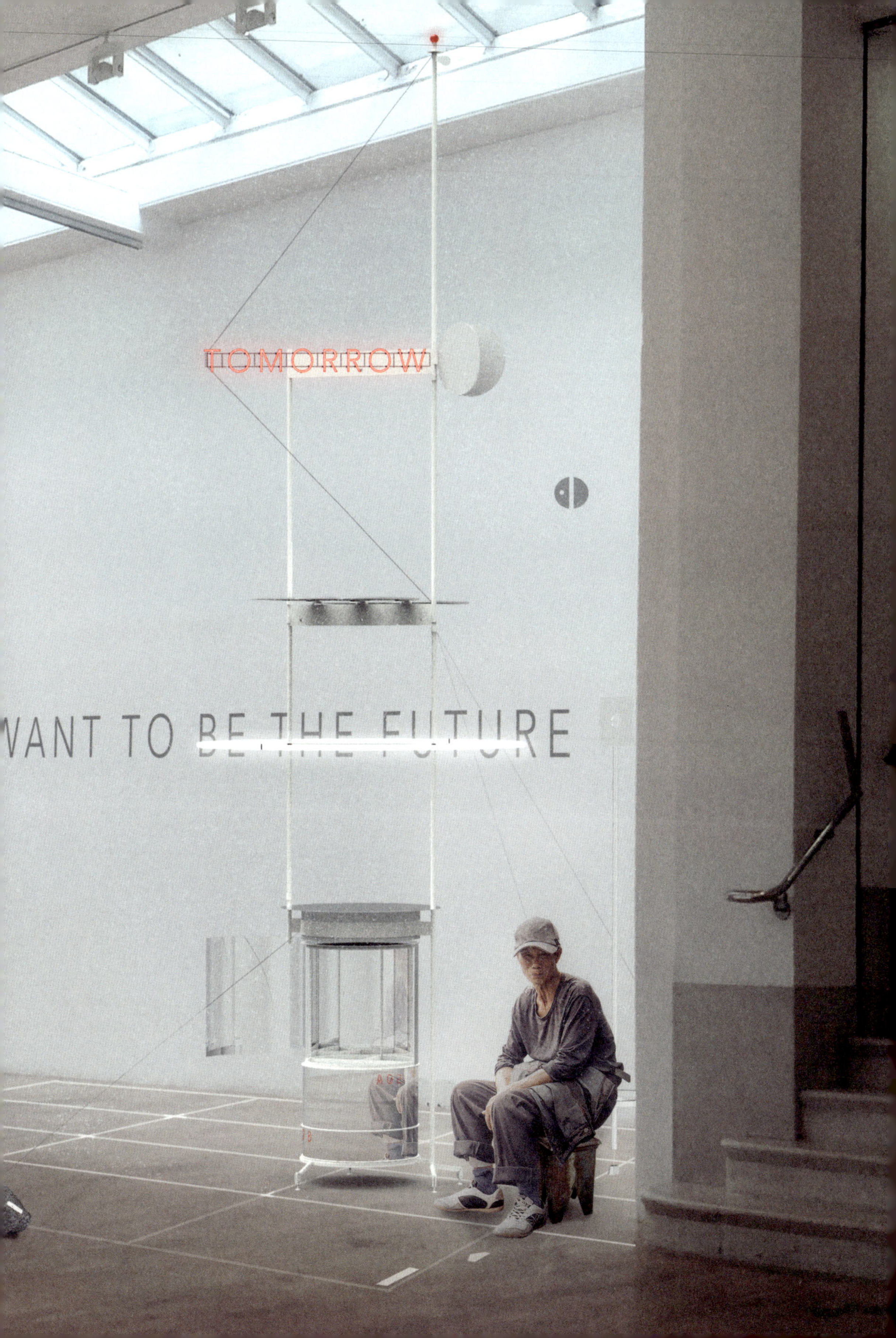

TOMORROW
VANT TO BE THE FUTURE

pp. 62–63
mono office, initial ideas for *I Want to be the Future*, 2018

p. 64
mono office, plan view of 'interaction space', 2019, digital rendering

p. 65
mono office, section view of 'interaction space', 2019, digital rendering

pp. 66–67
Left to right: Zhao Liqun, Miguel Esteban Alonso, Pablo Alfonso Resa Abad (mono office) and Cao Fei, Cao Fei Studio, Beijing, 2018

p. 68
Above: Cao Fei, still from *Whose Utopia*, 2006, video, 19 min 58 sec. Courtesy the artist

Below: Cao Fei, still from *Asia One*, 2018, multimedia installation with three color videos, 60 min 36 sec; 15 min, 29 sec; 13 min, 15 sec; dimensions variable. Courtesy the artist

p. 69
Cao Fei, stills from 11.11, 2018, video, 60 min 36 sec. Courtesy the artist. Commissioned by the Solomon R. Guggenheim Museum, New York for The Robert H. N. Ho Family Foundation Chinese Initiative

pp. 70–71
mono office, design for *I Want to be the Future*, 2019

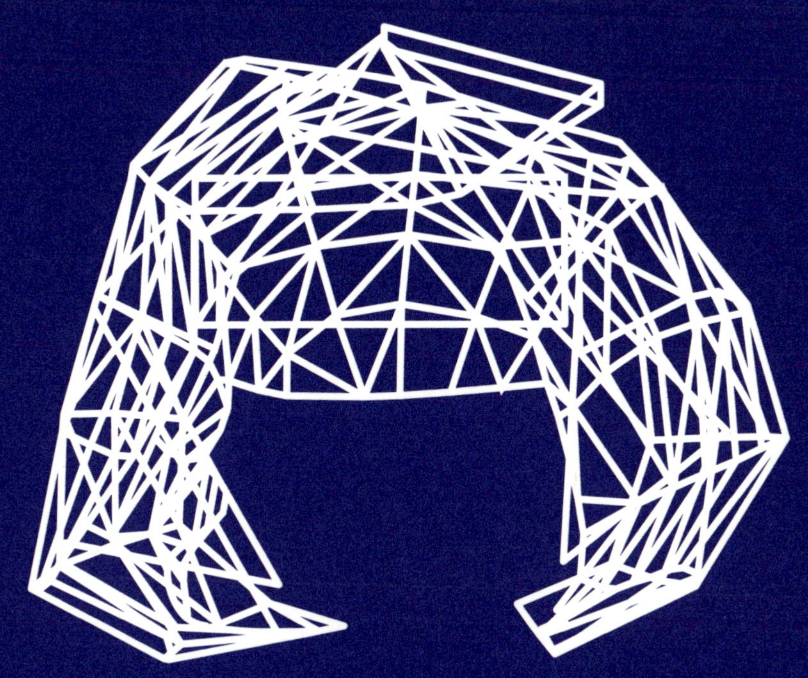

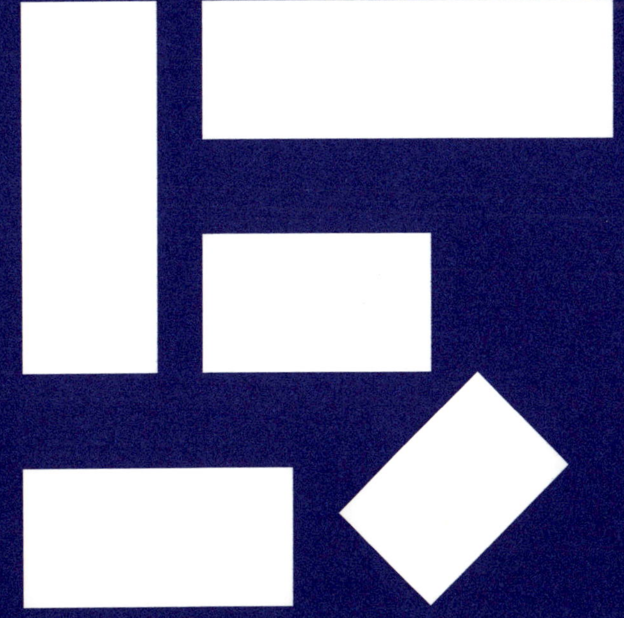

Andrés Jaque / Office for Political Innovation Jacolby Satterwhite

PROJECT TEAM

Alberto Heras
Roberto González García
Paola Pardo-Castillo
Andrés Jaque
Jacolby Satterwhite

Spirits Roaming The Earth

EPISODE I
Designing kind

In 2009, Sarah Jessica Parker and her partner Matthew Broderick released a photograph of themselves with their twin daughters, Marion Loretta and Tabitha Hodge, in their arms. This sweet scene was part of their strategy to counter tabloid descriptions of the twins' surrogate mother, Michelle Ross, as a 'tattooed, bisexual rocker'.[1]

In 2007, Dr John Zhang, the New York-based world leader of *in vitro* fertilisation implemented the three-parent baby technique, Mitochondrial Replacement Therapy, which involves assembling the intended parents' DNA with donated, young, healthy eggs, producing embryos from three people's sex cells.

According to Jennifer Garcia of Extraordinary Conceptions, couples pay twice as much for cells from tall, blond Ivy League donors. 'You can basically make a designer baby nowadays.'[2] The sex cells bank Cryobank developed Look-A-Likes, a service that sorts donors according to their resemblance to male celebrities such as James Franco or Ji Jin-hee.

New Hope screens composed embryos before they are placed in the surrogate uterus in order to eliminate those that might carry conditions such as sickle cell anemia, Tay-Sachs disease, or muscular dystrophy. The pre-implantation genetic screening makes selecting the embryo's gender possible.

At an average cost of $150,000, gender selection, combined with *in vitro* fertilisation and overseas surrogacy, has become part of an increasingly popular scheme among affluent couples worldwide to design human genetics and the placement of embryos in order to reduce future uncertainty, gain transnational citizenship and style their children as transcontinentally seductive.

'Dr Zhang, why did you place your office in the corner where you can see Columbus Circle?'. 'New York City definitely is one of the centres of the world and I think Columbus Circle, with the Times Warner Center next to us, is the centre of the centre. That is why we are here.'[3]

1 Daily Mail Reporter, 'Pictured: The tattooed, bisexual rocker who is pregnant with Sarah Jessica Parker's twins', *Mail Online,* 8 May 2009.

2 Alexandra Harney, 'Wealthy Chinese seek US surrogates for 2nd child, green card', *Reuters,* 22 September 2013.

3 Dr John Zhang recorded in conversation with Andrés Jaque, September 2017.

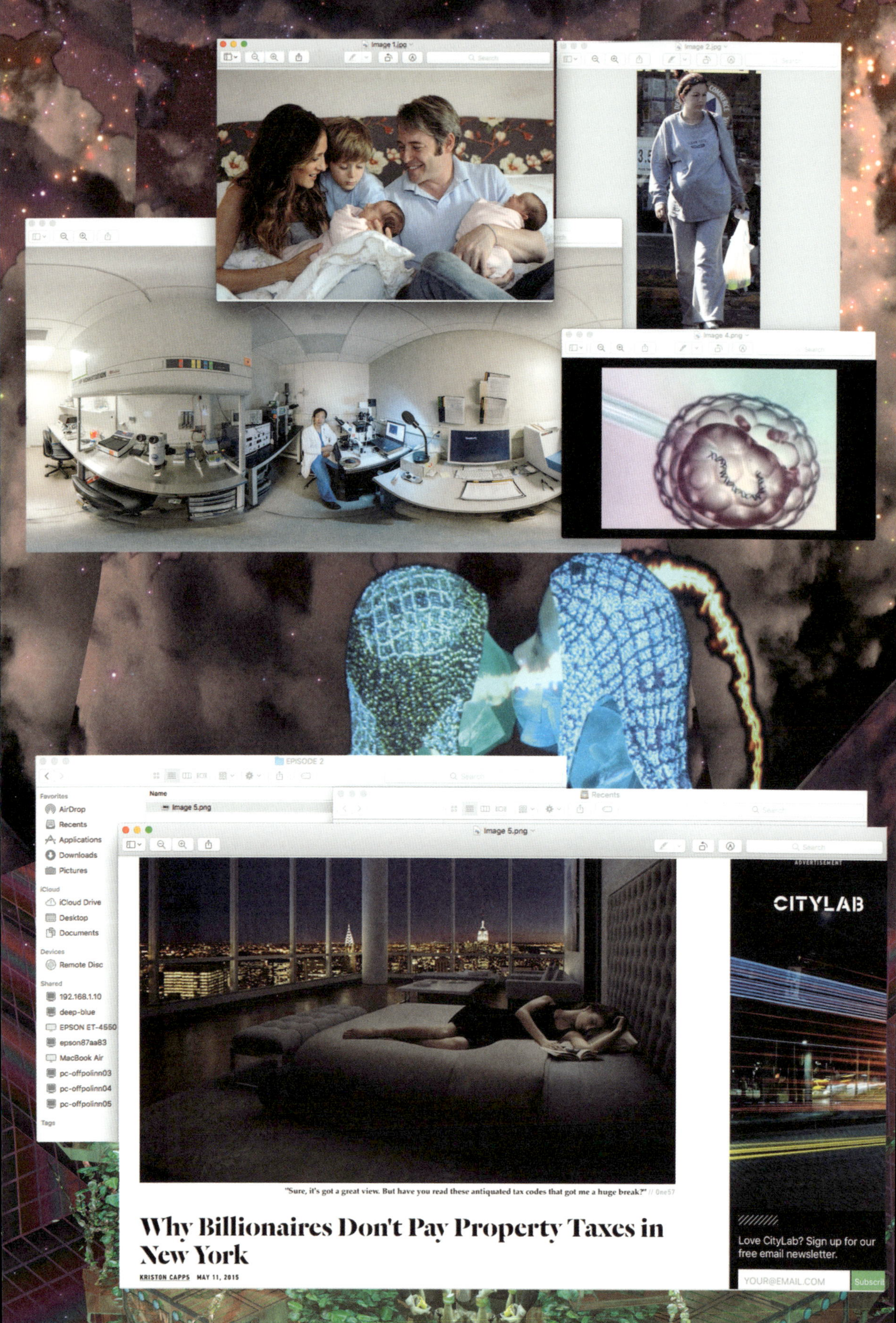

Image 1.jpg
Image 2.jpg
Image 4.png
EPISODE 2
Favorites
AirDrop
Recents
Applications
Downloads
Pictures
iCloud
iCloud Drive
Desktop
Documents
Devices
Remote Disc
Shared
192.168.1.10
deep-blue
EPSON ET-4550
epson87aa83
MacBook Air
pc-offpolinn03
pc-offpolinn04
pc-offpolinn05
Tags
Name
Image 5.png
Recents
Image 5.png
"Sure, it's got a great view. But have you read these antiquated tax codes that got me a huge break?"
Why Billionaires Don't Pay Property Taxes in New York
KRISTON CAPPS MAY 11, 2015
CITYLAB
Love CityLab? Sign up for our free email newsletter.
YOUR@EMAIL.COM

EPISODE II
Billionaires as godsends

The Time Warner Center opened in 2003, two years after Michael Bloomberg was elected mayor of New York City. At that time, a new interpretation of air rights law came into being. Air rights between lots with at least a ten-foot adjacency could be traded, which enabled The Related Companies, a real-estate firm, and Apollo Real Estate Advisors to replace a zoning-permitted twenty-six-storey building with a seventy-five-storey compound. 57% of the condominiums in Bloomberg Tower were bought through LLC shell companies. In 2013, Bloomberg stated: 'If we could get every billionaire around the world to move here, it would be a godsend.'[4]

This air-rights trading was combined with the use of limited-liability companies in New York as shell companies to hide the identity of real estate owners, and with the 1971 421-a New York exemption programme that reduced the tax imposition of top-priced apartments to 1/100 of the average New York property-tax payment. All three of these were enacted and coordinated by a newly coined architectural invention: the high-end tower, such as the Time Warner Center and Bloomberg Tower. These high-end towers have not only attracted, but have actually established a new body and transnational regime: HIGHENDCRACY, based on the decoupling of demarcations where fortune concentrates and the geo-political zone that sustains them.

EPISODE III
Apartments replace gay clubs

In 2015, the West Village's Westway Club closed, to be replaced by condominiums. Savyon Zabar, owner of the Latino club La Escuelita, claimed that his club had been shut down after forty-five years because 'minorities did not fit into the gentrification plans of the city'.[5] In 2016, the apartment towers of Chelsea, East Harlem and Greenpoint, with their floor-to-ceiling-glassed apartments, were Grindr users' favourite locations to meet lovers worldwide.

Historic 1980s and 90s match-making disco venues, such as La Escuelita, were replaced by apartment towers, just as smoky, lofty, night interiors were replaced by open-plan apartments as the number-one desired architecture for love. These gentrified

4 Michael Howard Saul, 'Mayor Says More Billionaires Would Ease City's Economic Situation', *Wall Street Journal*, 20 September 2013.

5 'Drag-out court fight over liquor license', *New York Daily News*, 4 January 2012.

parts of the city have attracted investment while at the same time becoming a laboratory for online-mediated romance.

EPISODE IV
Snowden and the CockyBoys

In 2013, the same year that Bloomberg stated New York's adoption of the new regime of LLC-encrypted HIGHENDCRACY, Edward Snowden disclosed more that 50,000 files on massive surveillance programmes run by the US National Security Agency and the Five Eyes intelligence alliance. He found shelter in room 1014 of Hong Kong's The Mira hotel. In the coverage that artist and filmmaker Laura Poitras and lawyer, journalist, civil rights blogger and media consultant Glenn Greenwald made of Snowden's seclusion, one can see how he kept the curtains of his floor-to-ceiling-windowed room drawn to avoid being spotted. New York is not a city, but a relational enactment where activist disclosure, encryption-based properties and pornography are in dialogue.

In 2002, gay porn star Jake Jaxson asked Glenn Greenwald, 'What do you hope to accomplish?' His answer: 'To change the world.'[6] In 2002, Jaxson offered Greenwald a partnership in Master Notions Inc., an online street and viral marketing company that ended up making CockyBoys the most successful gay porn platform, and which sexualised New York condo windows. Breaking from adult films' avoidance of window backlighting, CockyBoys' photography director R.J. Sebastian's cinematography brought sex to impressive apartment windows, where young models have sex suspended in New York's clear sky, framed by refined architectural interiors with catchy artworks.

EPISODE V
Blue skies and windows getting involved

In 2006, John Heilemann wrote in *New York Magazine*: 'In the past few years, architecture has become the sexiest of arts and DBOX are its pornographers.' Even though most people identify Rafael Viñoly and Deborah Berke as the architects of 432 Park Avenue, DBOX was the communications agency that was hired in 2012 by CIM Group and Macklowe Properties to deal with the most relevant part of the building's design: inventing the way in which the social ecosystem of the tower would be imagined and desired.

In 2013, as part of the tower's promotional campaign, a full-colour *432 Park Avenue* magazine was placed, together with Dior's

6 Jerry Portwood, 'Glenn Greenwald's Friend and Former Business Partner Defends Him', *Out*, 3 July 2013.

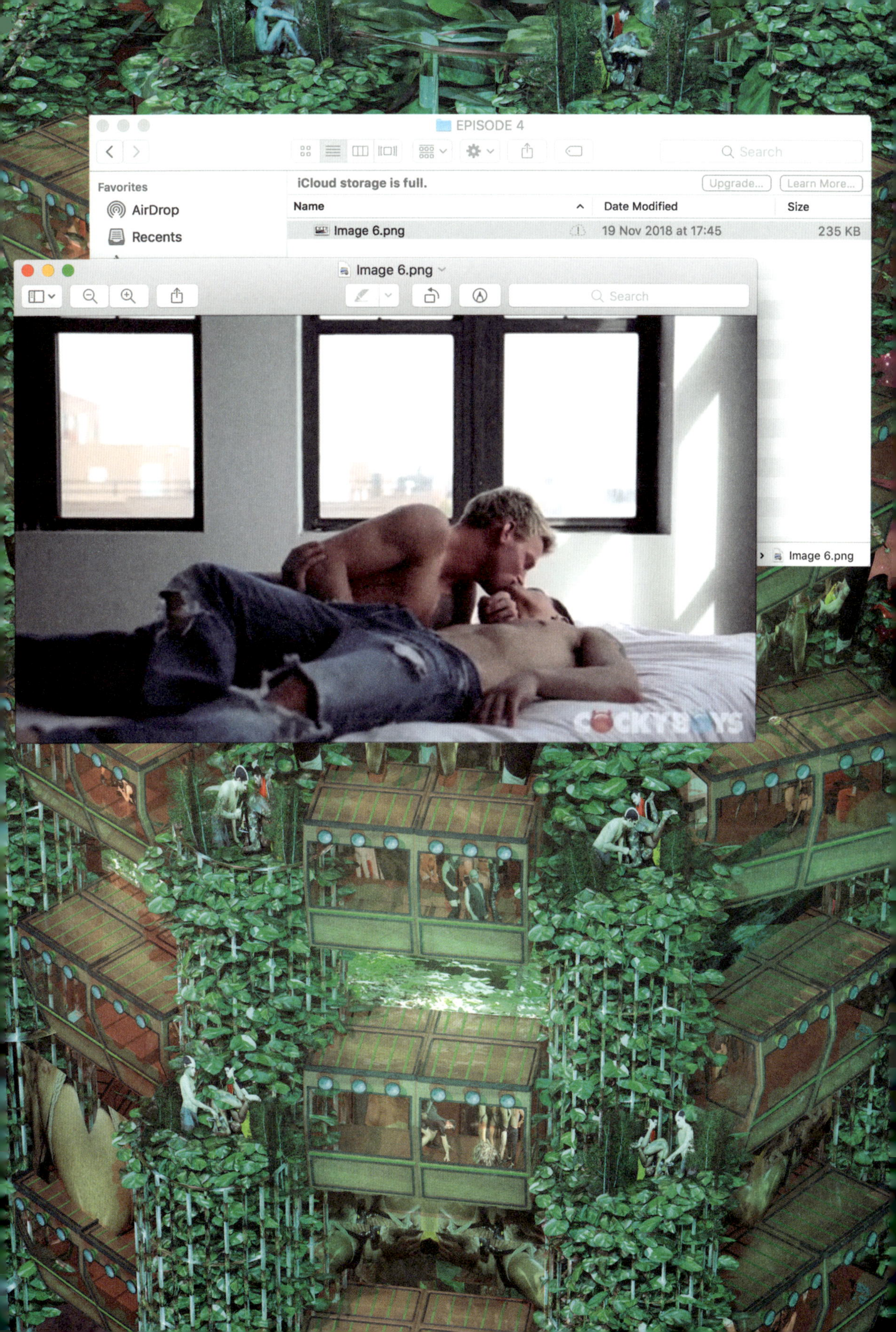
EPISODE 4
Search
Favorites
AirDrop
Recents
iCloud storage is full.
Upgrade...
Learn More...
Name
Date Modified
Size
Image 6.png
19 Nov 2018 at 17:45
235 KB
Image 6.png
Search
Image 6.png

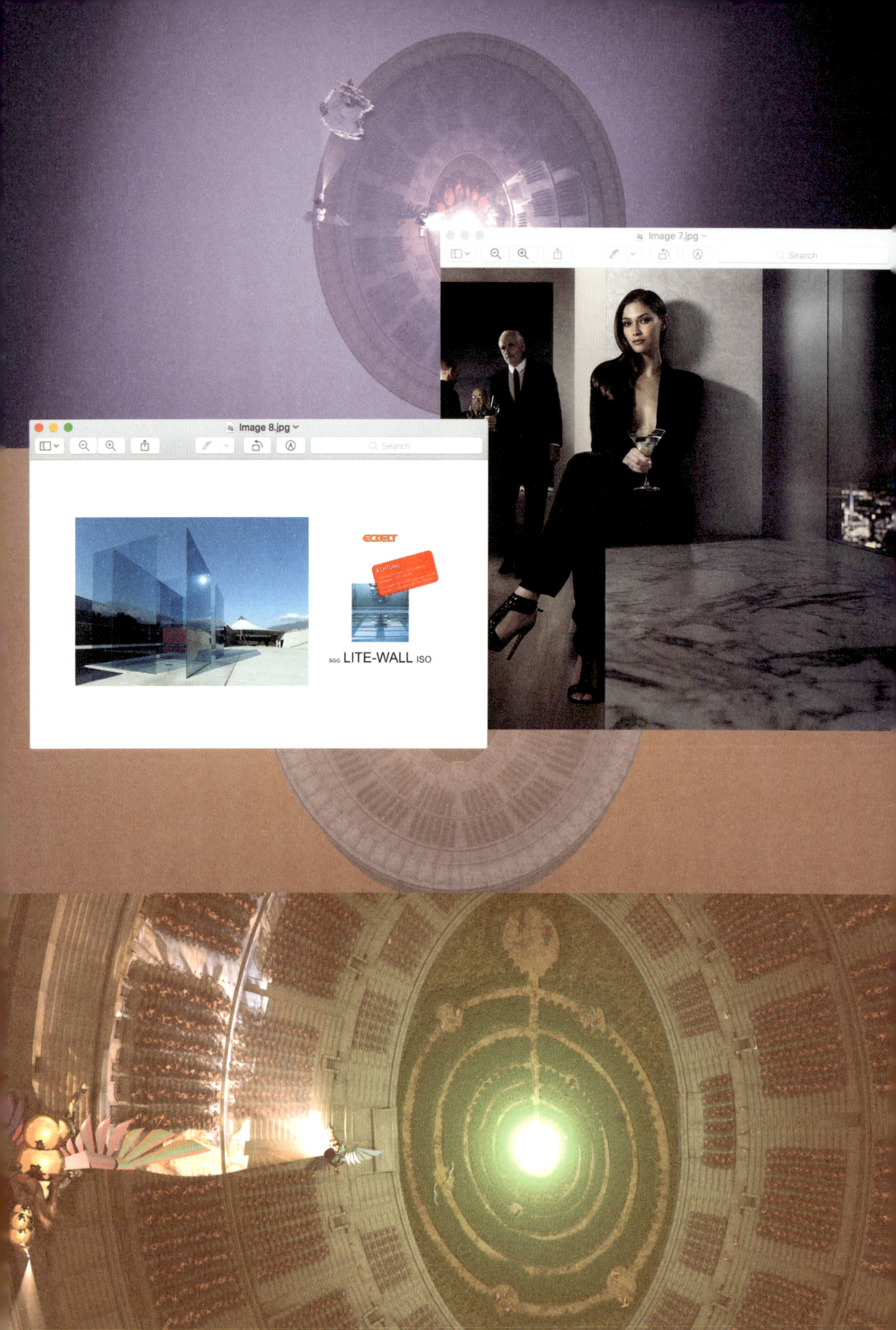
Image 7.jpg
Search
Image 8.jpg
Search
ECKELT
ACHTUNG!
SGG LITE-WALL ISO

catalogue, on the desk of each room at the Ritz-Carlton Hotel in Moscow. On its cover, Austrian ballet dancer Vik Tory posed elegantly in a digital 3D model of 432's 10 × 10 foot window frame.

The magazine's interior recreates the story of a cool, affluent, middle-aged heterosexual couple, together with their two slender children, entertaining for dinner a chubby businessman in a 432 apartment. Whereas the family members are performed by professional models, the chubby guy is a real businessman from New Jersey, a close friend of DBOX's CEO Matthew Bannister. He is a character whom the DBOX team call the 'Danny DeVito Guy' and who was meant to make the story more relatable to potential investors who might find themselves opening the 432 magazine during a bout of insomnia at the hotel. The 2016 *Sports Illustrated* bathing suit model Christina Makowski, sitting in the window frame, seduces the businessman while wearing a respectable version (designed by Armani) of Kim Kardashian's famous Lanvin shirtless suit.

Developer Harry Macklowe claims to be the inventor of the term 'helicopter views' to refer to the kind of distant views only unique apartment towers, tall enough to stand above the urban fabric, can provide.

The most expensive component of 432 Park Avenue is not its structure, nor its finishing, nor its services, but its glass. An Austrian-made Eckelt Lite-Wall glass covers the building's 2,136 10 × 10 foot fixed windows designed to polarise natural light and thus intensify the blue part of the daylight colour spectrum. Windows are fixed and not openable, so that the artificial spectrum they provide cannot be discovered by the people inside. The windows are a high-cost and accurate material adjustment that synchronises the architectural detailing of the tower with the city's territorial project of displacing its consumption's environmental cost to rural locations in neighbouring states.

EPISODE VI
Displacing pollution

In June 2012, the New York City Department of Environmental Protection announced a $100 million plan to convert New York oil-based heating infrastructures to natural gas. The New York City Clean Heat programme dropped the city's sulphur dioxide level by 68%, its nitric oxide levels by 24%, nitrogen dioxide by 21% and particulate matter by 16%.

It is nitrogen dioxide that renders skies into gradients of yellow to brown. Its progressive disappearance from New York skies scales up to a territorial dimension of what DBOX renderings and 432 Park Avenue Lite-Wall glass anticipated. Sex, sex cells, billions of dollars and blue skies are all coordinately redistributed by means of architectural adjustments and technologies to segregate newly produced social types and newly produced subjectivities.

Since 2010, based on severe concerns for public health, fracking has been fully banned in New York State. Paradoxically, following that moment, the percentage of energy consumed in New York fuelled by natural gas has continued to grow, now reaching an increase of 50%. It is not extracted in New York, but elsewhere, mainly in Pennsylvania.

Since 2010, the volume of natural gas extracted in Pennsylvania has multiplied by ten. With 9,775 active unconventional wells operating in the Marcellus Shale, the state now extracts an annual volume of 5,313,258 million cubic feet of natural gas. In 2015, Pennsylvania Department of Environmental Protection issued an air quality alert in Susquehanna Valley.

As air quality in New York has increased since 2012, it has decreased in Pennsylvania: nitrogen dioxide levels increased by 20%, sulphur dioxide levels by 30%, and fine particulate matter by 56%.

EPISODE VII
Fracking Susquehanna. The architecture of ghost houses confronted by gardens for activism

Vera Scroggins become the best-known anti-fracking activist when she started the Yahoo group, Citizens For Clean Water, in 2001. She has intensively documented and broadcast from her YouTube channel the violations operated by her neighbouring fracking industry. During the initial four months of her first injunction, she was banned from accessing all land where mineral rights had been leased to Cabot Oil & Gas Corporation, which constituted 40% of Susquehanna County's public space. Nowadays, she is not allowed to get closer than 100 feet from any Cabot facility.

Together with an extensive network of associated activists, she has composed a complex heterogeneous archive of fracking-related evidence that she preserves in piles around her home. This independent use of available technologies provides collective accountability to the most invisible actor in this story: namely, Susquehanna's disputed undergrounds. But are they really so invisible? Are they equally invisible to everyone?

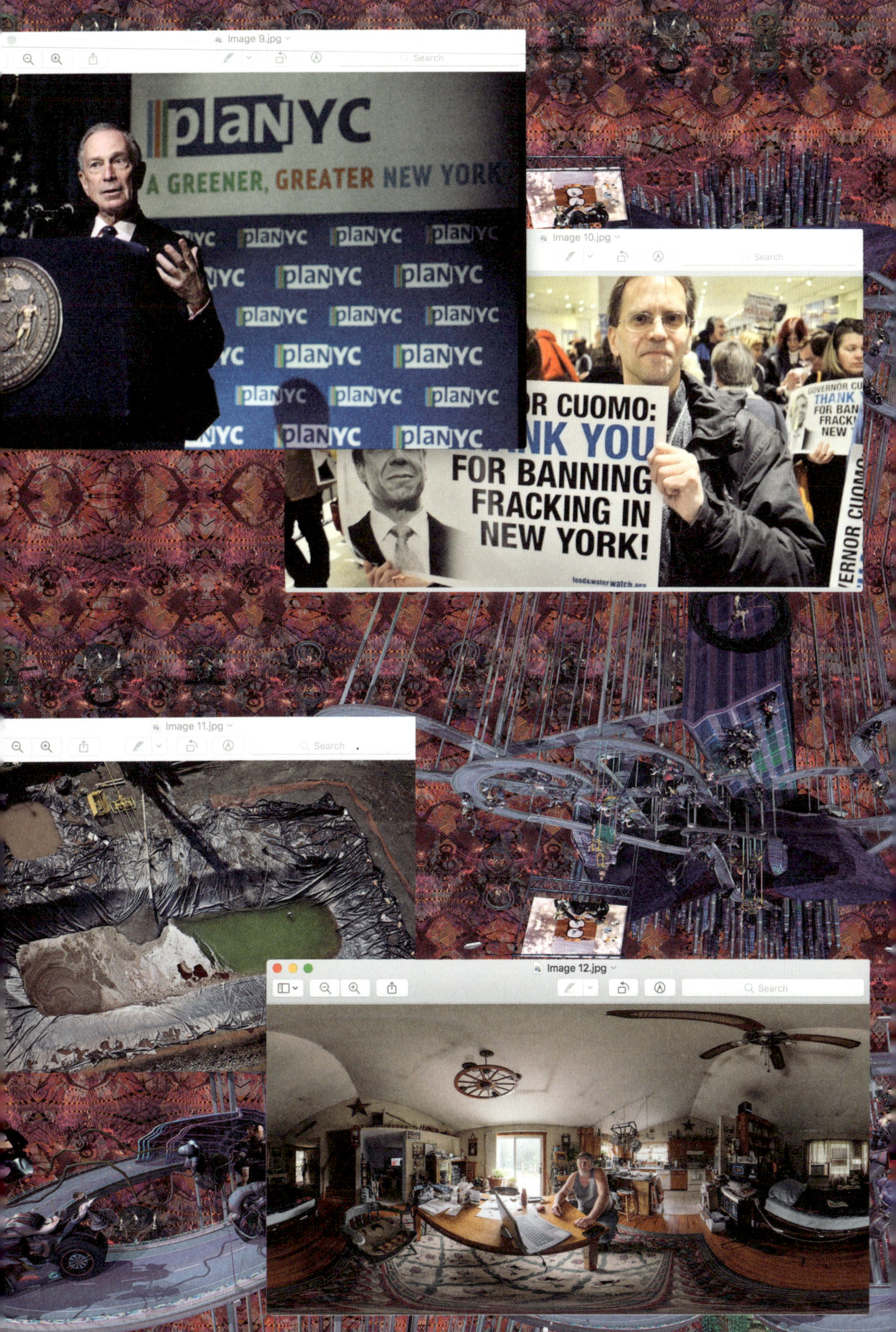
Image 9.jpg
planYC
A GREENER, GREATER NEW YORK
Image 10.jpg
R CUOMO:
NK YOU
FOR BANNING
FRACKING IN
NEW YORK!
foodandwaterwatch.org
Image 11.jpg
Image 12.jpg

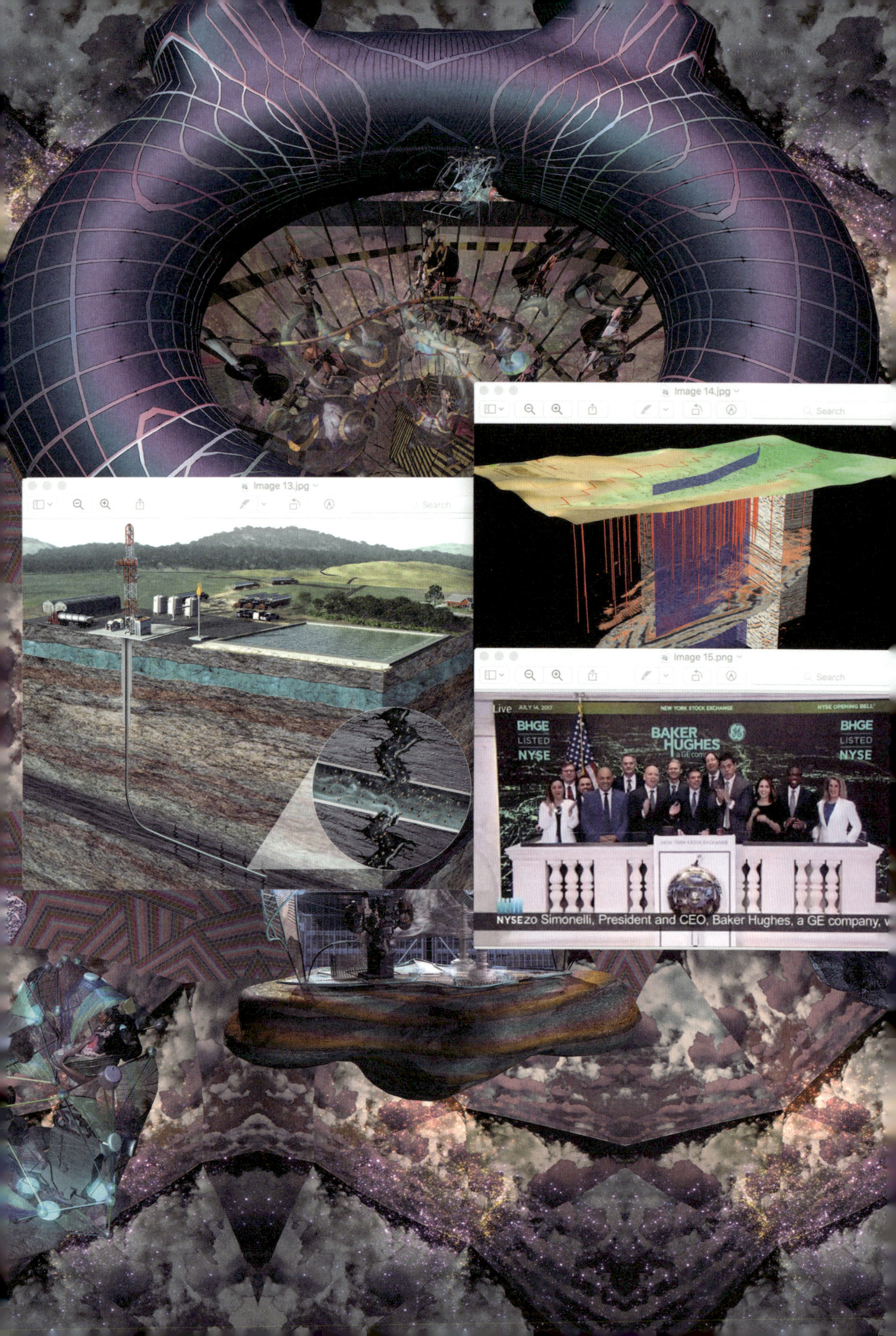

Image 14.jpg
Search
Image 13.jpg
Search
Image 15.png
Search
Live
JULY 14, 2017
NEW YORK STOCK EXCHANGE
NYSE OPENING BELL
BHGE
LISTED
NYSE
BAKER HUGHES
BHGE
LISTED
NYSE
NYSE zo Simonelli, President and CEO, Baker Hughes, a GE company,

EPISODE VIII

The techno-consolidation of the underground as a multimedia asset. From the Halliburton era to Baker Hughes

6 June 1998 was the day when the first episode of *Sex and the City* was broadcast in the US. That was precisely the time when the first 'land-men', agents trained to trade mineral rights leasing agreements with individual property owners, arrived in Susquehanna County. They would mainly act as individual brokers, and would later transfer their agreements to larger agencies, and so on, until the small and fragmented tissue of divided lots in the surface would progressively be consolidated as a large underground mineral property concentration.

Between 1990 and 2008, the stock price of Halliburton's oil and gas field competitor Baker Hughes tripled. It was the effect of the commercialisation of AutoTrak, a rotary steerable drilling system that pioneered the directional drilling tool that prompted the rapid expansion of fracking. The system enabled control of the angle of the drilling bit, bringing new levels of accuracy to the transition from vertical to horizontal well drilling.

In 1992, Baker Hughes purchased Teleco Oilfield Services Inc, a company dedicated to developing sensing Measurement-While-Drilling technologies, since the 1970s. Together, they developed a new generation of tri-cone bits that included a triple combo of sensors, which would transform the bits into a digital sensing device. Along with the Californian company Dynamic Graphics Inc., they developed the digital platforms CoViz 4D, a software to produce quantitative visualisation platforms of time-variant geospatial data. This 4D reconstruction of the consolidated mineral regions produced from the integration of big data, collected while drilling by the triple combo of sensors installed in the tri-cones drilling bits, turned gas into a new asset for liberal trading.

pp. 76, 79–80, 83–84
Foreground: Andrés Jaque / Office for Political Innovation, digital collages of found media images, 2018

Background: Jacolby Satterwhite, digital compositions, 2018

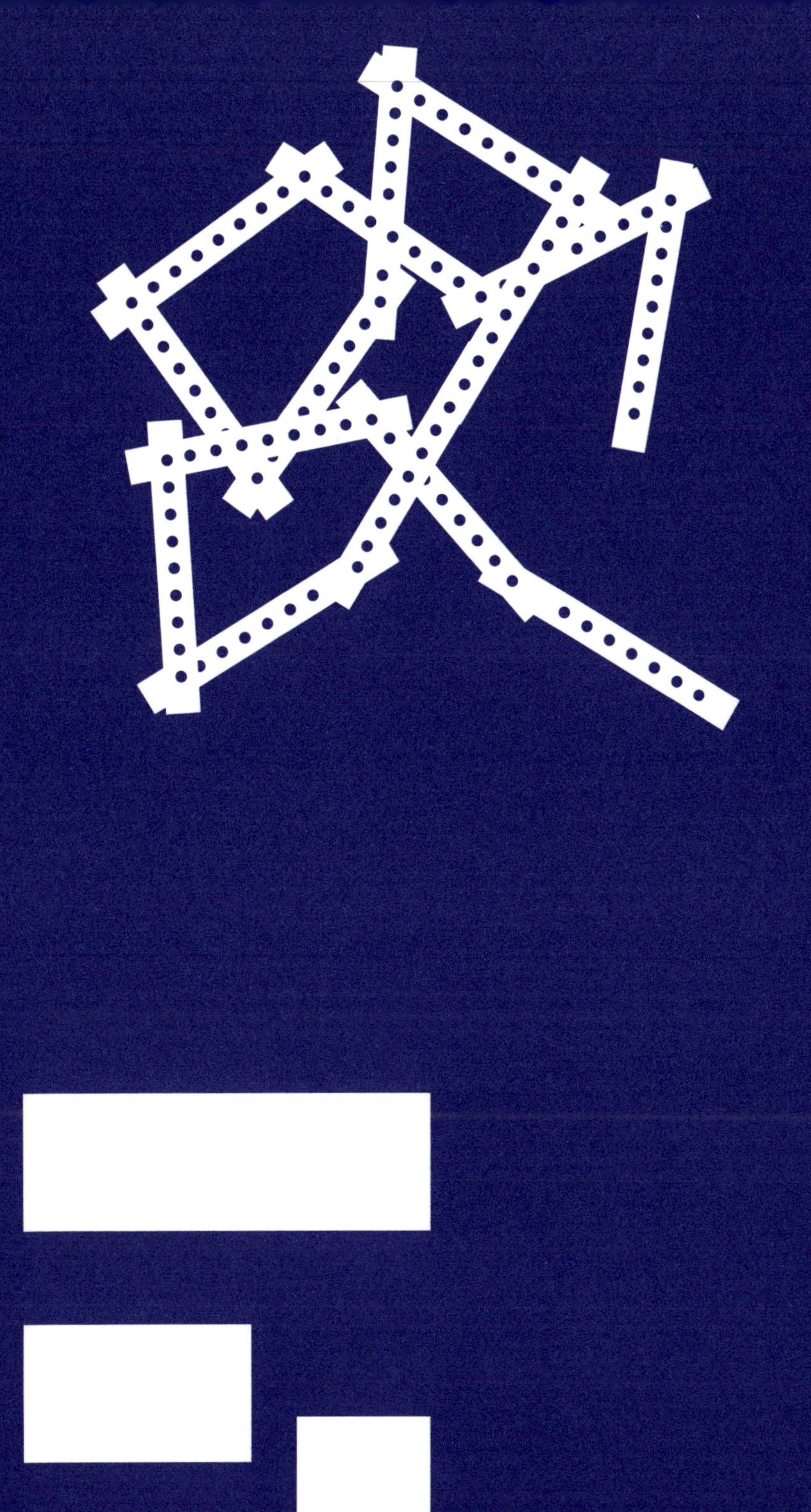

Mariana Castillo Deball
Tatiana Bilbao Estudio

PROJECT TEAM

Tatiana Bilbao
Alba Cortes
Mariana Castillo Deball
Sophie de Saint Phalle
Paulina Sevilla

Mind Garden, Heart Garden

To measure – whether distance or time – is to develop a material engagement with the world that is at once emotional and conceptual.

Mind Garden, Heart Garden is a reflection on our approach to time and space. It is a collaboration that brings together Mariana Castillo Deball's sculptural work on the Mesoamerican calendar, Tōnalpōhualli, with Tatiana Bilbao's *Ways of Life* project. *Mind Garden, Heart Garden* expands on how spaces are designed for living based on conviviality and shared activities, rather than on conventional living standards.

Spatial measurements in ancient Mesoamerica were based on the human scale. The most common measure was a 'heart', the distance from the middle of the chest to the outstretched fingertip. The measuring device used in agriculture and construction is called *octacatl*, which equals three hearts: 270 cm.

The Four Directions of the Universe depicted on the first page of the sacred Aztec document, the Codex Fejérváry-Mayer, represents a Tōnalpōhualli or count of the days. This ritual calendar presents 260 days formed by a combination of twenty names of days (*veintenas*) and thirteen numbers of days (*trecenas*). Each space coordinate refers to a colour: East – red, North – yellow, West – green and South – blue.

In *Mind Garden, Heart Garden*, the calendar of 260 days is transformed into twenty metal strips, each measuring three hearts. Every strip contains thirteen perforations, corresponding to a day in the calendar. The colours refer to spatial coordinates. The full sculptural intervention corresponds to a year, and this year provides a space of encounter between the individual and collective time-spaces.

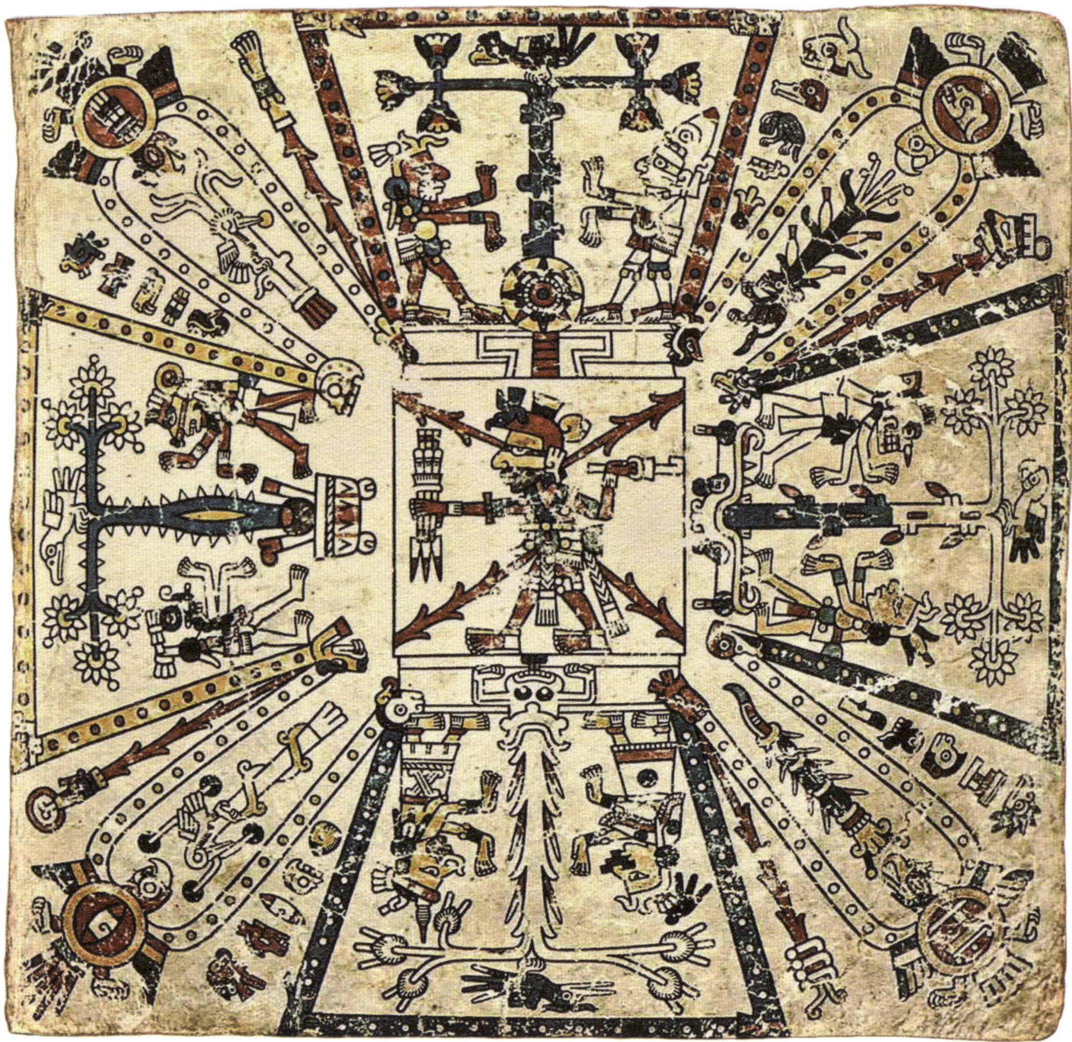

1

1 The four directions of the universe depicted on the first page of the Codex Fejérváry-Mayer (AD 1200–1521), represents a Tōnalpōhualli or count of the days, a ritual calendar of 260 days formed by the combination of twenty names of days (*veintenas*) and thirteen numbers of days (*trecenas*).
2 Each space coordinate refers to a colour: East – red, North – yellow, West – green and South – blue.
3 Tōnalpōhualli Size-Time units.

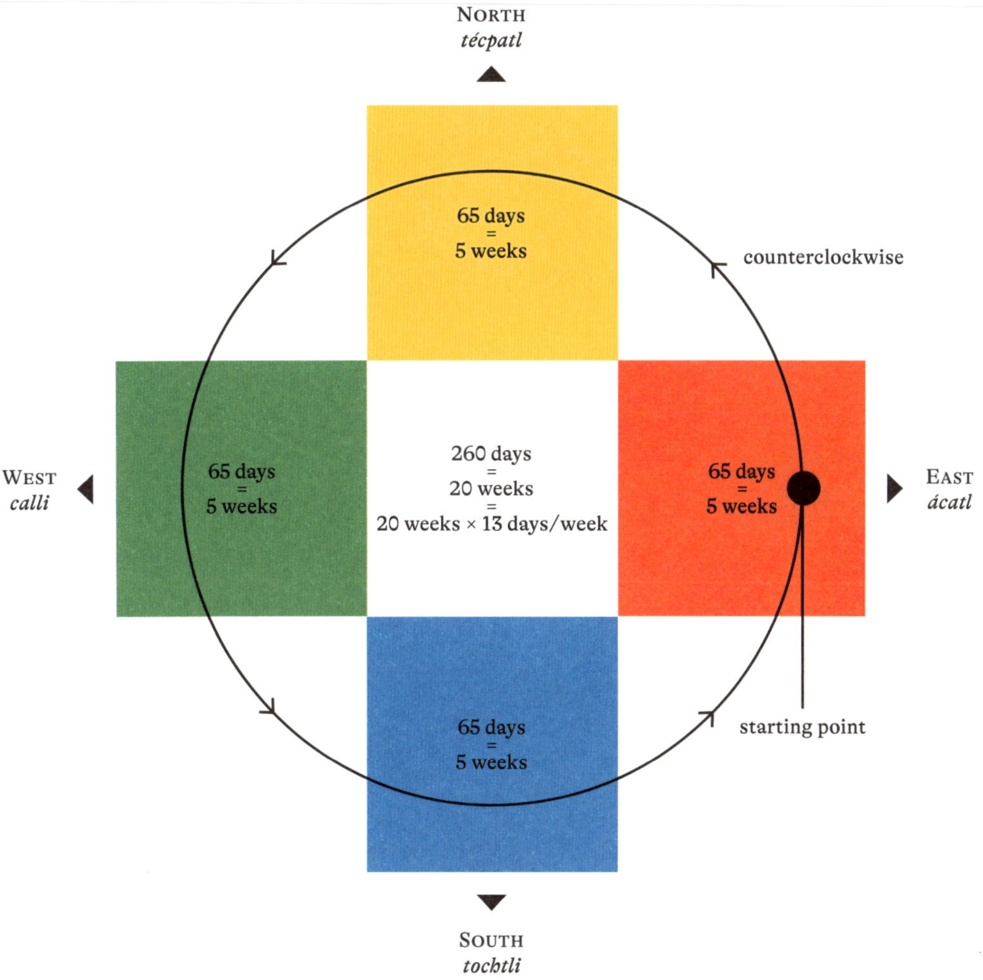

NORTH
técpatl

65 days = 5 weeks

counterclockwise

WEST
calli

65 days = 5 weeks

260 days = 20 weeks = 20 weeks × 13 days/week

65 days = 5 weeks

EAST
ácatl

starting point

65 days = 5 weeks

SOUTH
tochtli

2

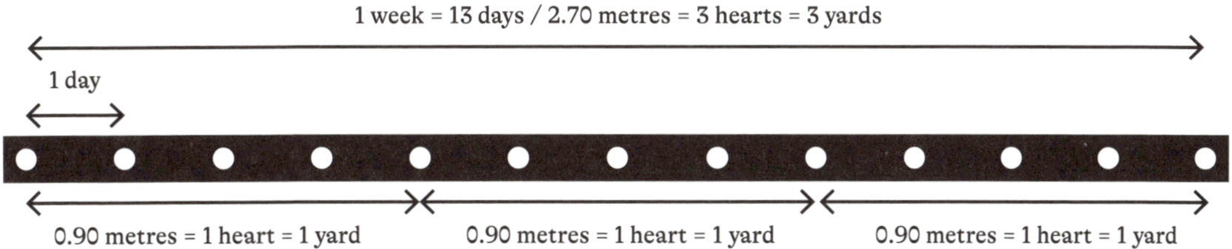

3

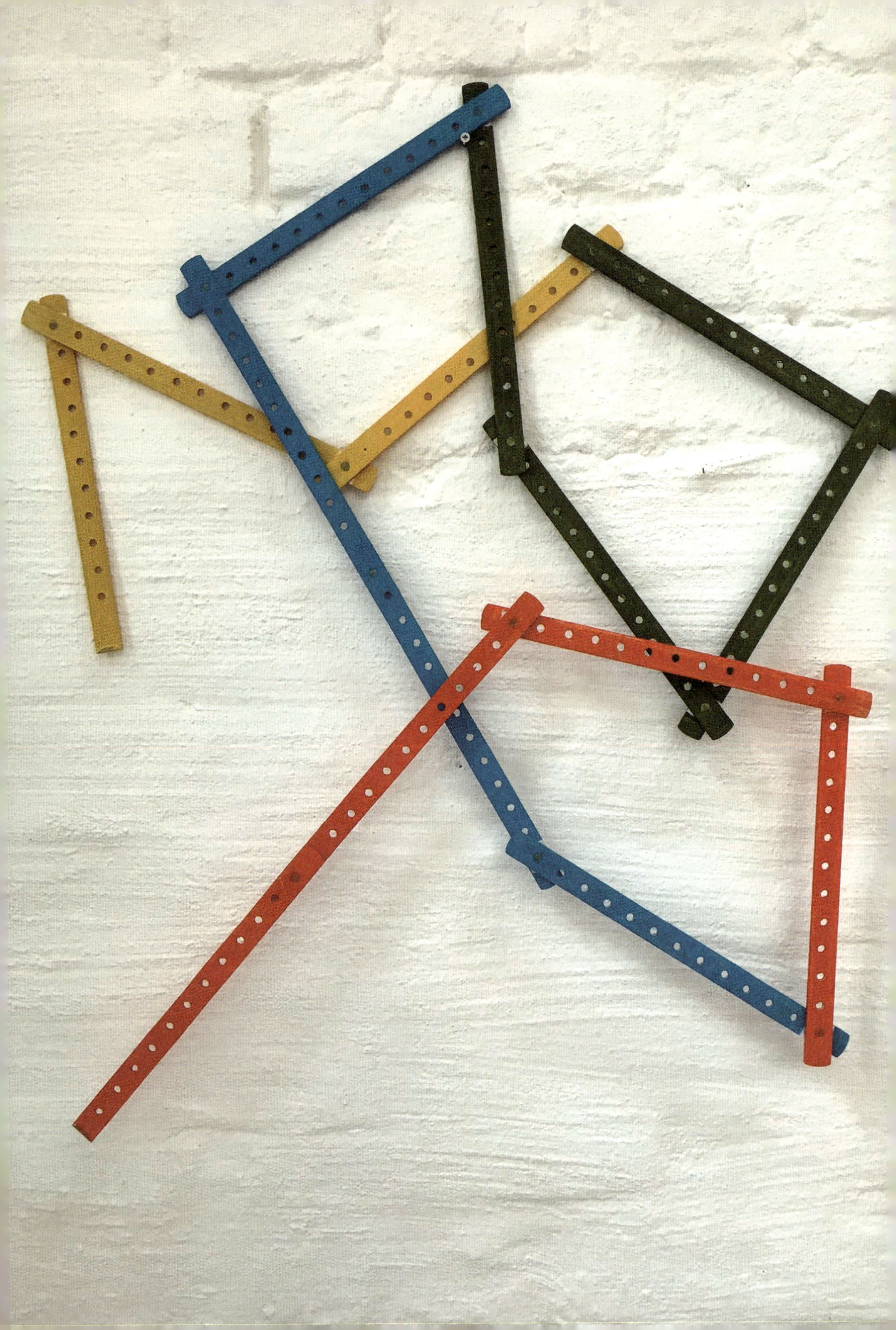

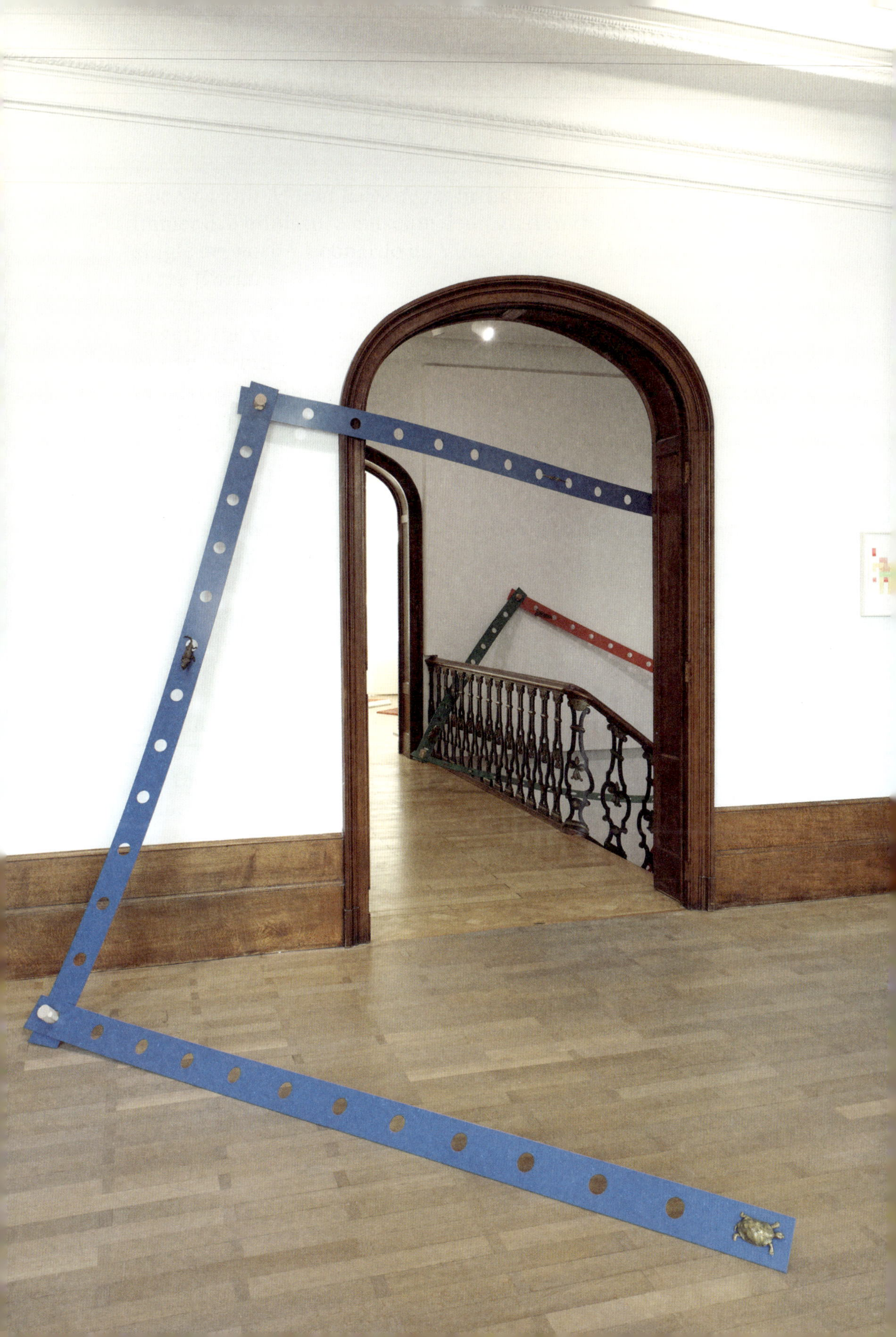

CONCEPT

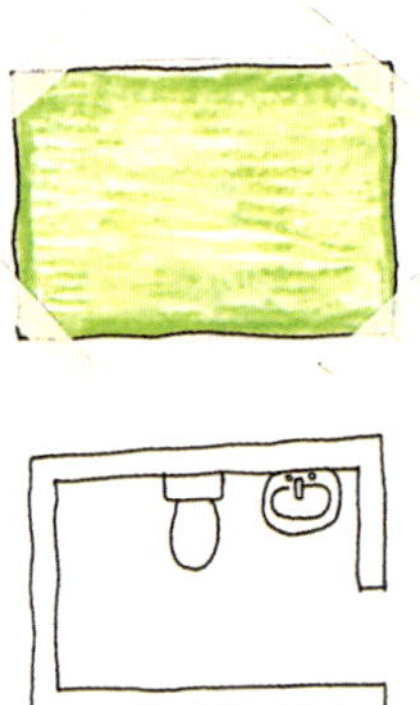

ONE UNIT
Individual and intimate spaces: with more individuality there is less time and less space.

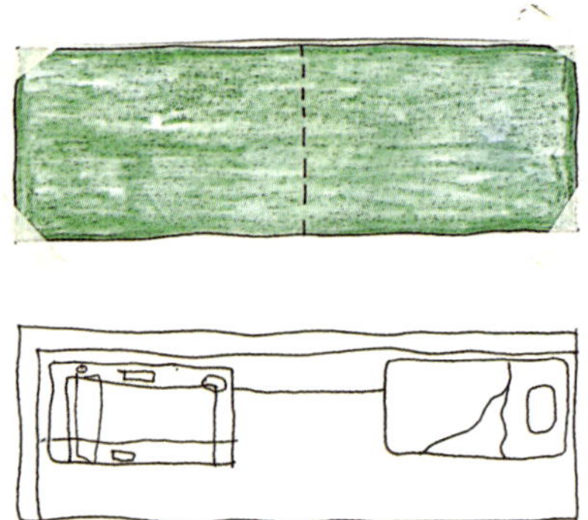

TWO UNITS
Sleep: semi-individual spaces.

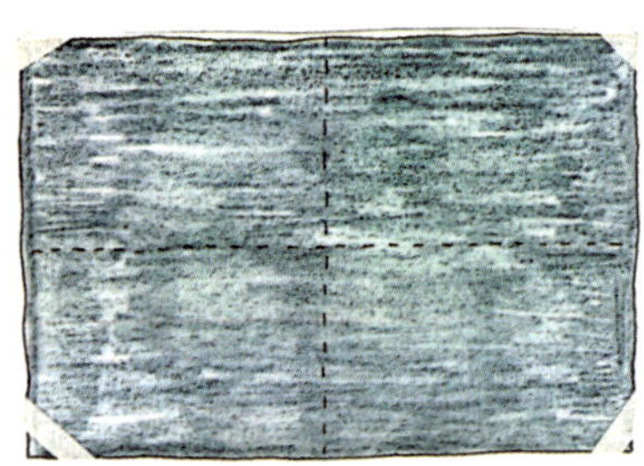

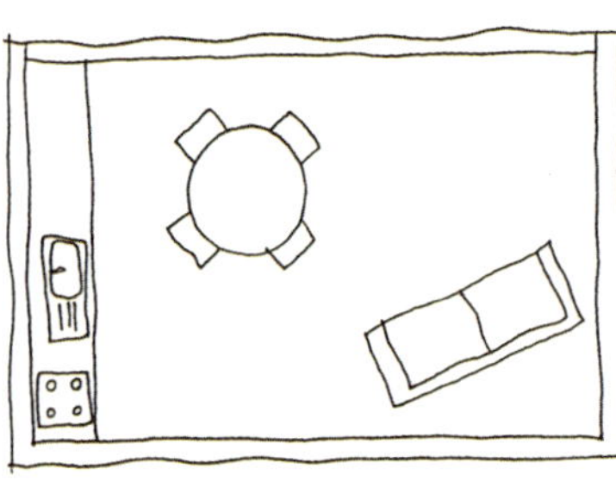

THREE UNITS
Kitchen / dining / living room: semi-individual spaces transformed according to user needs and temporality.

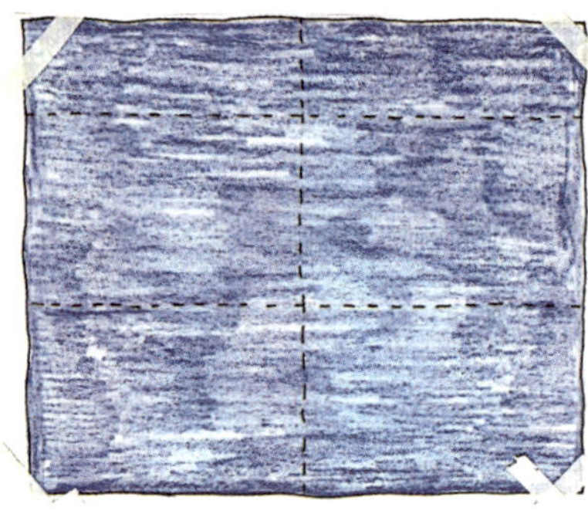

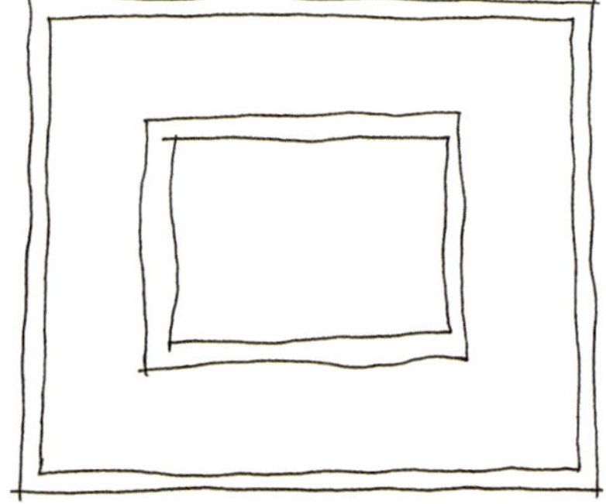

FOUR UNITS
Community spaces: connection spaces in between neighbours. They are the biggest spaces and users spend more time living in them.

CONCEPT

30 m2
5.40 m / 65 days
5.50 m.
5.40 m / 65 days
1 week
13 days
35 days
1.01
5.50

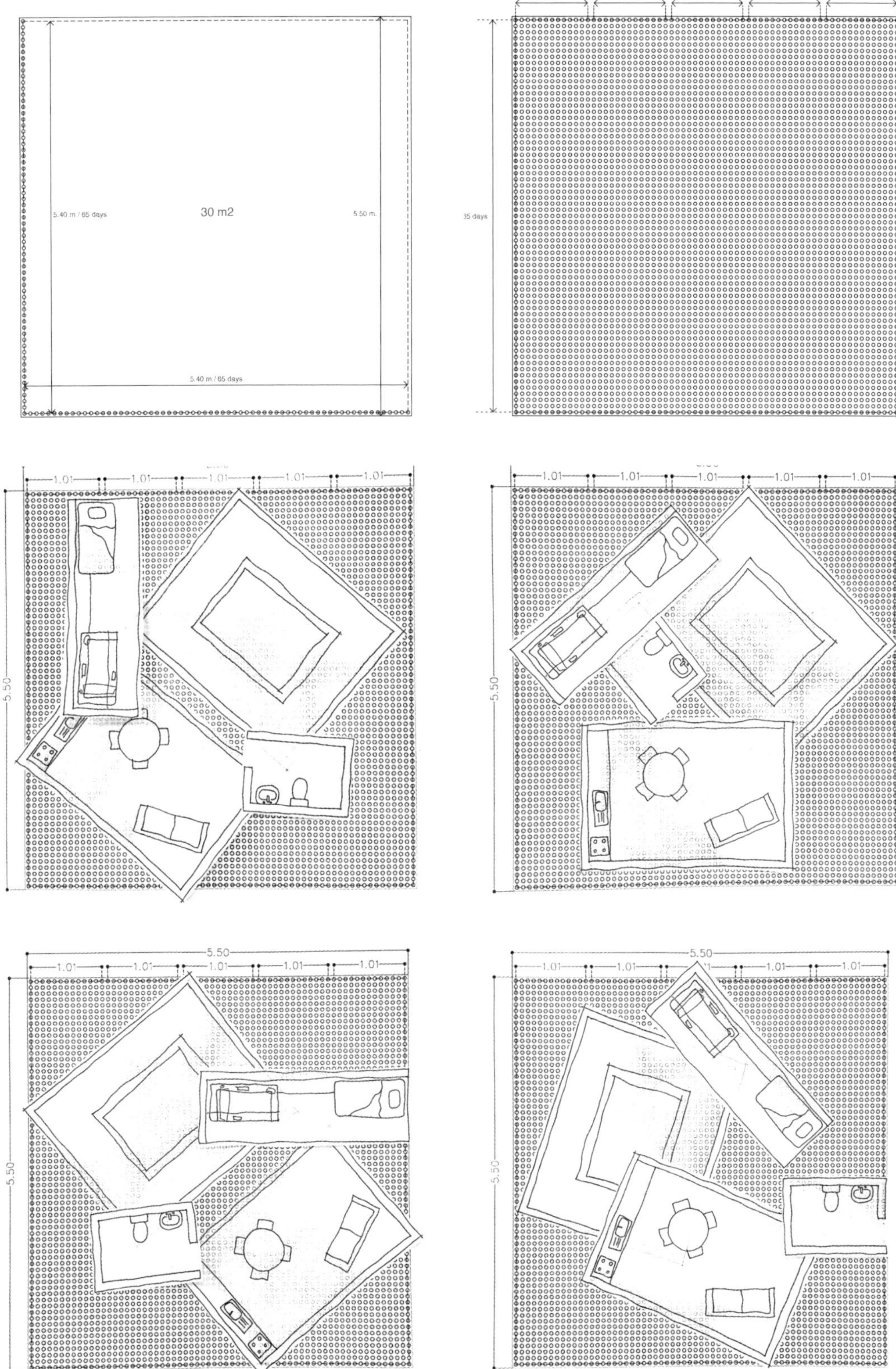

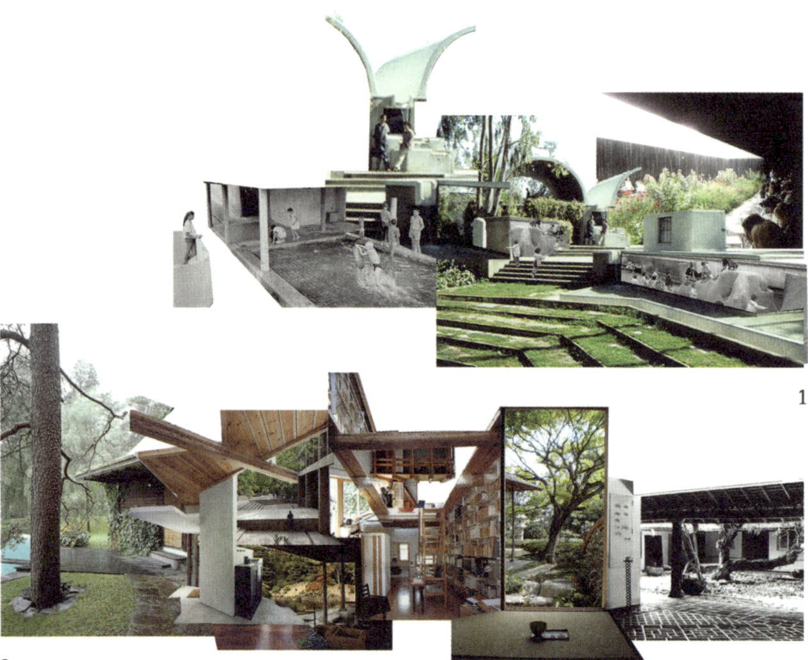

1

2

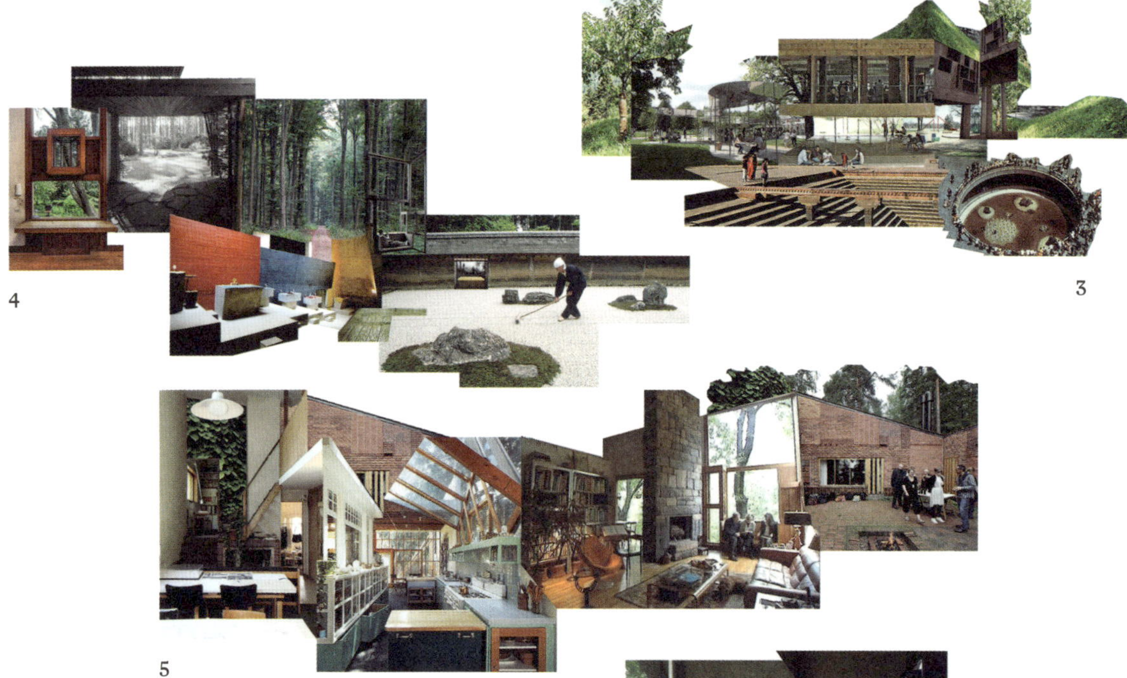

3

4

5

6

1 Individual spaces
2 Semi-individual spaces
3 Gathering spaces
4 Collective spaces
5 Family spaces
6 Temporary spaces

WAYS / EMOTIONS

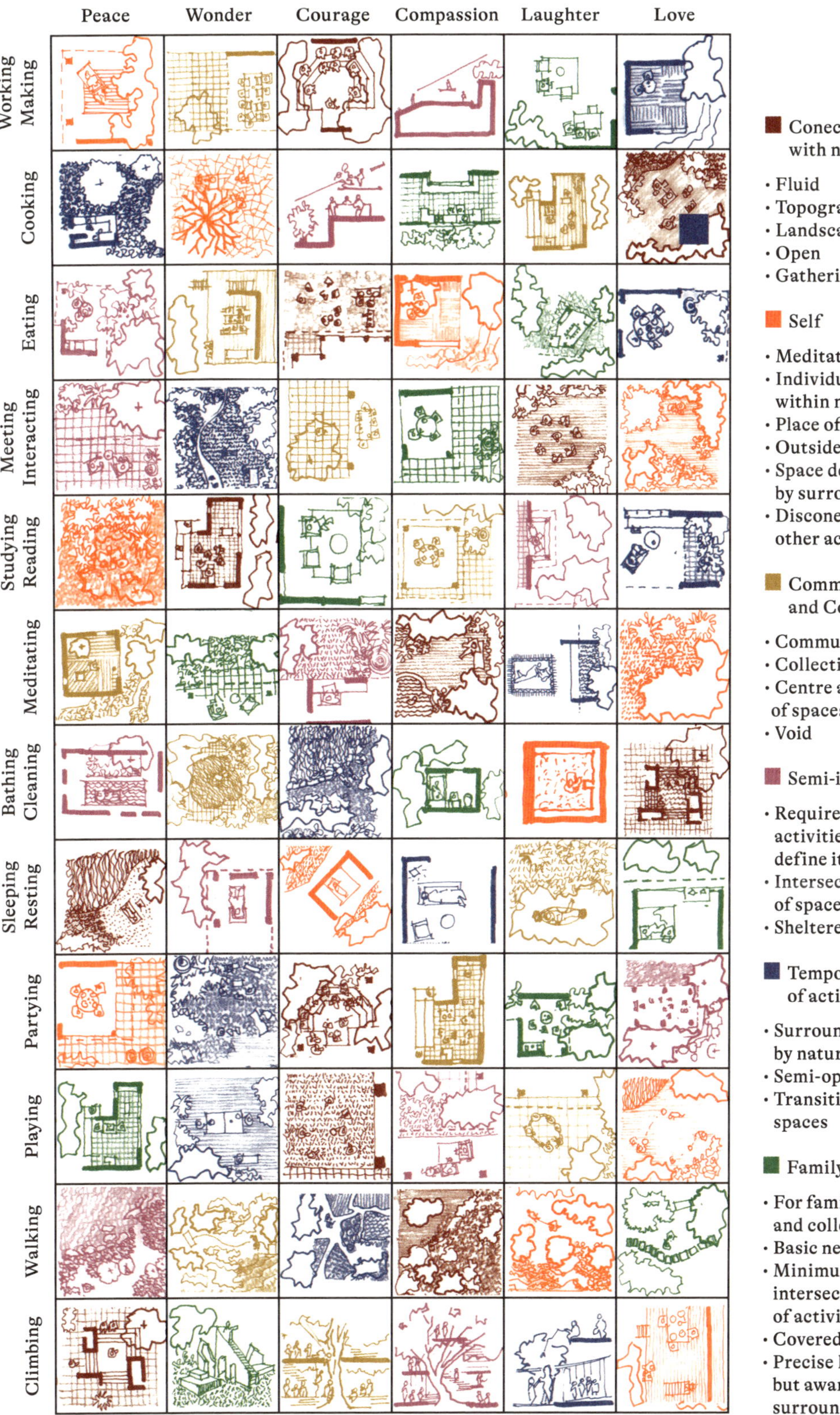

Conection with neighbours

- Fluid
- Topographical
- Landscaped
- Open
- Gathering

Self

- Meditative
- Individual within nature
- Place of pause
- Outside
- Space defined by surroundings
- Disconected from other activities

Communal and Collective

- Community scale
- Collective
- Centre and heart of spaces
- Void

Semi-individual

- Requires other activities to define itself
- Intersections of spaces
- Sheltered

Temporariness of activities

- Surrounded by nature
- Semi-open
- Transitional spaces

Family Scale

- For family, friends and colleagues
- Basic needs
- Minimum intersection of activities
- Covered
- Precise limits but aware of surroundings

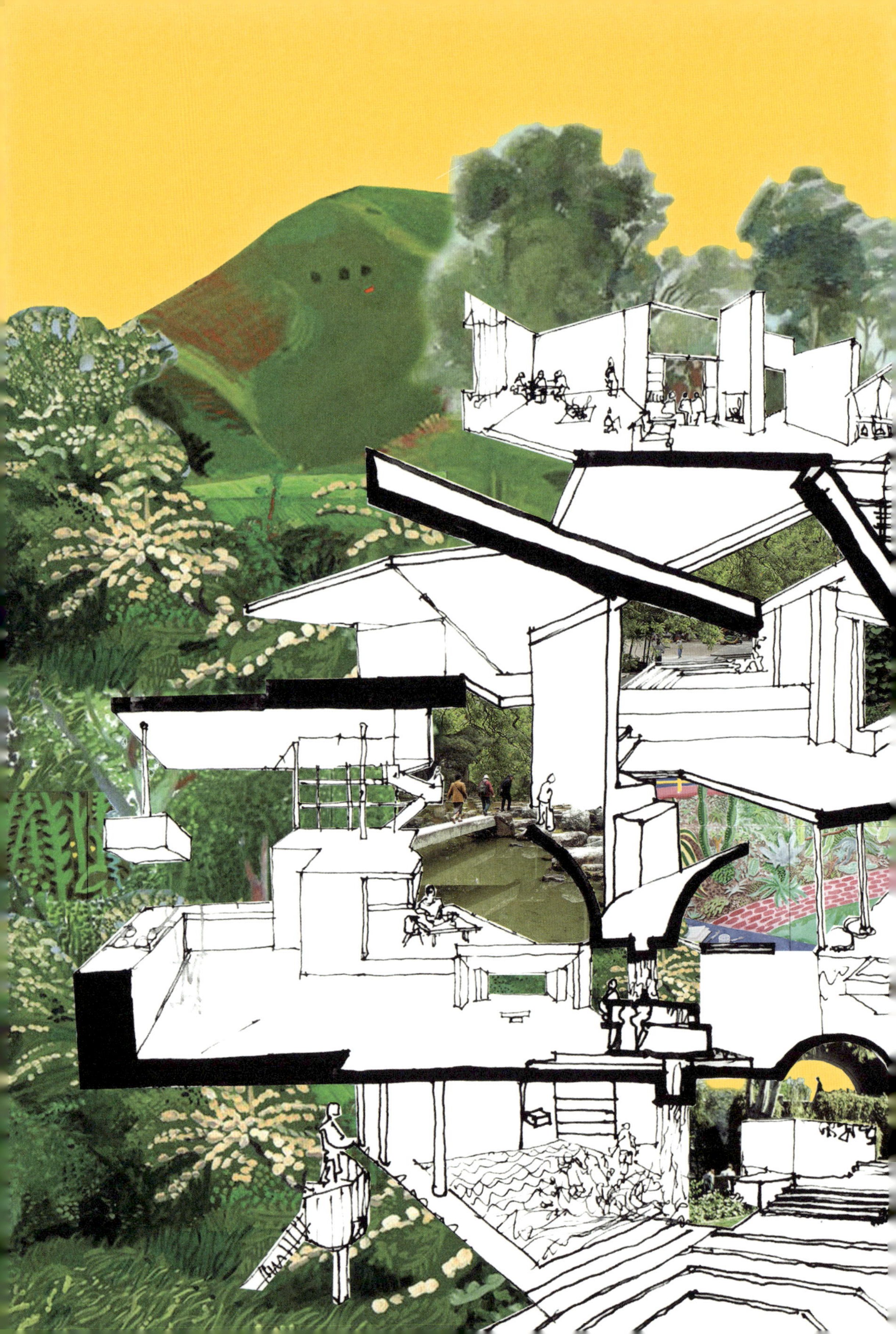

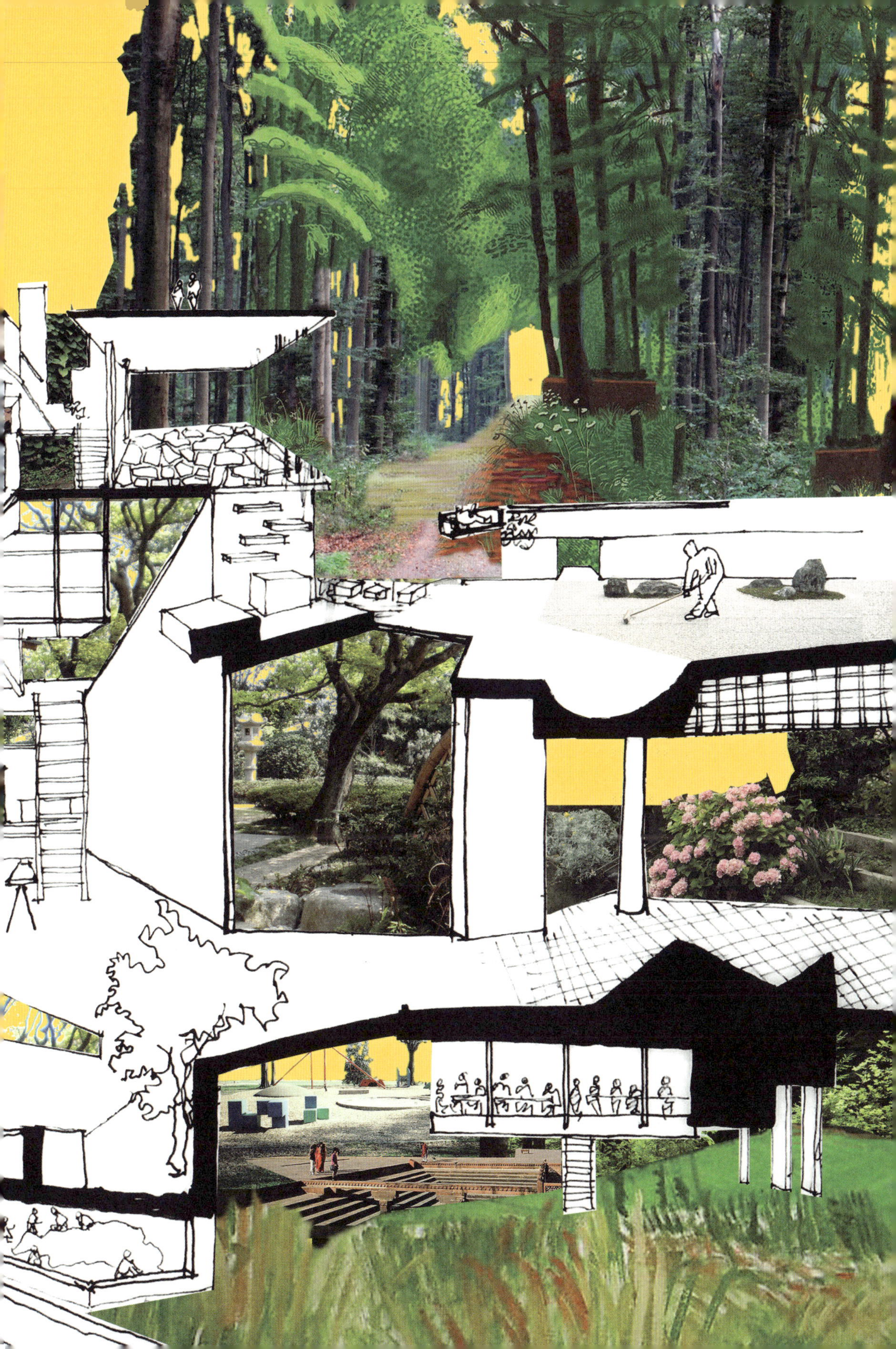

IMAGES

p. 90
Codex Fejérváry-Mayer (AD 1200–1521), first page. Collection of World Museum Liverpool

p. 91
Tatiana Bilbao and Mariana Castillo Deball, concept development diagram for *Mind Garden, Heart Garden*, 2018

p. 92
Mariana Castillo Deball, *Tonalpohualli Zollstock*, 2018, four adapted folding rulers, each: 100 cm long. Courtesy Mariana Castillo Deball

p. 93
Mariana Castillo Deball, *Tonalpohualli Blue*, 2017, powder coated aluminum, wood, bronze, each: 270 × 12 × 0,3 cm, installation view Mendes Wood DM, Brussels, 2017. Courtesy Mariana Castillo Deball and Mendes Wood DM, Brussels

pp. 94–99
Tatiana Bilbao and Mariana Castillo Deball, concept development diagrams, photo-montages, sketches and collages for *Mind Garden, Heart Garden*, 2018

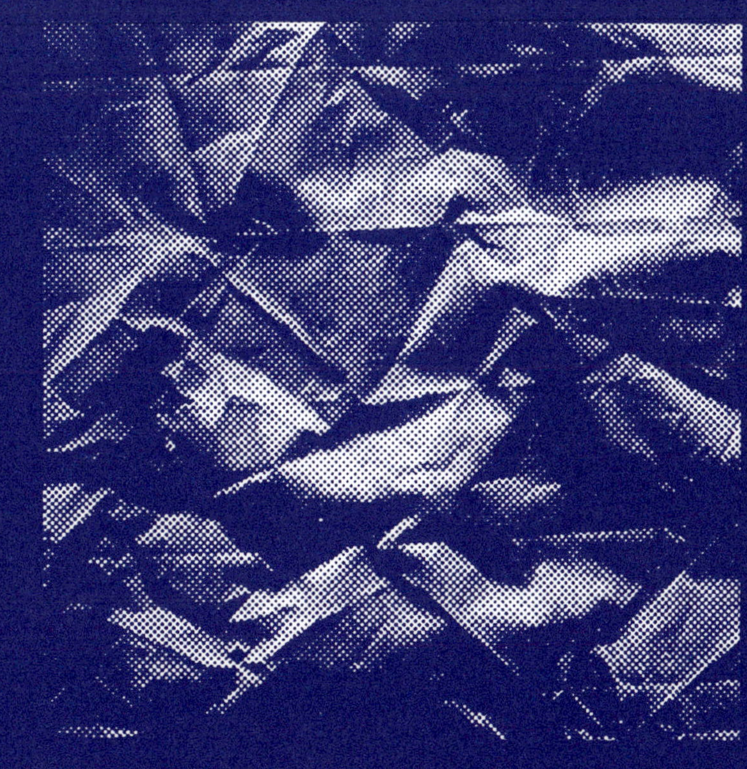

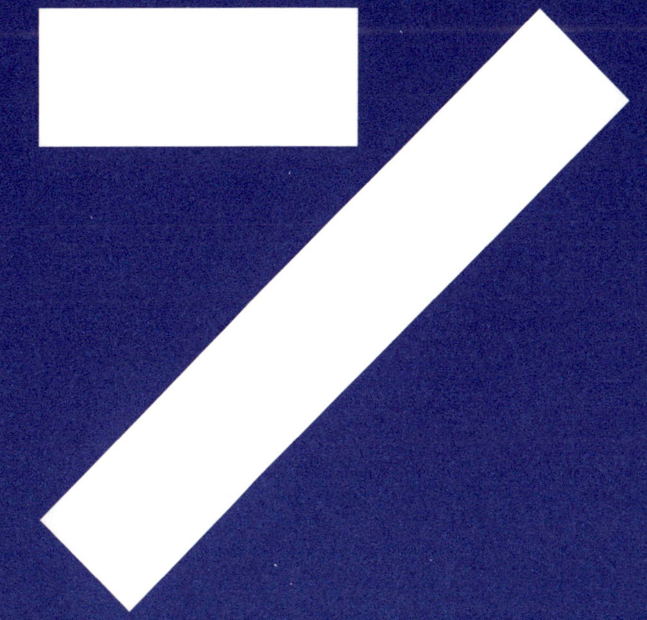

Rana Begum
Marina Tabassum Architects

PROJECT TEAM

Rana Begum
Tasneem Farah Siddique
Argha Shaha
Marina Tabassum

Phoenix Will Rise

A banal hard exterior, almost repulsing,
until the colour catches the eye –
Only the curious will enter into the depth of its void.

Two hopeless 'todayers' beaming a light on tomorrow's hope:
Yet again Phoenix will rise from the ashes
beyond the horizon,
Born with renewed wisdom,
healing, repairing what is lost …

What have we lost?
Humanity.

Dear tomorrow,
hope is all in your hands.

> *'They may*
> *defeat you,*
> *burn you,*
> *insult you,*
> *injure you,*
> *abandon you,*
> *but they*
> *will not*
> *and cannot*
> *destroy you.*
> *For you,*
> *like Rome,*
> *were built*
> *on ashes,*
> *and you,*
> *like a phoenix,*
> *know how*
> *to resurrect.'*
>
> *– Nikita Gill*

Marina Tabassum

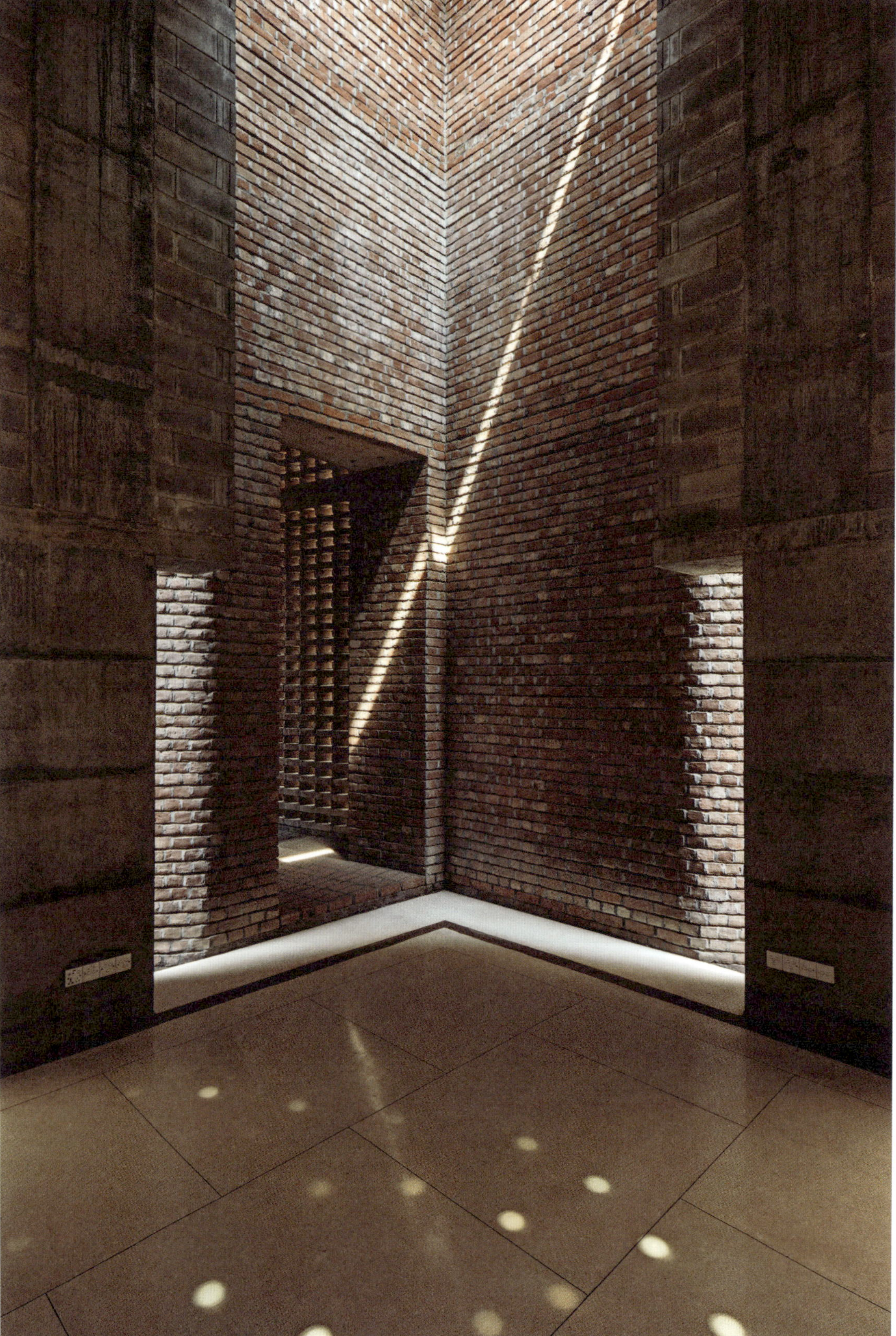

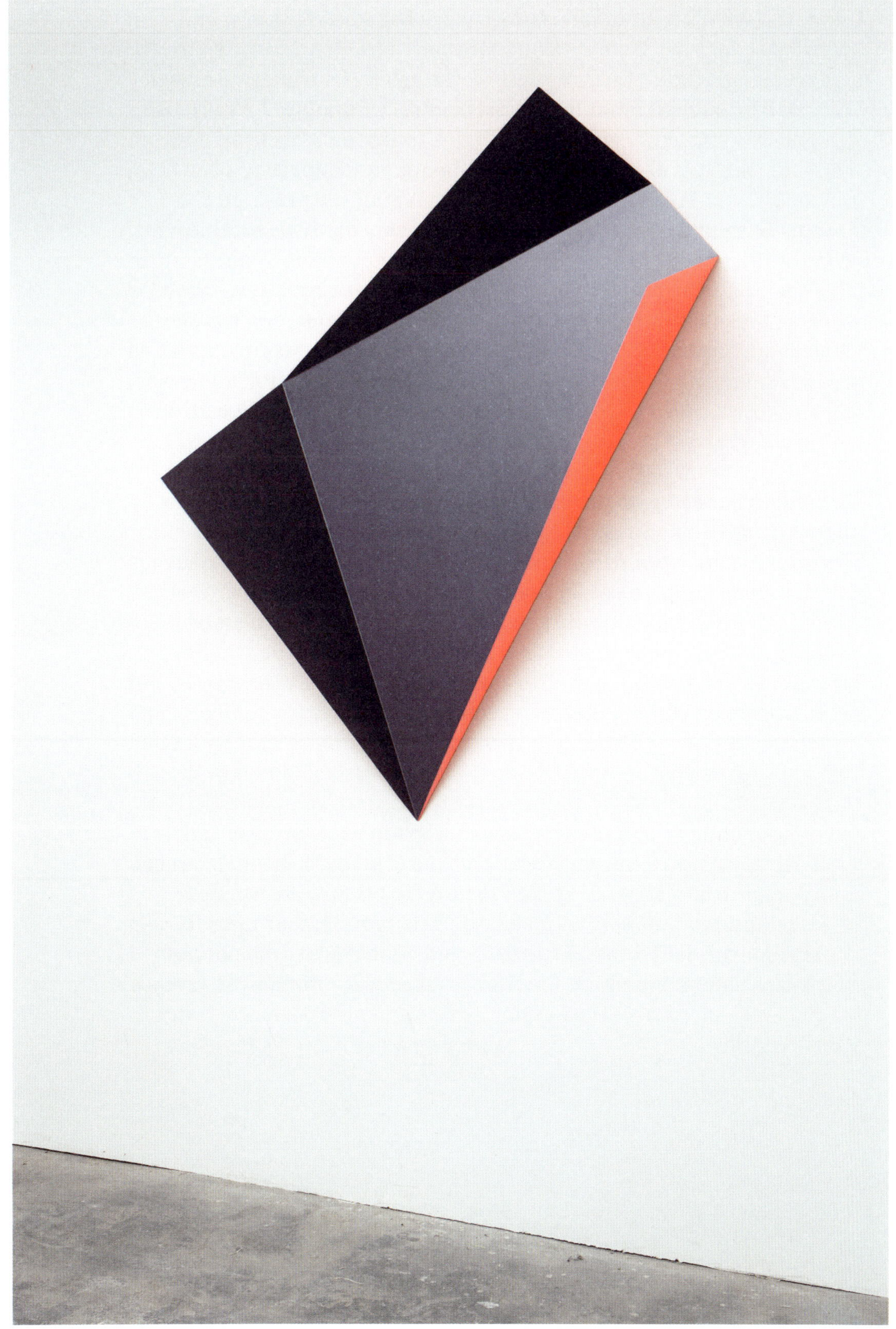

I have followed Marina Tabassum's work for several years, and recently visited her Bait Ur Rouf Mosque (The Red Mosque), in Dhaka, Bangladesh. I was moved by the space, by the raw, honest approach to material and how light becomes tangible. I could feel goose bumps rising up through this experience of light and material coming together to create a space for thought, calm and meditation. Light is a fundamental part of my practice too. Alongside colour and form, it exists simultaneously in each work.

There are other parallels between our practices that I recognised instantly. Marina and I are clearly drawn to and respond to the same colours and materials. There was an obvious need for us to create something tangible together. It has been challenging to work together from two different countries, making sure we don't call each other in the middle of the night!

Our immediate response to the exhibition brief was to create an environment that people can experience. We began to explore the idea of building a space led by contrasting experiences – at once brutal and ethereal, hard and sensitive, grey and colourful, dark and light, intense and meditative. The focus soon became more about the experience of the present (exterior) and future (inside). How do we imagine space? How do we imagine architecture to protect us and still connect us to the outside world, to reality?

The piece is constructed with a plain and untouched exterior. On the inside, the surfaces are covered with a layer of relief sprayed in vibrant colours. The very physical and plain exterior is initially uninviting, but glimpses of the colour and texture inside can be seen underneath. Light is picked up on the faceted surfaces that seem to describe an otherworldly landscape. The space encourages us to consider the benefits of a spiritual and contemplative place, and grants the visitor a moment to think of a better tomorrow, to escape.

Rana Begum

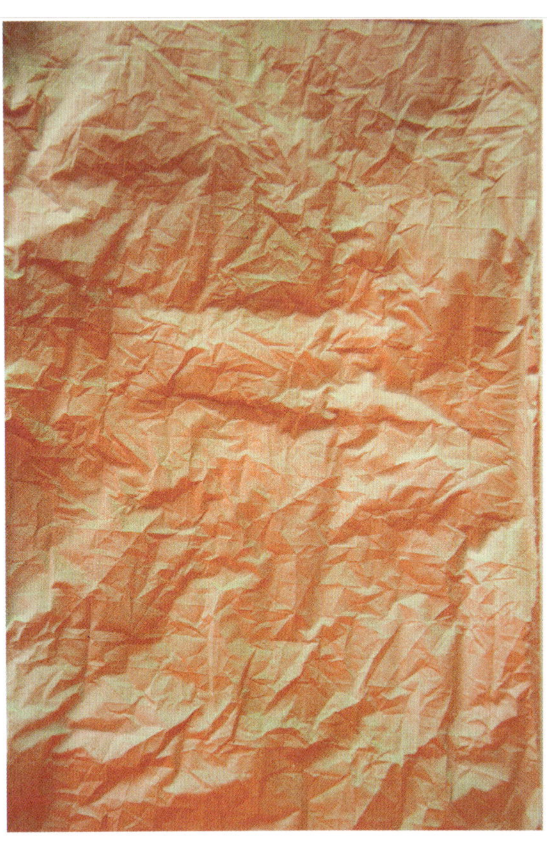
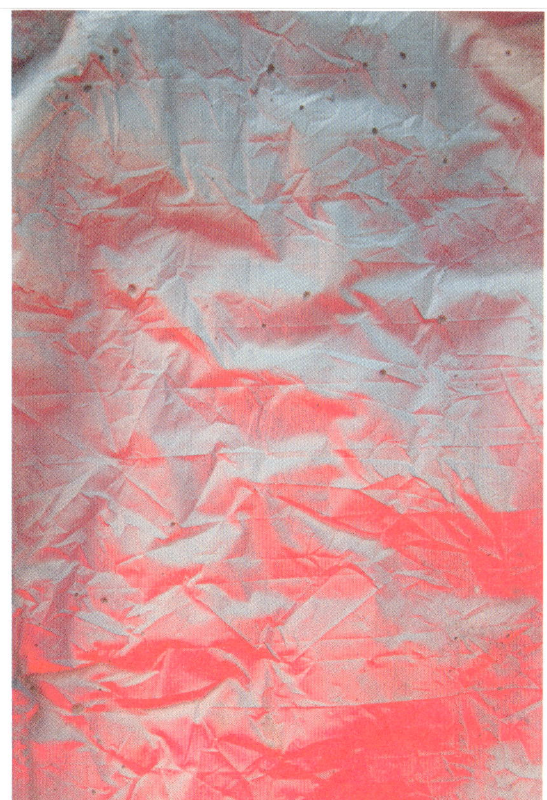
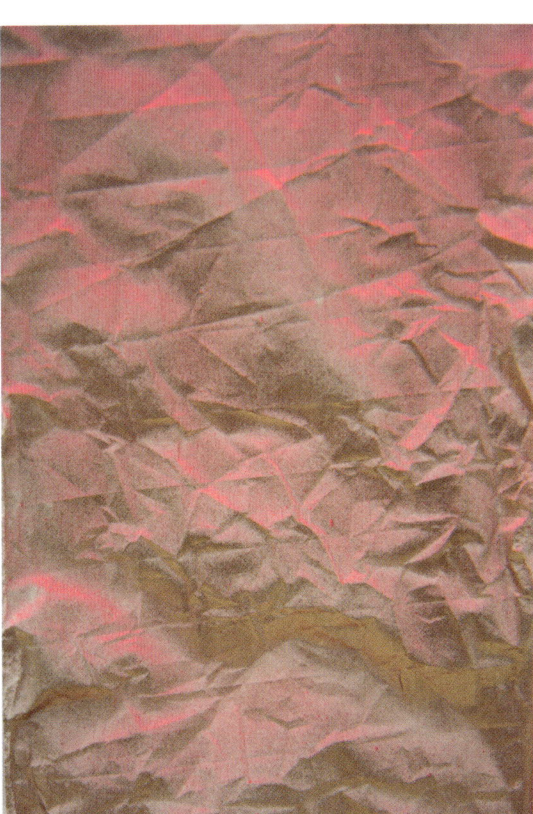
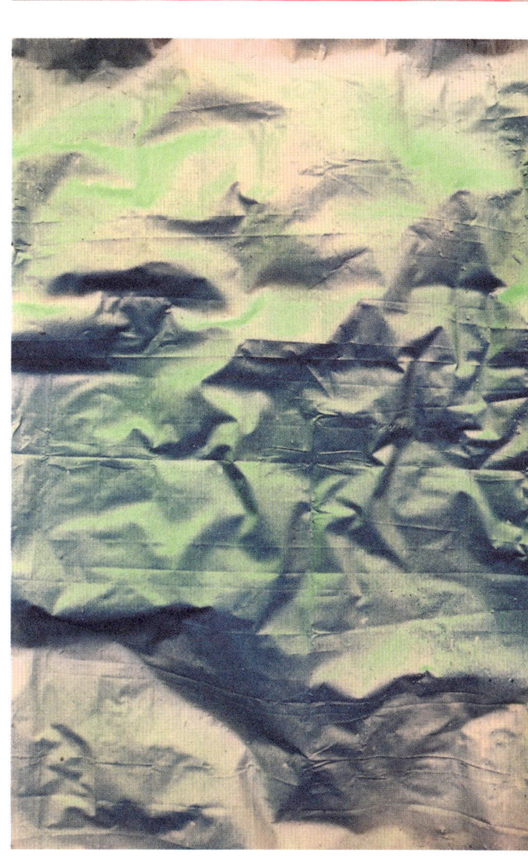

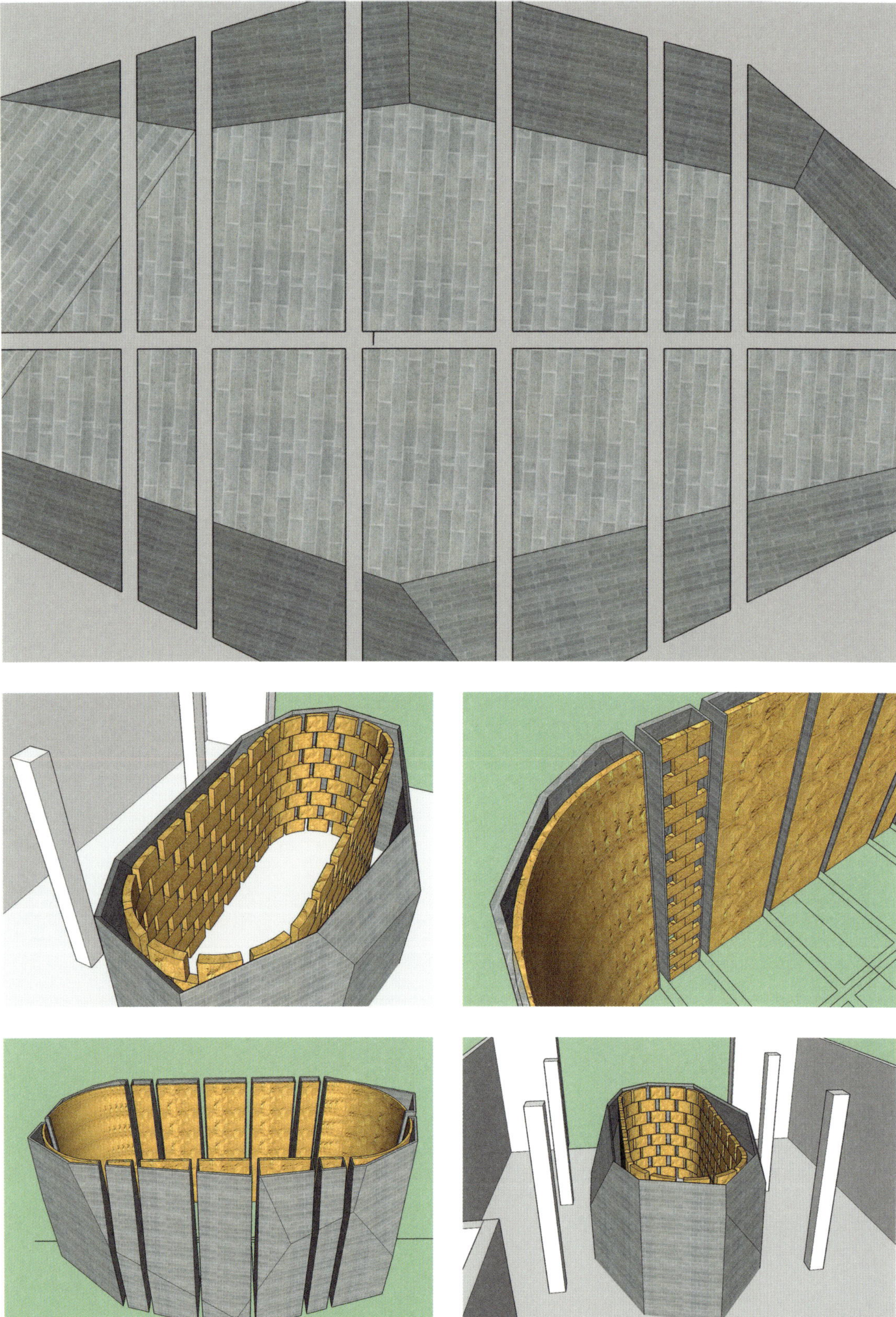

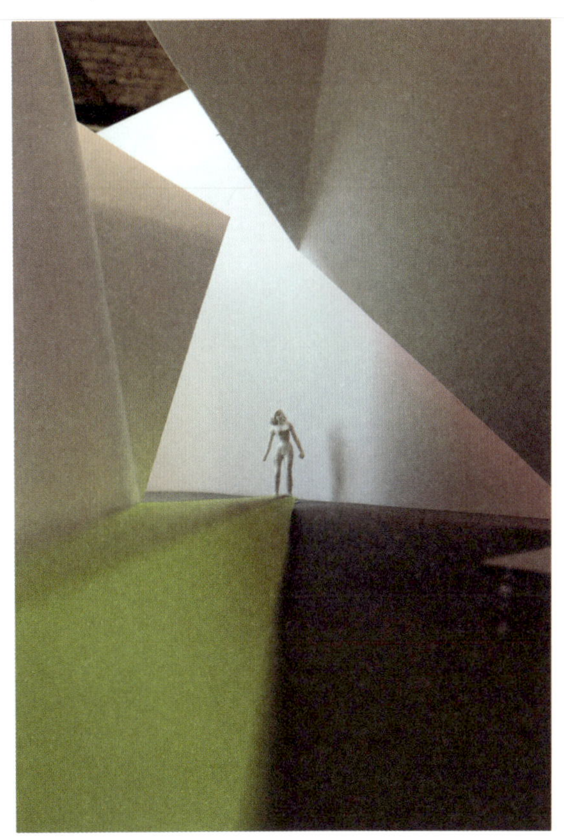
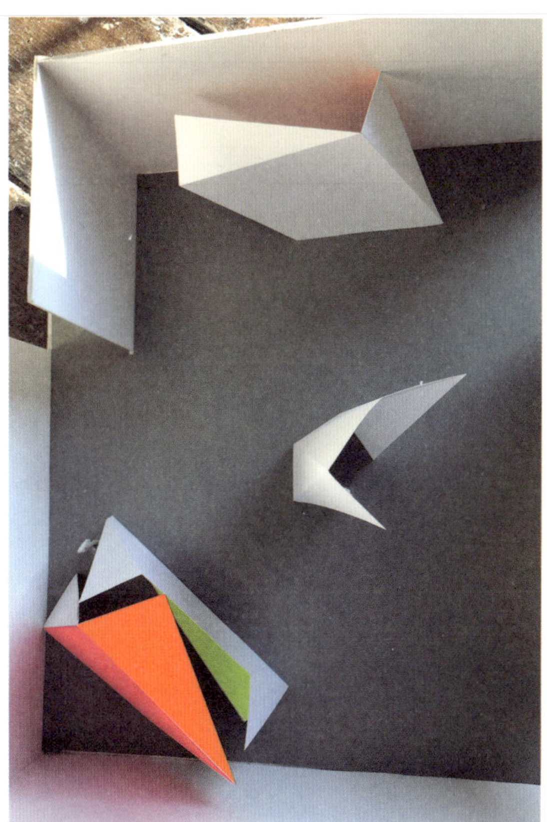
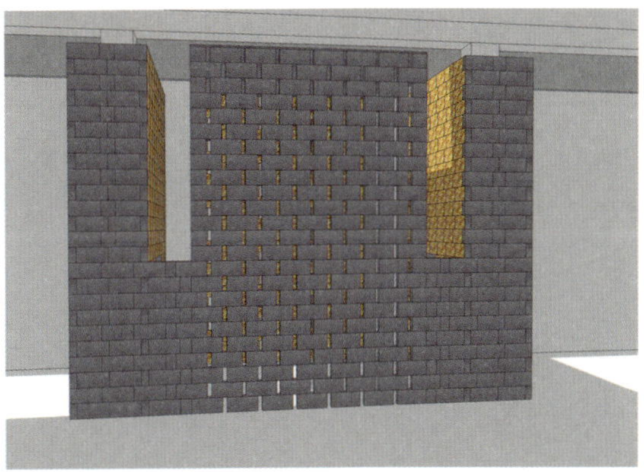
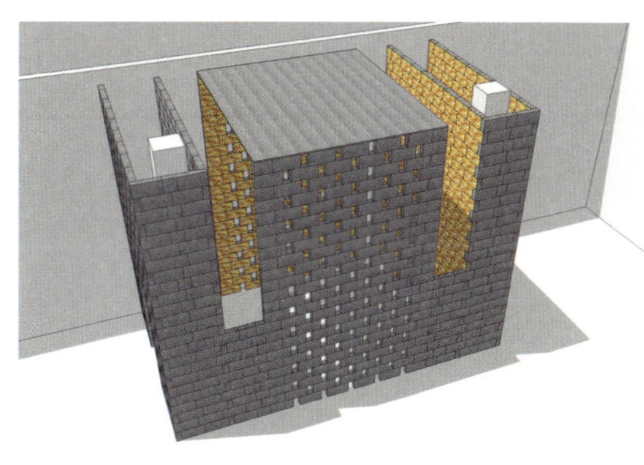
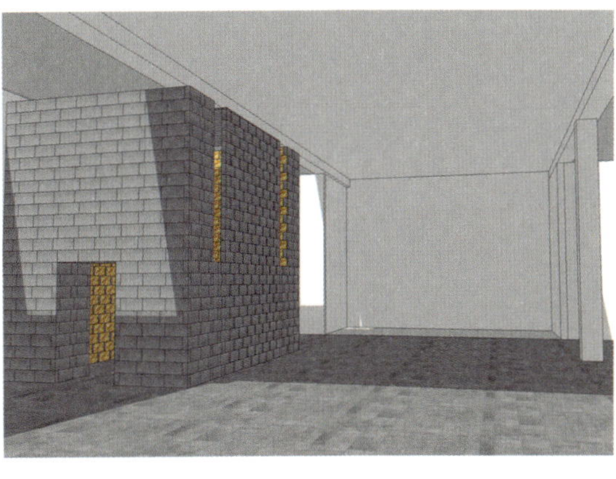
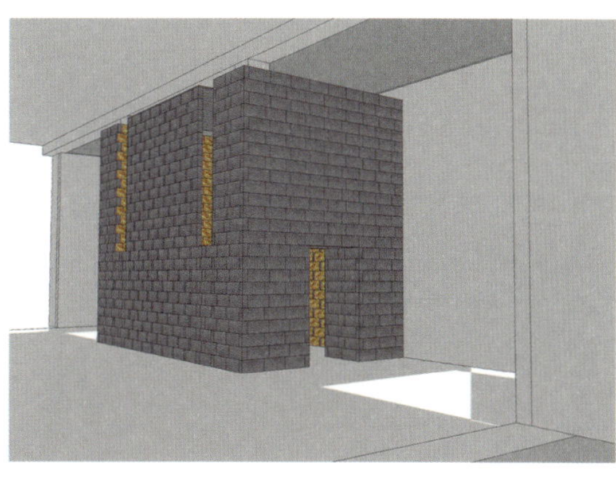

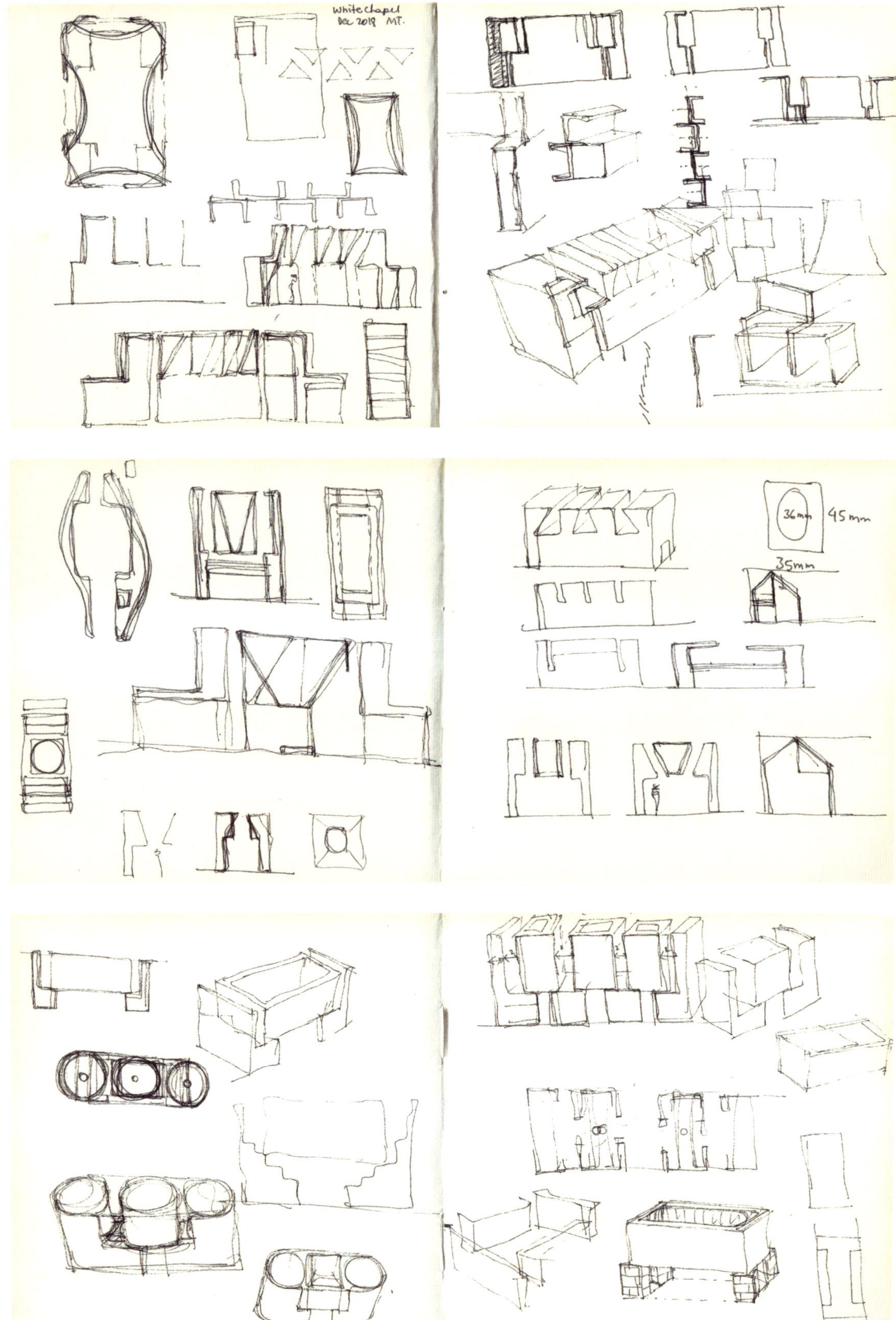
Whitechapel
Dec 2018 MT.
36mm
45mm
35mm

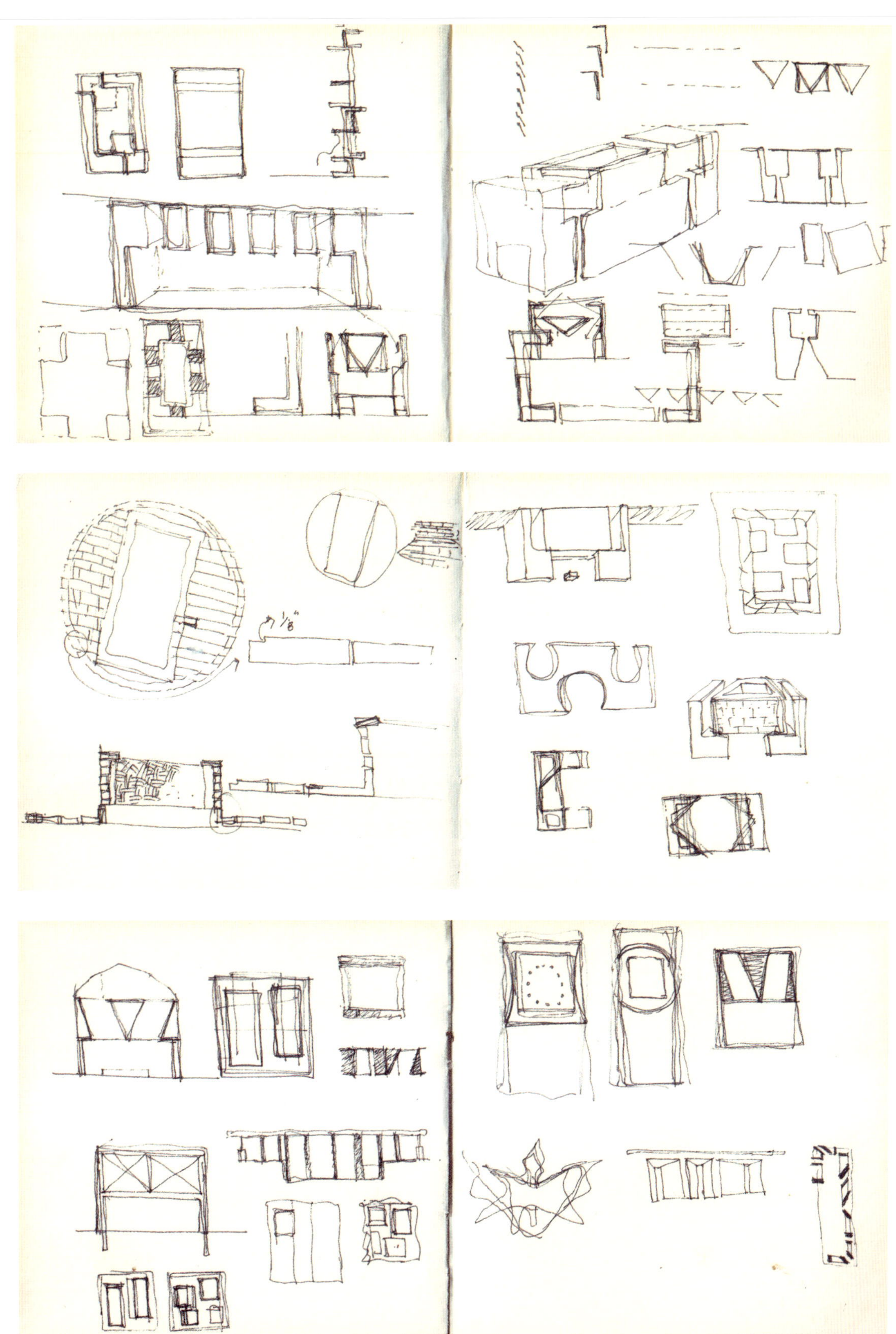
1/8"

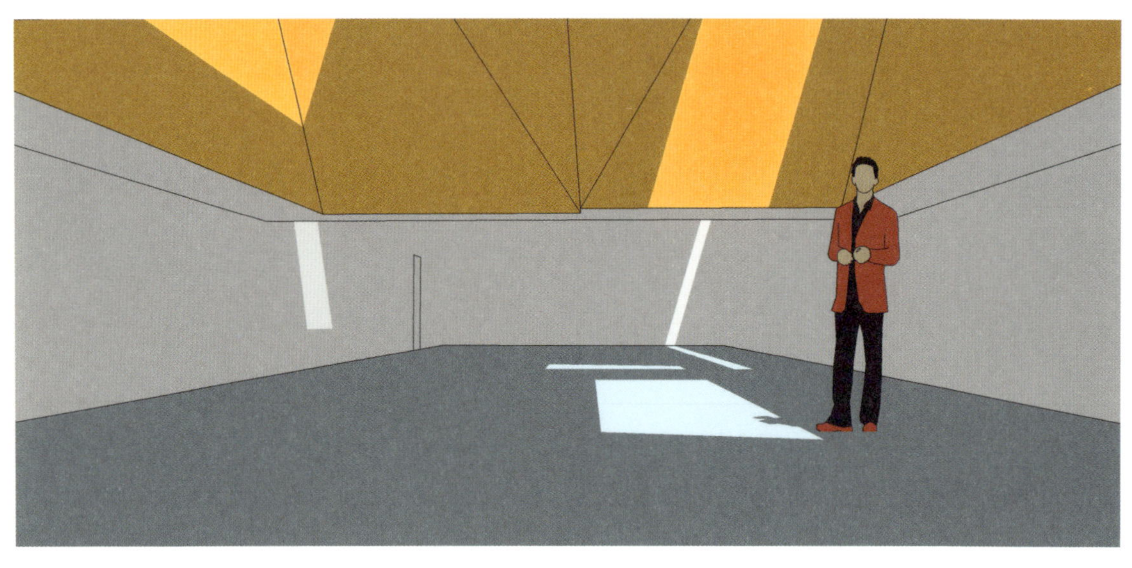

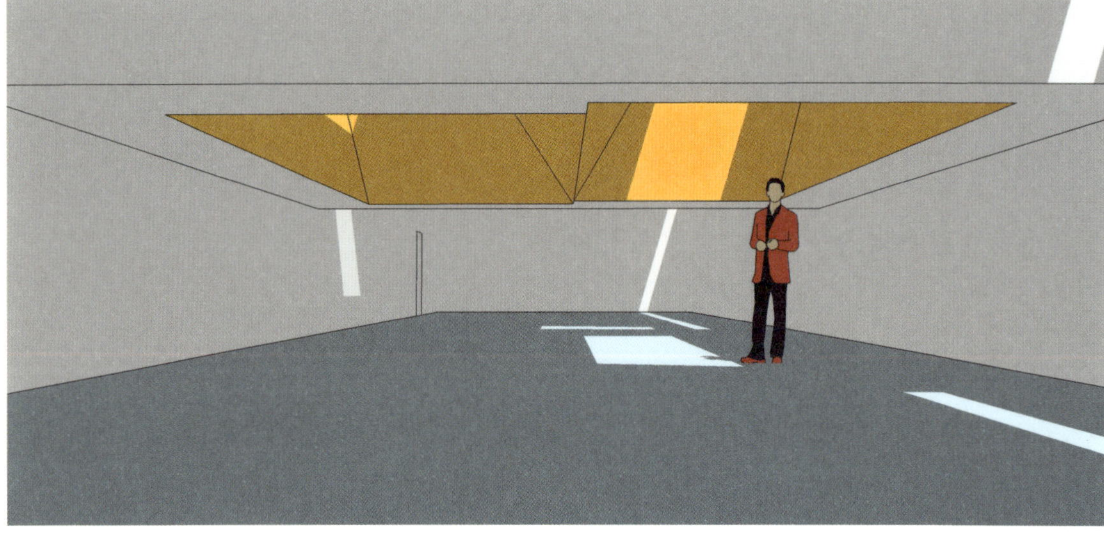

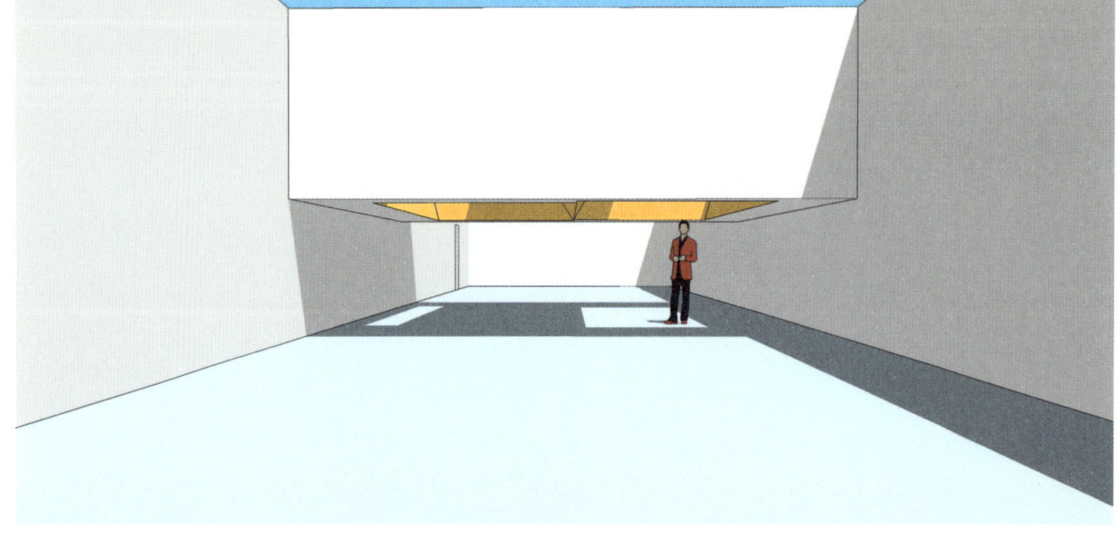

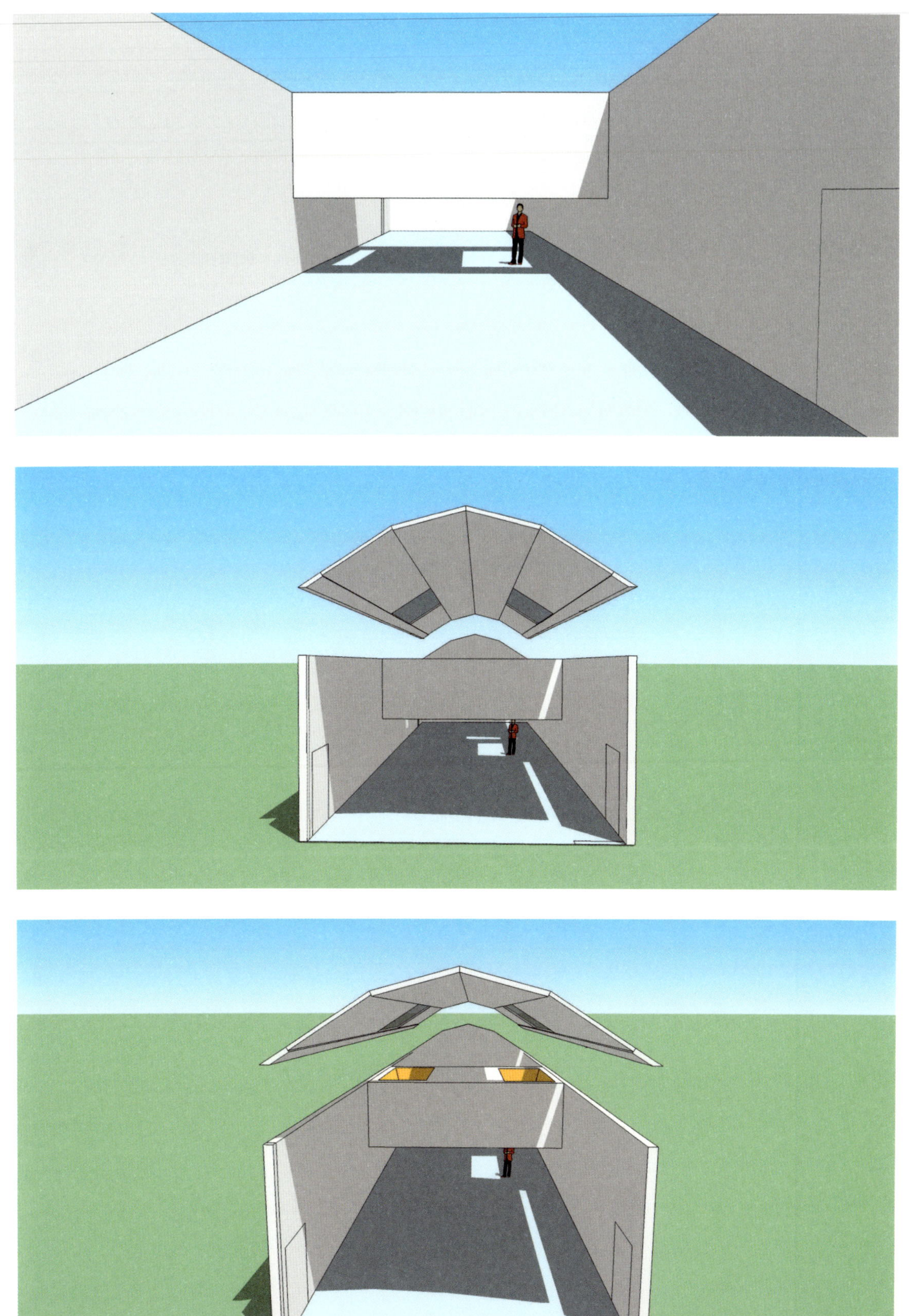

p. 104
Marina Tabassum Architects, *Bait Ur Rouf Mosque (The Red Mosque)*, Dhaka, Bangladesh, completed 2012. Exterior view of corner light court and vertical linear gap indicating the qibla direction. Courtesy Aga Khan Trust for Culture. Photo: Rajesh Vora

p. 105
Rana Begum, *No. 850 L Fold*, 2018, paint on mild steel, 160 × 90 × 40 cm. Photo: Philip White

p. 107
Rana Begum, test samples for *Phoenix Will Rise*, 2018, spray paint on paper

p. 108
Marina Tabassum Architects, design development sketches for *Phoenix Will Rise*, 2018, digital rendering

p. 109
Above: Rana Begum, design development model for *Phoenix Will Rise*, 2018, paper, card and glue

Below: Marina Tabassum Architects, design development sketches for *Phoenix Will Rise*, 2018, digital rendering

pp. 110–11
Marina Tabassum, design development sketches for *Phoenix Will Rise*, 2018, ink on paper

pp. 112–13
Marina Tabassum Architects, design development sketches for *Phoenix Will Rise*, 2018, digital rendering

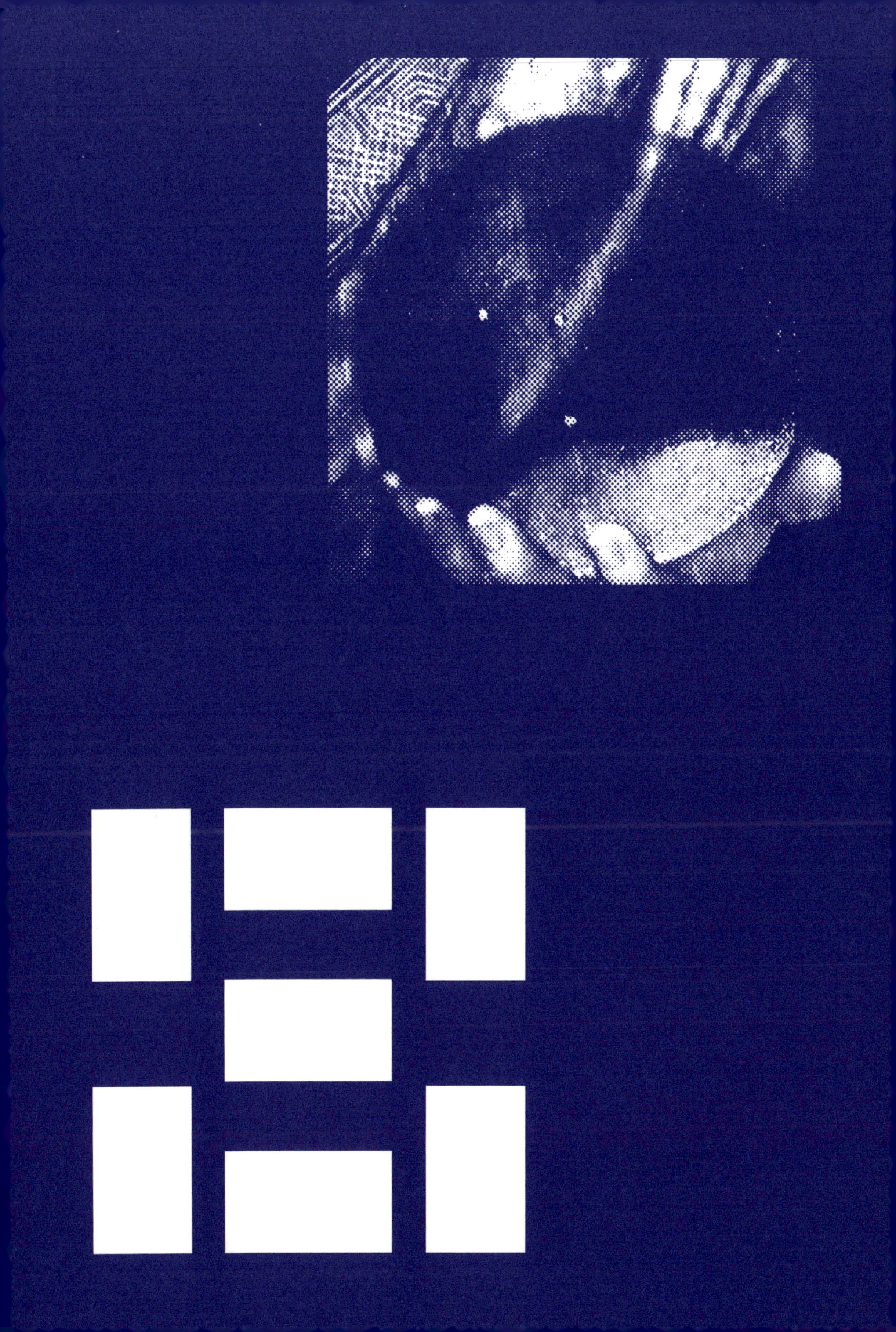

David Kohn Architects
Simon Fujiwara

PROJECT TEAM

Mungo Adam-Smith
Elva Choi
Simon Fujiwara
David Kohn
Jessica Lyons
Maria Bartau Madariaga
Bushra Mohamed

The Salvator Mundi Experience

The Salvator Mundi Experience brings visitors, one by one, into an immersive miniature museum dedicated to the presentation of a single artwork – Leonardo da Vinci's *Salvator Mundi* or *Saviour of the World.*

In 2017, the work – once thought to be a copy and disfigured by over-painting – broke world records for the highest ever auction price reached for an artwork. In part due to a vigorous marketing campaign that saw the painting tour the globe, *Salvator Mundi* became a highly mediated image, canonised as an 'instant masterpiece' through its replication, and increasingly described as a male counterpart to the Mona Lisa. The painting was acquired by the Department of Culture and Tourism Abu Dhabi, with the intention of displaying it in the newly opened Louvre Abu Dhabi.

As part of our research, we travelled to Abu Dhabi to experience the spatial and cultural contexts in which the painting would be exhibited. Visits to the Louvre, the Heritage Village, the theme park Ferrari World and Dubai's Burj Khalifa (the world's tallest building), informed our desire to create our own mass tourist attraction in which visitors would experience not the painting itself but the *story* of the painting – its transformation from discarded, valueless image to iconic masterpiece through mass mediation.

Created at a scale large enough to immerse a single visitor, *The Salvator Mundi Experience* is both a miniature proposal for an attraction and an attraction in itself. Within the context of *Is This Tomorrow?*, *The Salvator Mundi Experience* considers a future shaped by the logic of hypercapitalism, in which both art and architecture are expected to deliver ever higher levels of spectacle and offer more extreme, more individualised and more immersive experiences. *The Salvator Mundi Experience* is a melancholic yet anthropologically plausible vision of a near future in which humanity itself is placed on display as a dwindling resource.

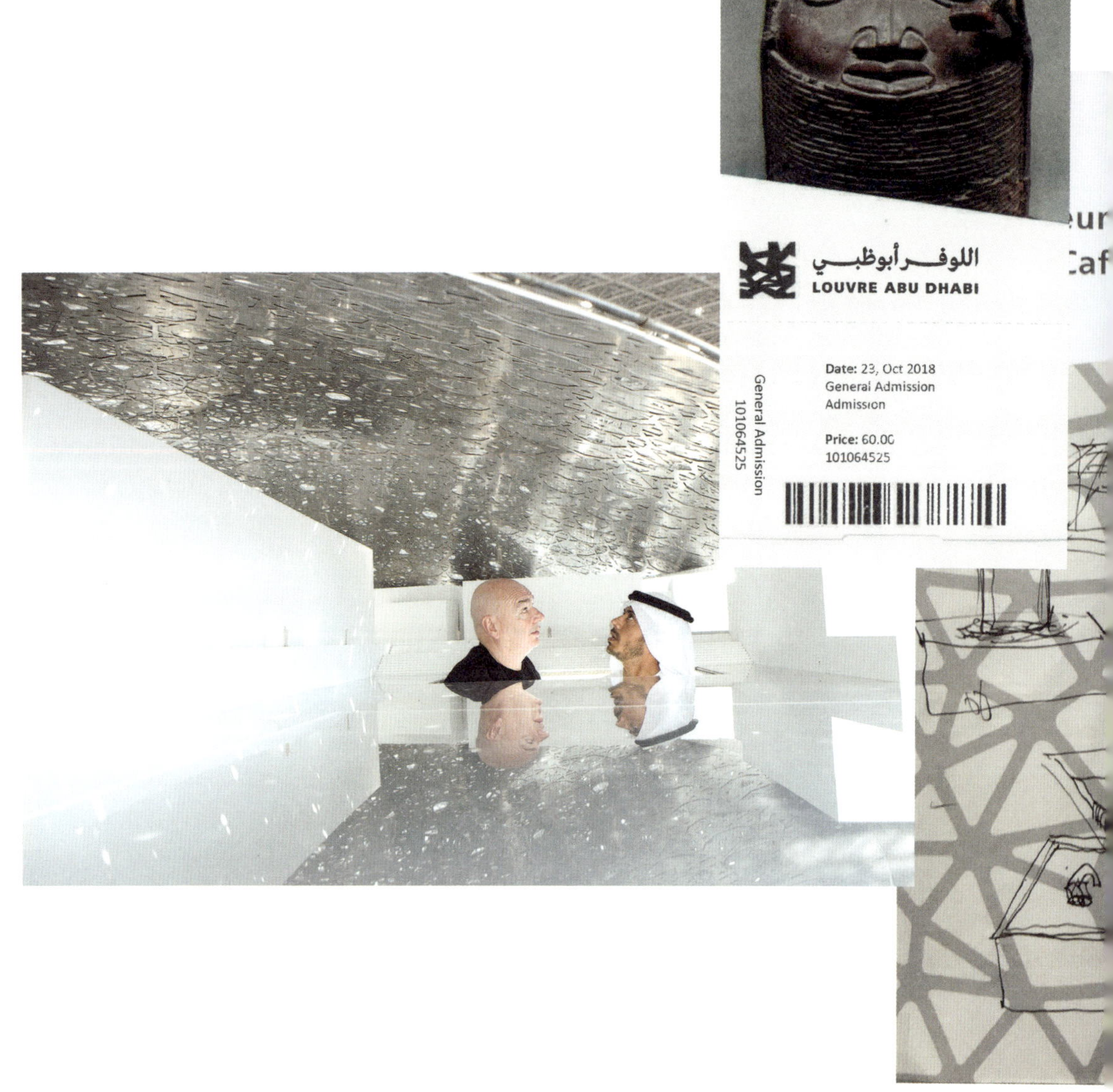
اللوفر أبوظبي
LOUVRE ABU DHABI
General Admission
101064525
Date: 23, Oct 2018
General Admission
Admission
Price: 60.00
101064525

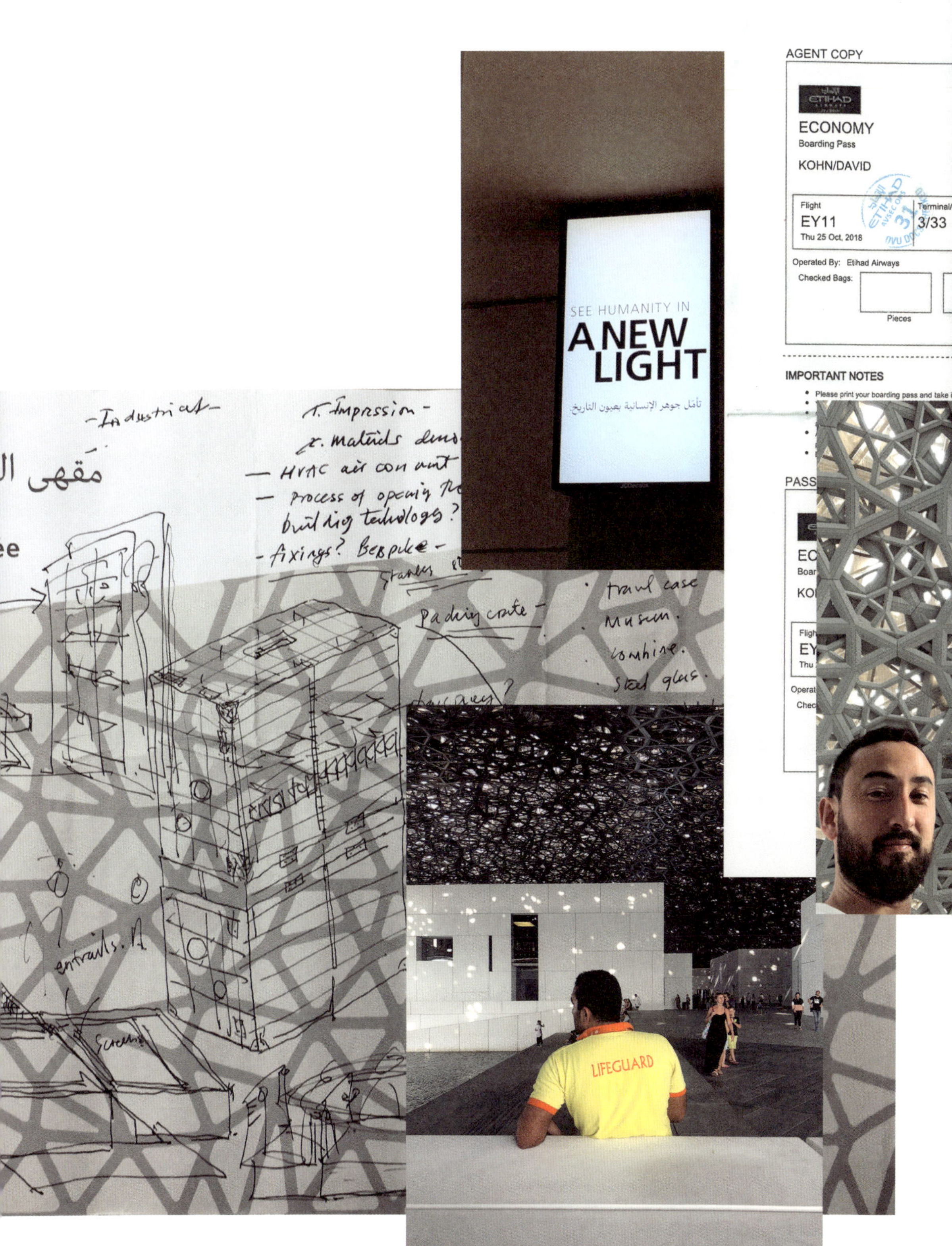

SEE HUMANITY IN
A NEW
LIGHT
تأمل جوهر الإنسانية بعيون التاريخ
AGENT COPY
ETIHAD
ECONOMY
Boarding Pass
KOHN/DAVID
Flight
EY11
Thu 25 Oct, 2018
Terminal/
3/33
Operated By: Etihad Airways
Checked Bags:
Pieces
IMPORTANT NOTES
-Industrial-
1. Impression -
2. materials
- HVAC air con
- process of opening
building technology?
- fixings? Bespoke -
packing crate
travel case
Museum.
combine.
Steel glass.
entrails.
LIFEGUARD

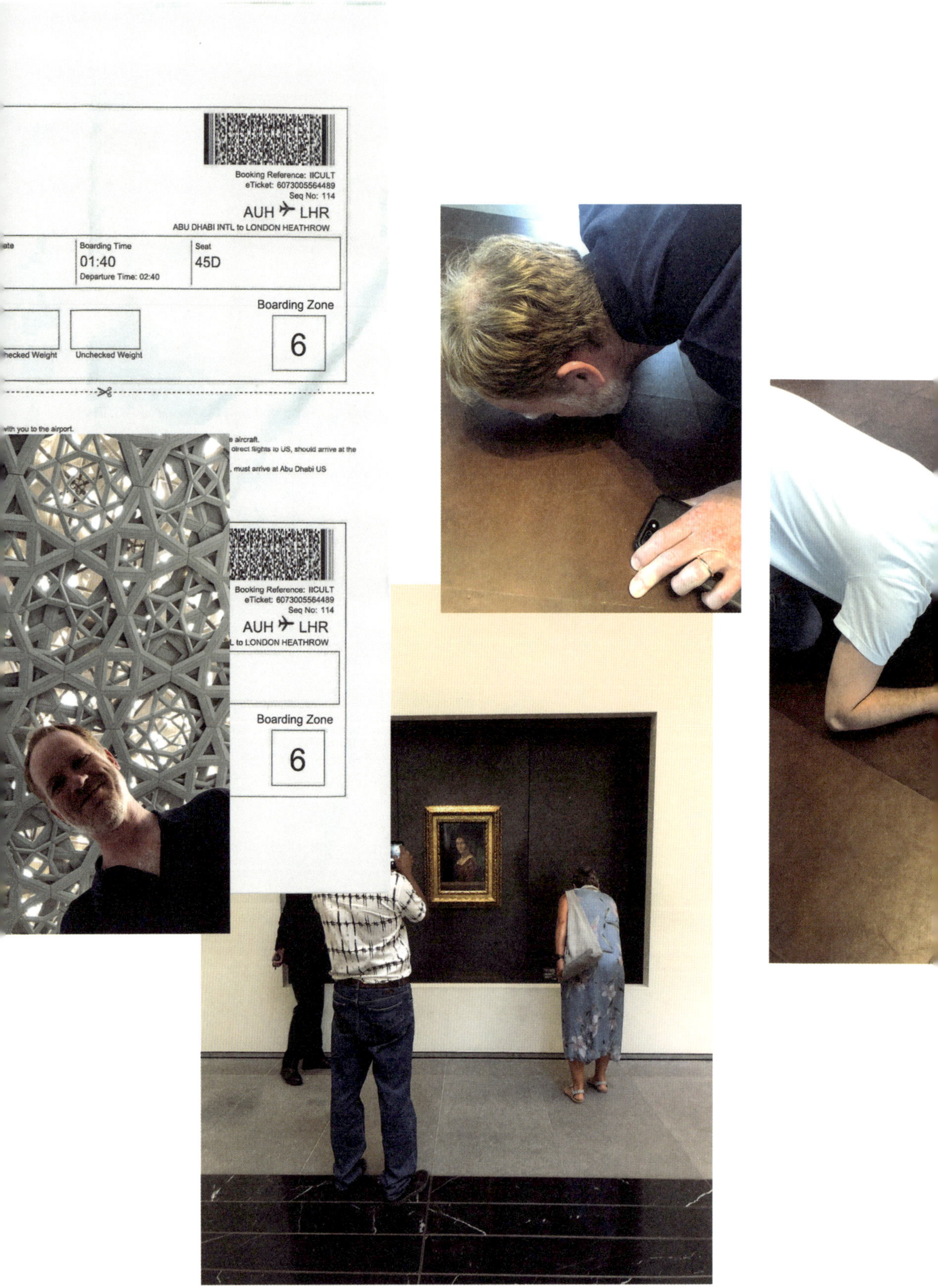

Booking Reference: IICULT
eTicket: 6073005564489
Seq No: 114

AUH ✈ LHR

ABU DHABI INTL to LONDON HEATHROW

ate	Boarding Time	Seat
	01:40 Departure Time: 02:40	45D

Boarding Zone

6

hecked Weight

Unchecked Weight

with you to the airport.

e aircraft.

direct flights to US, should arrive at the

, must arrive at Abu Dhabi US

Booking Reference: IICULT
eTicket: 6073005564489
Seq No: 114

AUH ✈ LHR

L to LONDON HEATHROW

Boarding Zone

6

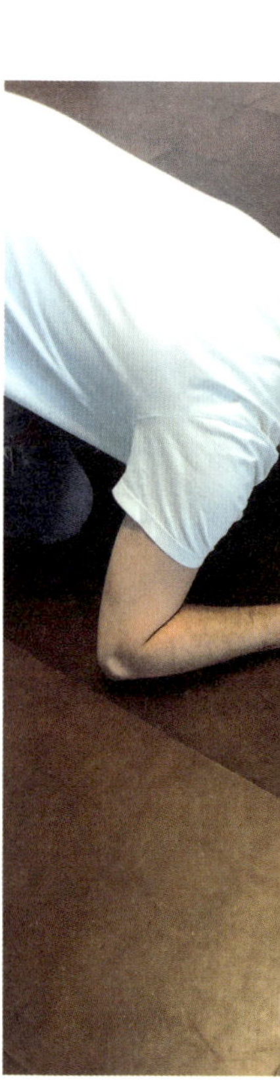

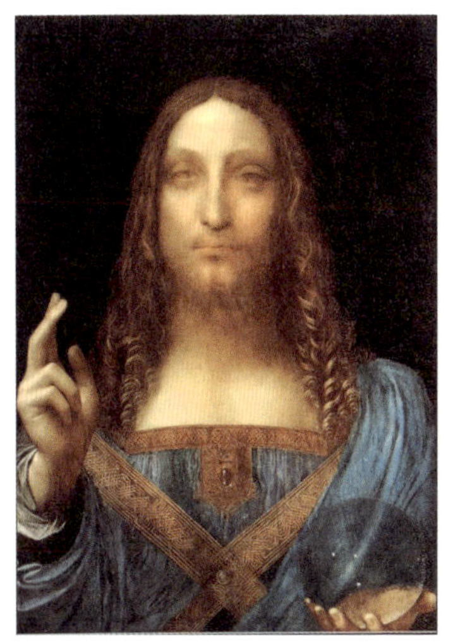
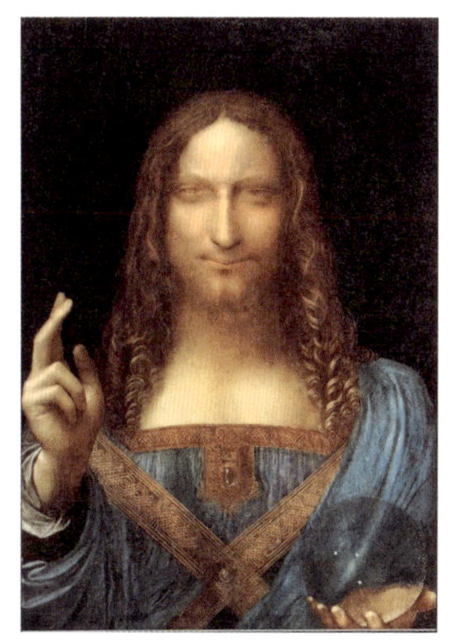
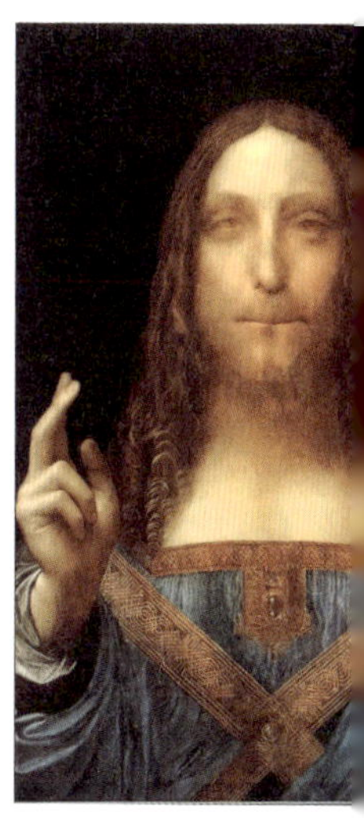
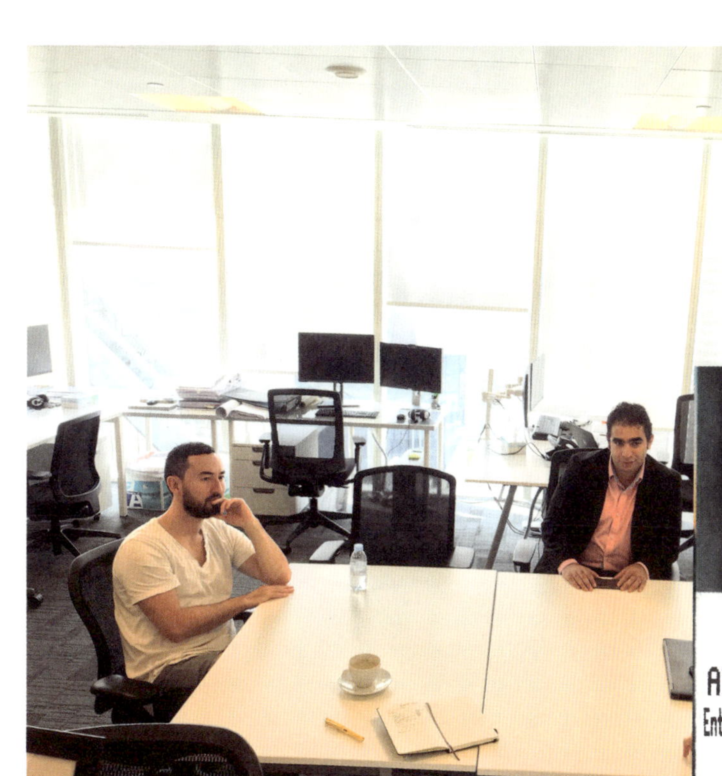
AT
B
Valid for ON
AT THE TOP
Entry Date & Time: 2
10:39 24/10/2018

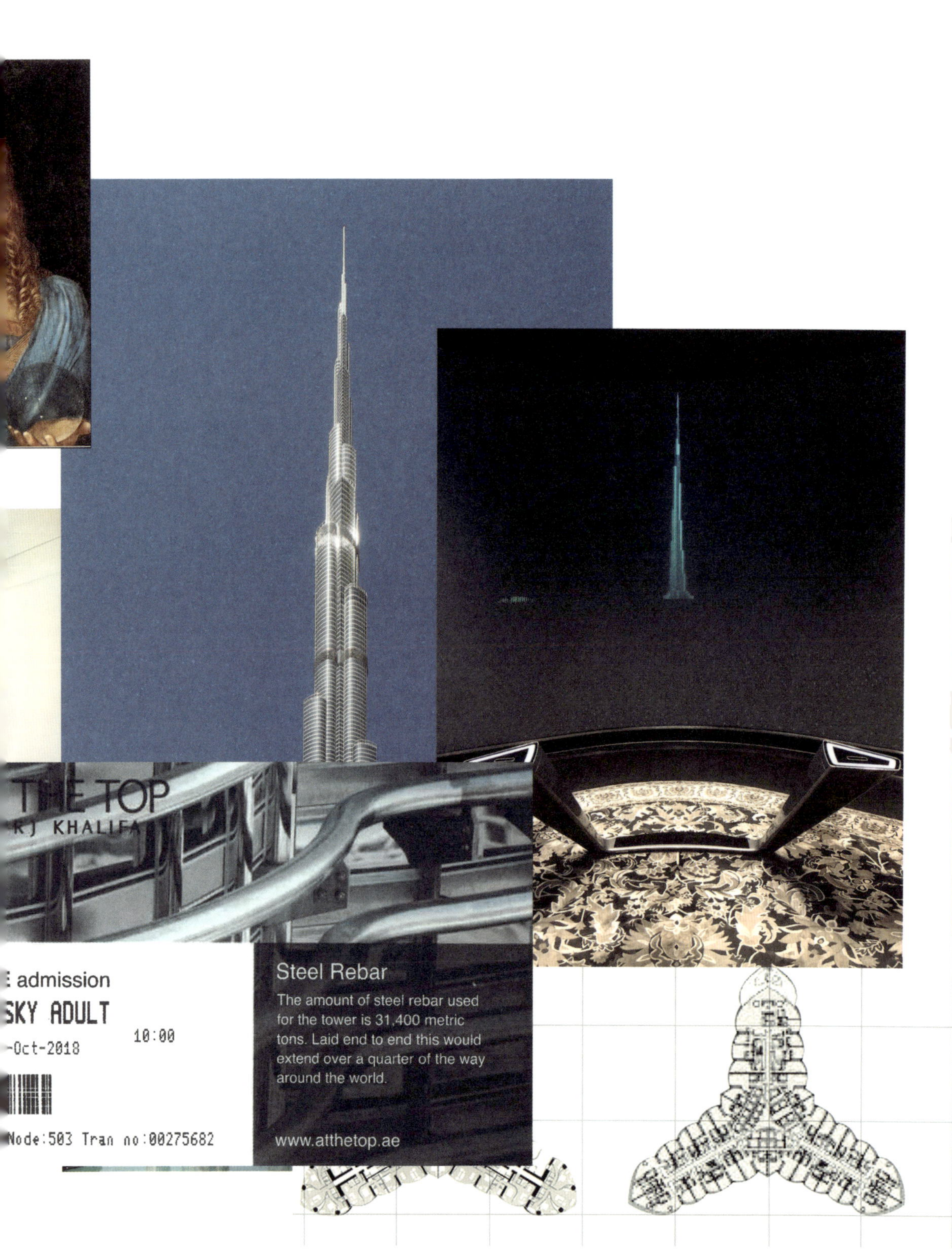
THE TOP
RJ KHALIFA
admission
SKY ADULT
10:00
-Oct-2018
Node:503 Tran no:00275682
Steel Rebar
The amount of steel rebar used for the tower is 31,400 metric tons. Laid end to end this would extend over a quarter of the way around the world.
www.atthetop.ae

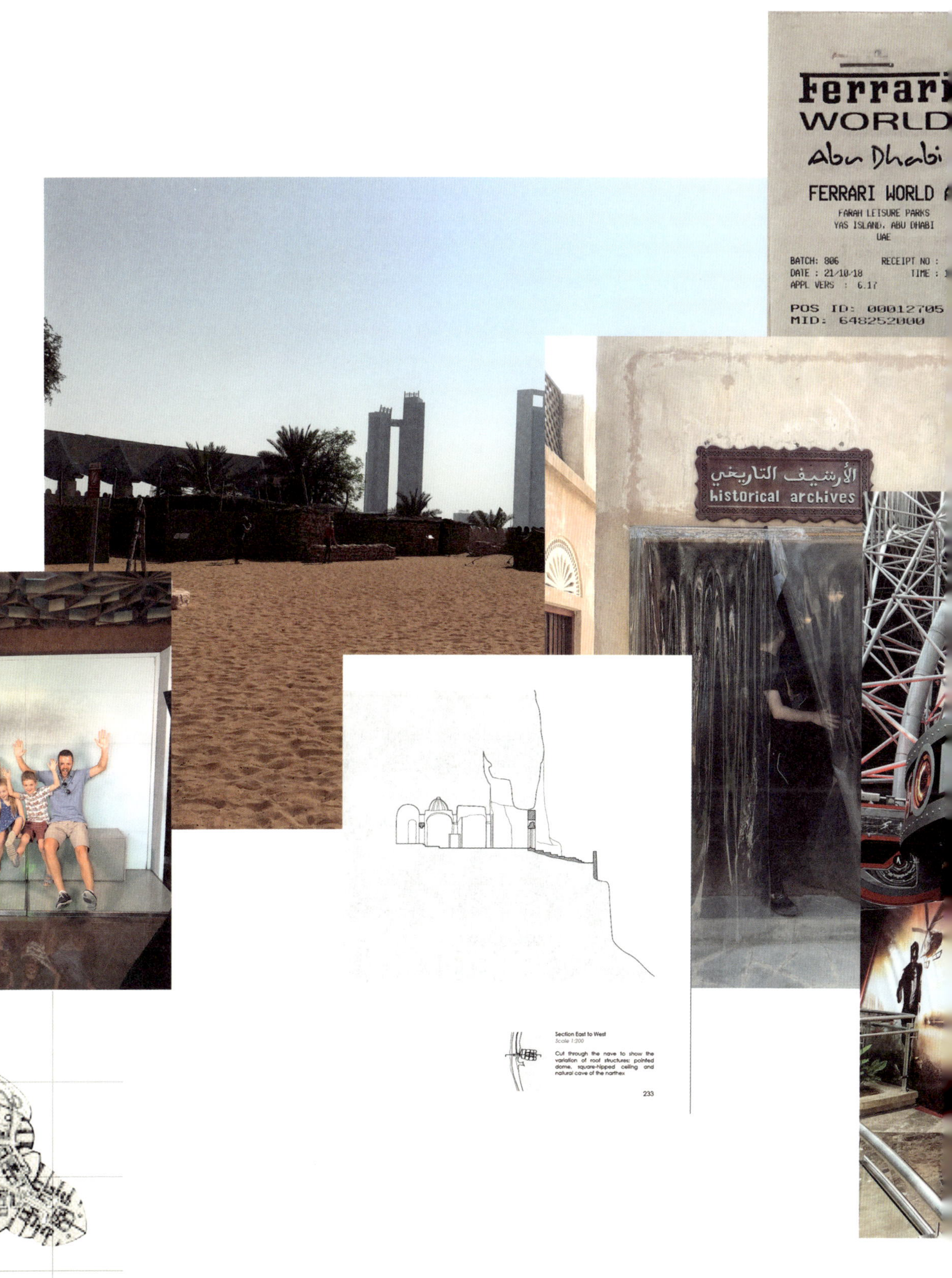
Ferrari
WORLD
Abu Dhabi
FERRARI WORLD
FARAH LEISURE PARKS
YAS ISLAND, ABU DHABI
UAE
BATCH: 806
RECEIPT NO :
DATE : 21/10/18
TIME :
APPL VERS : 6.17
POS ID: 00012705
MID: 648252000
الأرشيف التاريخي
historical archives
Section East to West
Scale 1:200
Cut through the nave to show the variation of roof structures: pointed dome, square-hipped ceiling and natural cave of the narthex
233

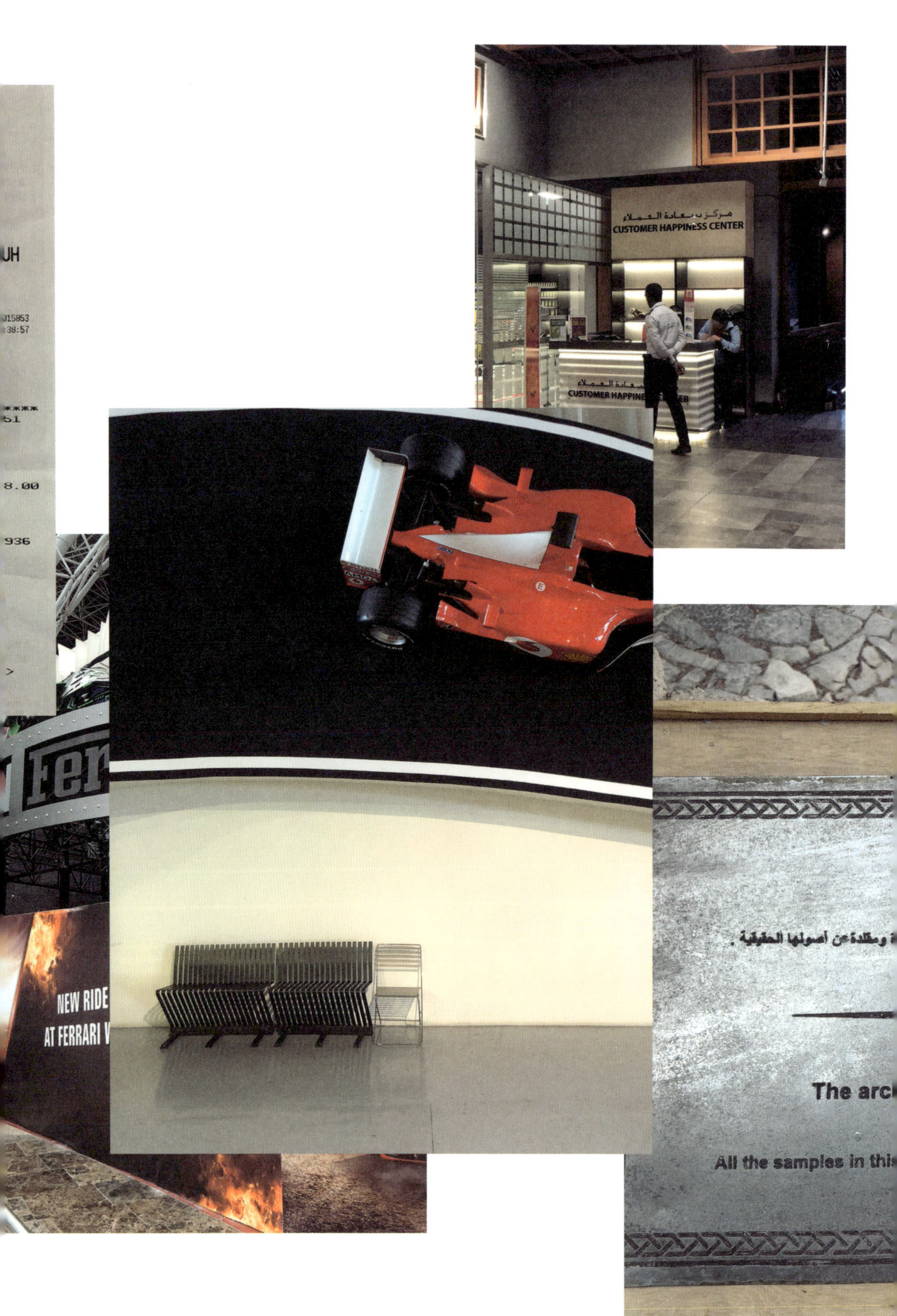
مركز سعادة العملاء
CUSTOMER HAPPINESS CENTER
NEW RIDE
AT FERRARI
All the samples in this

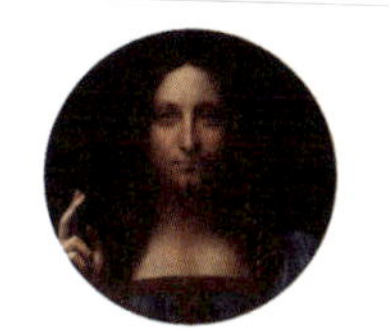

thelastdavinci Follow

110 posts 980 followers 0 following

The Last da Vinci
A portrait of real people through the eyes of Leonardo's Salvator Mundi.

POSTS TAGGED

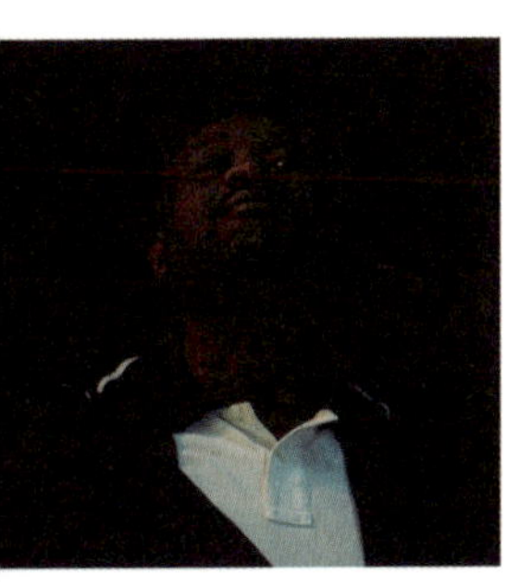

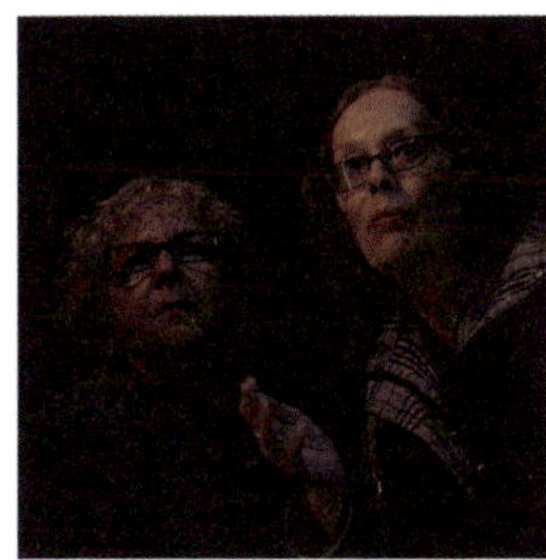

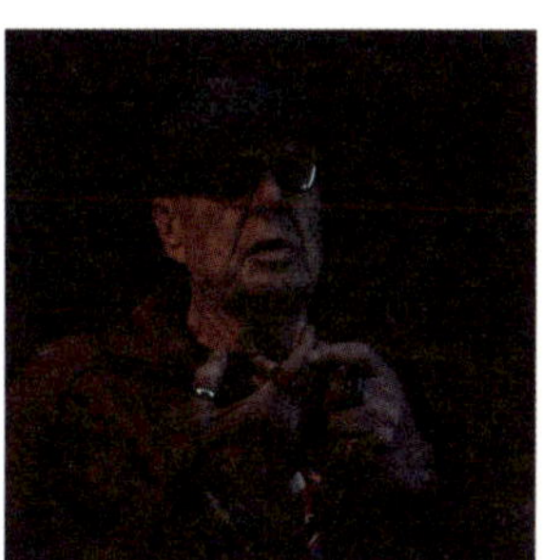

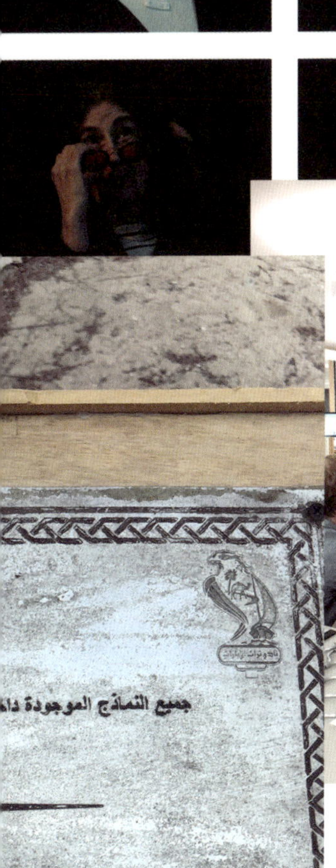

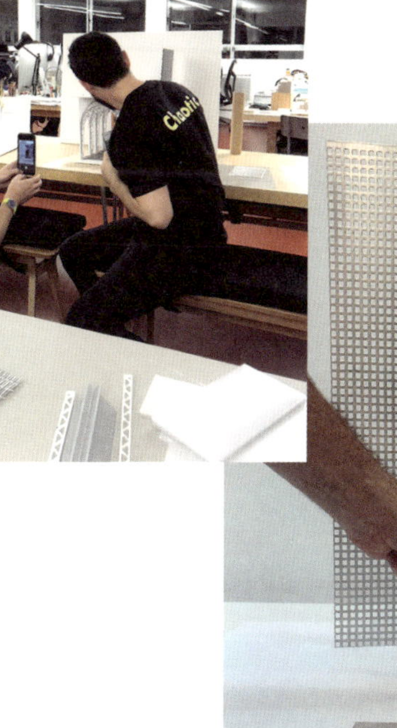

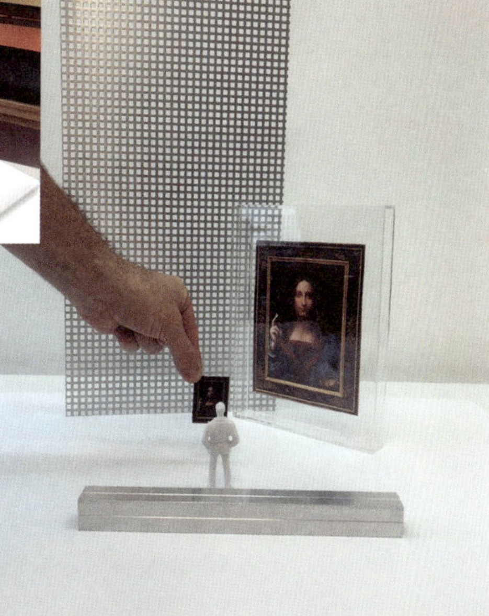

IMAGES

p. 118
Left: Architect Jean Nouvel and H.E. Sheikh Sultan Bin Tahnoon Al Nahyan, chairman of Department of Culture and Tourism Abu Dhabi, examine scale model of Louvre Abu Dhabi. Photo: Gerry O'Leary/www.gerryoleary.com

p. 122
Above centre: Burj Khalifa, Dubai. Photo: Donald Y. Tong

pp. 122–23
Below: Comparison of floorplans for Burj Khalifa, Dubai, with other tall skyscrapers. Image: Paul C. Martens

p. 123
Tarn Philipp, Cross-section drawing of Arbatu Ensesa, Freweyni, 2018

pp. 118–125
All other images: Simon Fujiwara and David Kohn

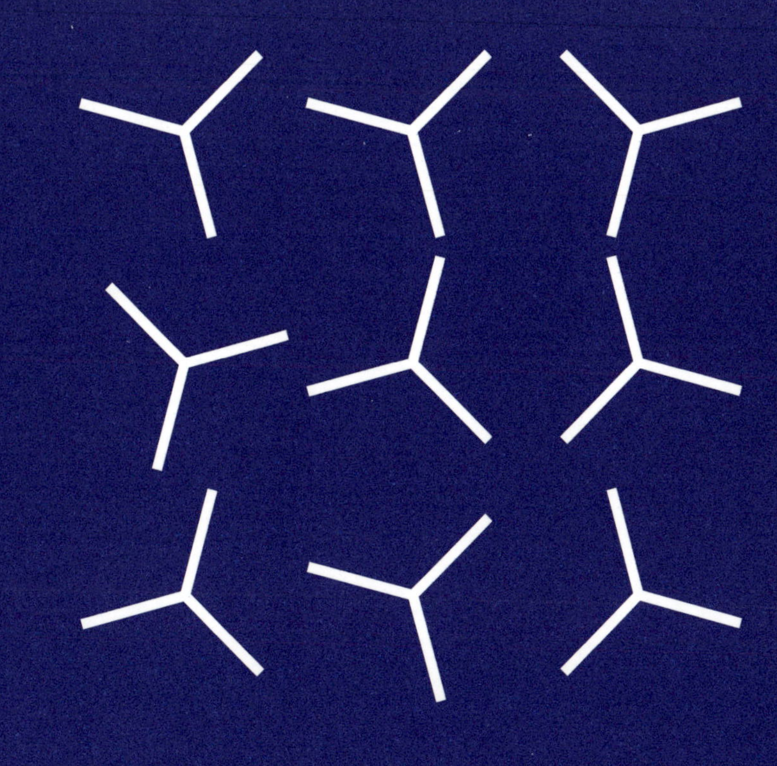

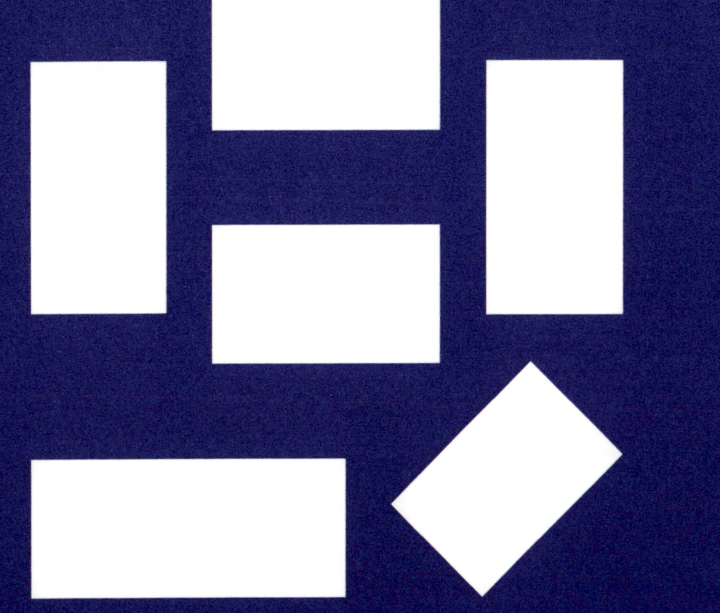

Farshid Moussavi Architecture
Zineb Sedira

PROJECT TEAM

Farshid Moussavi
Zsuzsa Peter
Zineb Sedira

Borders / Inclusivity

The world is defined by diversity: different ideas, people and things. Borders between countries that have become sites of contention during the last two decades – such as the border between Mexico and the USA, between Spain and Morocco, between China and North Korea, between Iran and Pakistan, between India and Burma, between Kuwait and Iraq – intend to eliminate diversity by blocking free movement. And there are many proposals for new borders – between Morocco and Algeria, between Hungary and Serbia, between Hungary and Croatia, between Turkey and Syria, between Turkey and Iran, between Brazil and Argentina, between Russia and Ukraine, between Malaysia and Indonesia and between the United Kingdom and Europe.

These macro-borders block free movement but cannot create homogeneous societies. A diversity of ideas, people and things exists at a molecular scale in every city. In response, urban spaces, their streets as well as their built forms, are increasingly defined by borders: red routes, turnstiles, swing gates, bollards, metal-detector gates, swivel gates, retractable belt barriers, crowd-control barriers and so on. These make the experience of inhabiting the city tedious. It takes ever more time to traverse the streets, office buildings, subway stations, airport terminals and museums. Mobility can be fluid, congested or non-existent depending on where you are.

But the very presence of these borders is a space of hope too. There is, underlying all these borders, the acceptance that the city is a multiplicity. Its diversity of ideas, people and things cannot be erased. It may need to be controlled, but cannot be homogenised. For a brief time, as we are channelled through red routes or turnstiles, we become united as urban subjects, leaving our differences – of religion, ethnicity or political belief – aside, to subscribe to the city as a space for all.

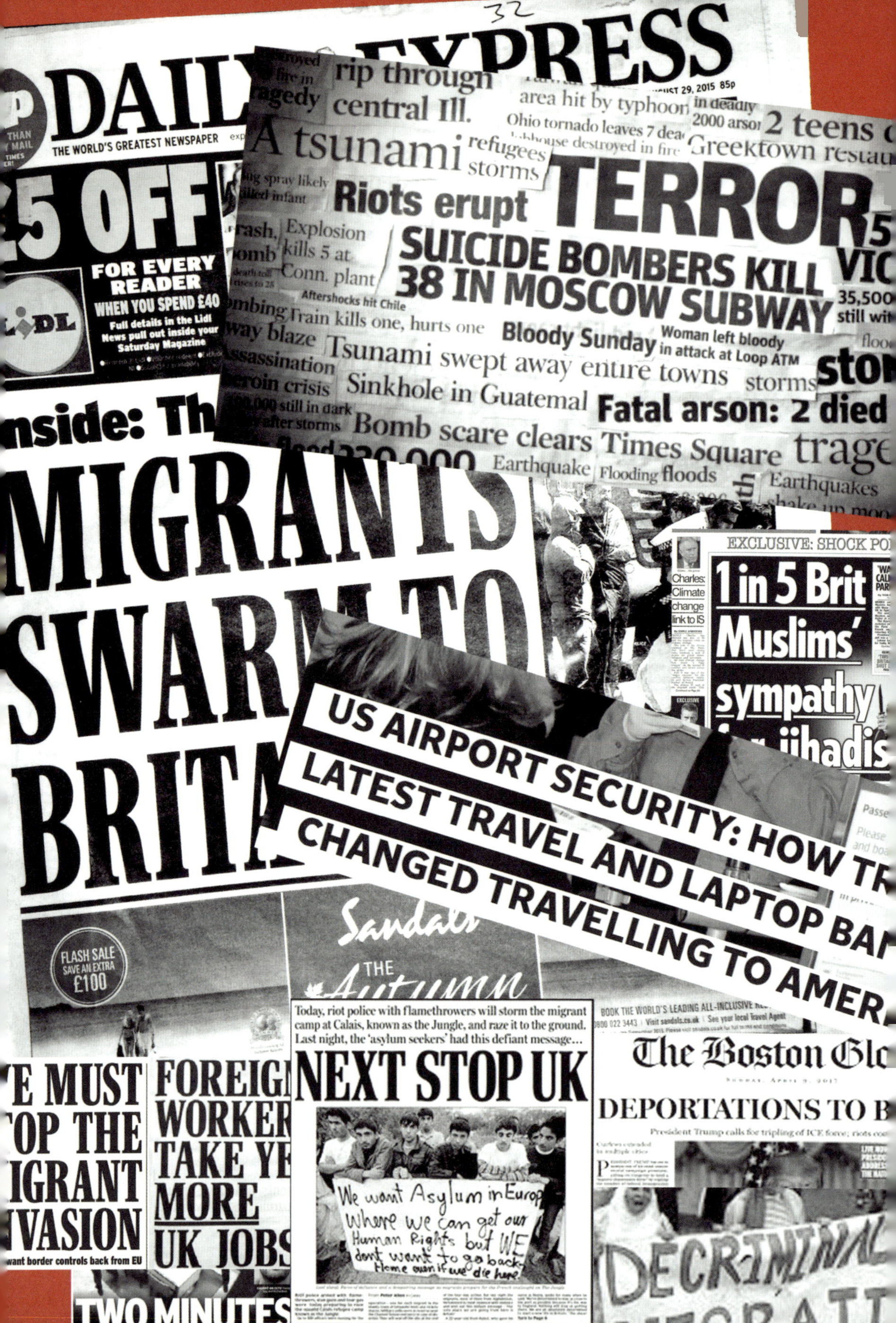

DAILY EXPRESS
THE WORLD'S GREATEST NEWSPAPER
AUGUST 29, 2015 85p
£5 OFF
FOR EVERY READER
WHEN YOU SPEND £40
Full details in the Lidl News pull out inside your Saturday Magazine
LIDL
rip through central Ill.
area hit by typhoon
in deadly 2000 arson
2 teens
Ohio tornado leaves 7 dead
Greektown restau
A tsunami
refugees storms
Riots erupt
TERROR
Explosion kills 5 at Conn. plant
SUICIDE BOMBERS KILL 38 IN MOSCOW SUBWAY
Aftershocks hit Chile
Train kills one, hurts one
Bloody Sunday
Woman left bloody in attack at Loop ATM
35,500 still wit
Tsunami swept away entire towns
Sinkhole in Guatemal
storms
Fatal arson: 2 died
Bomb scare clears Times Square
Earthquake
Flooding floods
Earthquakes
trage
Assassination
heroin crisis
inside: Th
MIGRANTS SWARM TO BRITA
EXCLUSIVE: SHOCK PO
Charles: Climate change link to IS
1 in 5 Brit Muslims' sympathy for jihadis
US AIRPORT SECURITY: HOW TR
LATEST TRAVEL AND LAPTOP BA
CHANGED TRAVELLING TO AMER
FLASH SALE SAVE AN EXTRA £100
Sandals
THE Autumn
BOOK THE WORLD'S LEADING ALL-INCLUSIVE
0800 022 3443 | Visit sandals.co.uk | See your local Travel Agent
Today, riot police with flamethrowers will storm the migrant camp at Calais, known as the Jungle, and raze it to the ground. Last night, the 'asylum seekers' had this defiant message…
NEXT STOP UK
We want Asylum in Europ Where we can get our Human Rights but WE dont want to go back Home even if we die here
The Boston Gl
DEPORTATIONS TO B
President Trump calls for tripling of ICE force; riots co
E MUST TOP THE IGRANT VASION
want border controls back from EU
FOREIGN WORKER TAKE YE MORE UK JOBS
TWO MINUTES
DECRIMINAL

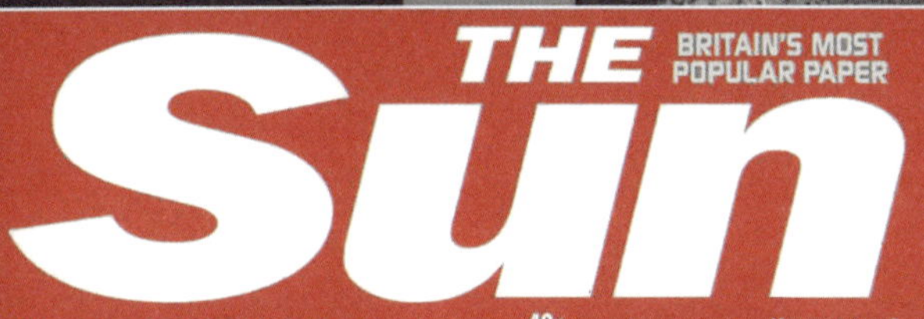

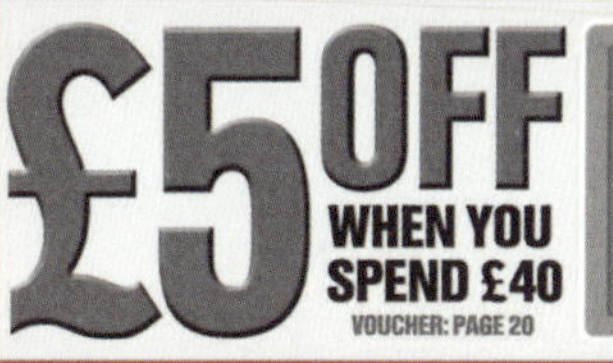

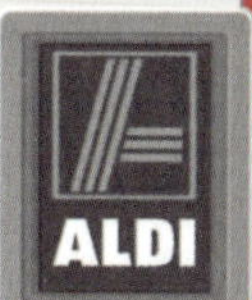

Wednesday, December 18, 2013 40p thesun.co.uk

UK

AS PM FLIES TO MEET EU LEADERS, YOU TELL HIM:

DRAW A RED LINE ON IMMIGRATION OR ELSE!

ROMANIA

BULGARIA

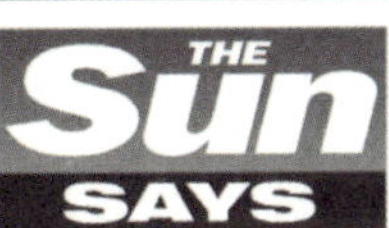

THE British people and The Sun today issue this red line demand to David Cameron: Win back our power to halt immigration from the EU.

If you can't stop the flood, PM, there's every chance the country will vote to get out altogether at your referendum.

On the eve of Mr Cameron's latest EU summit, a landmark poll for The Sun reveals how

Continued on Page Four

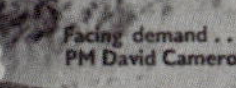

Facing demand . . .
PM David Cameron

SPECIAL REPORT: PAGES 4 & 5

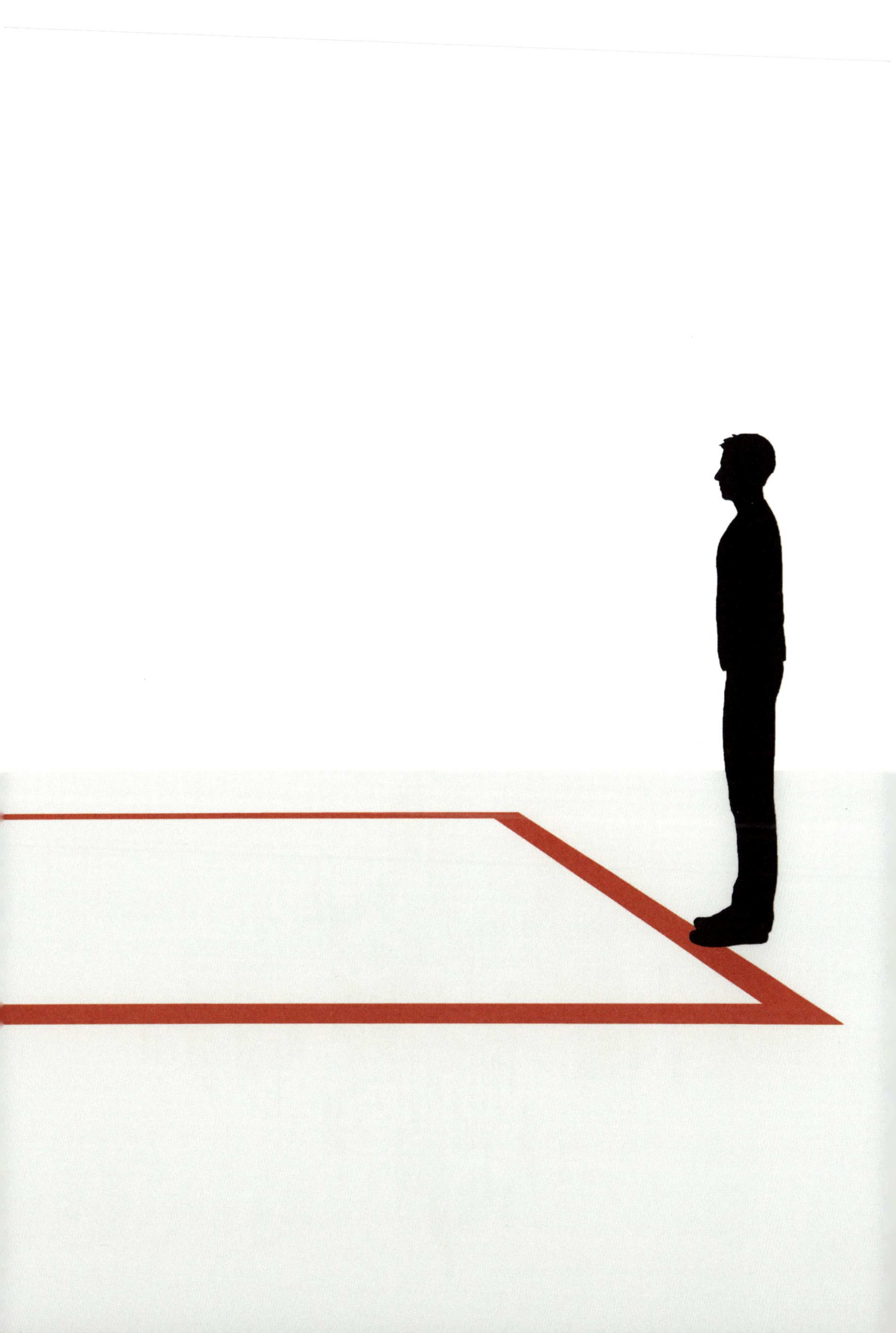

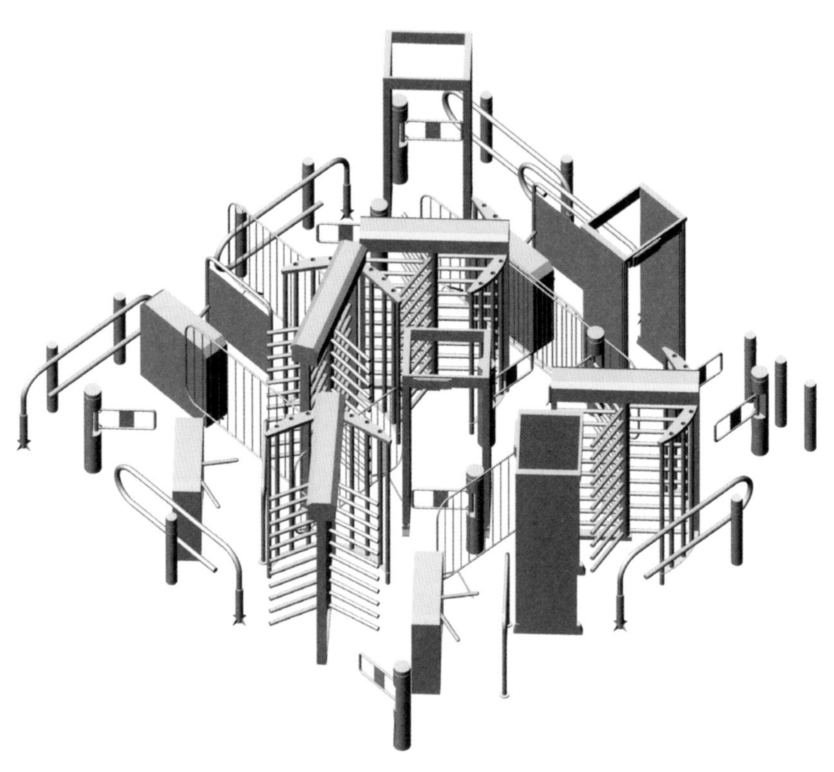

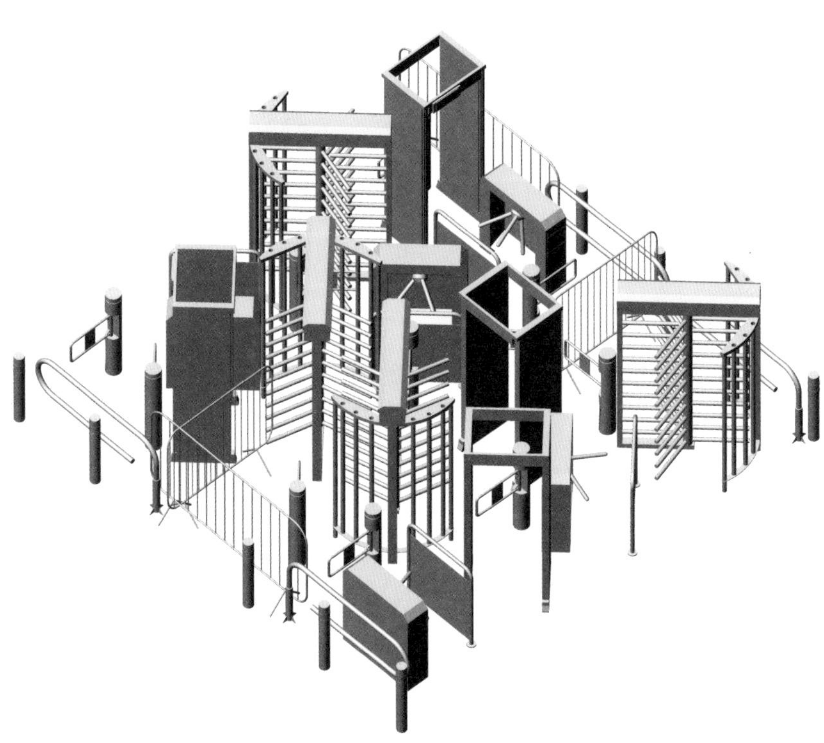

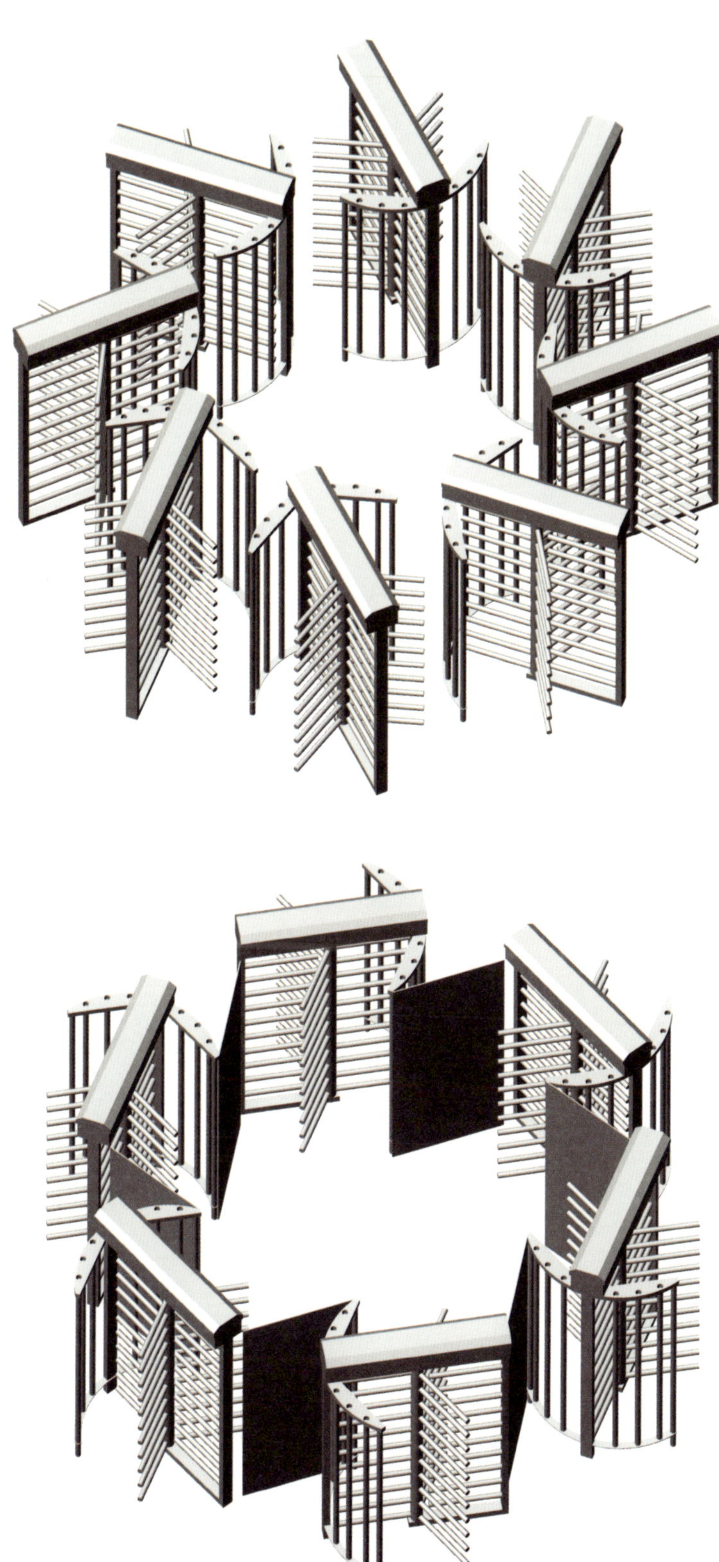

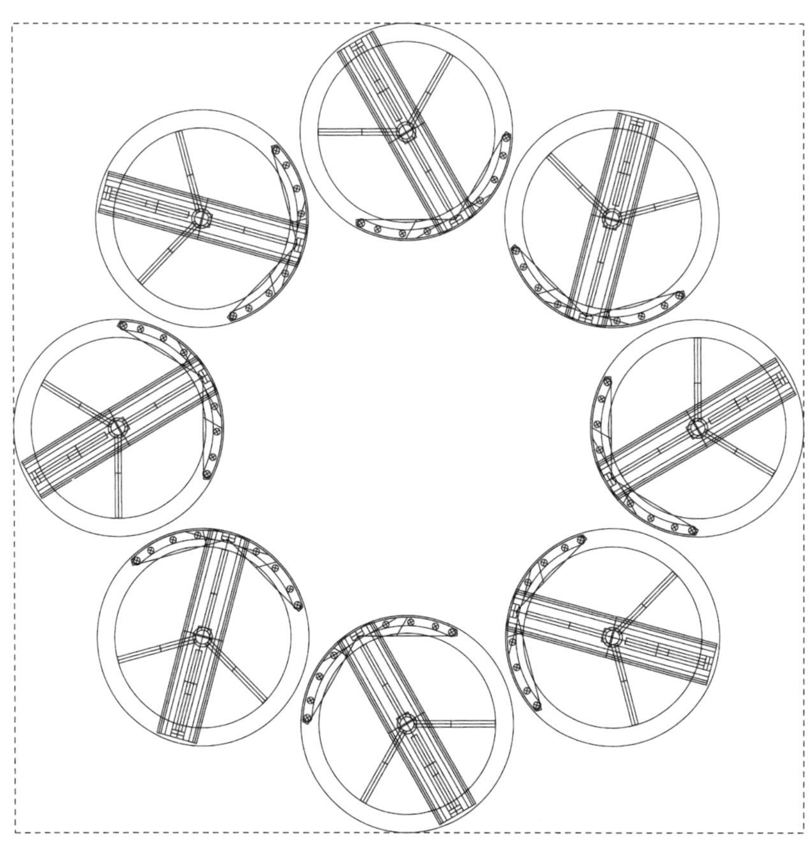

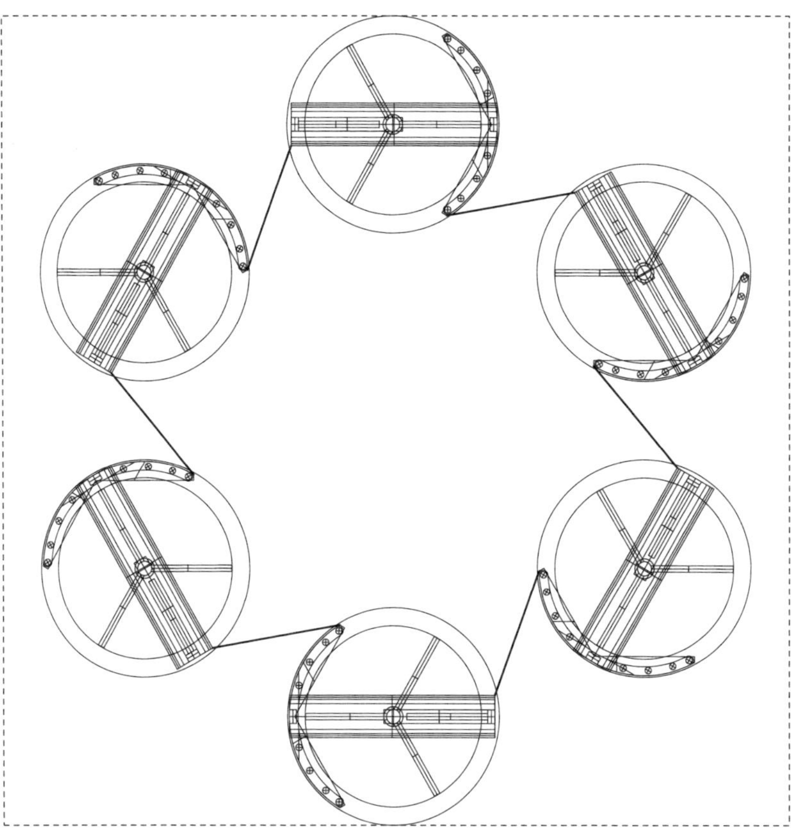

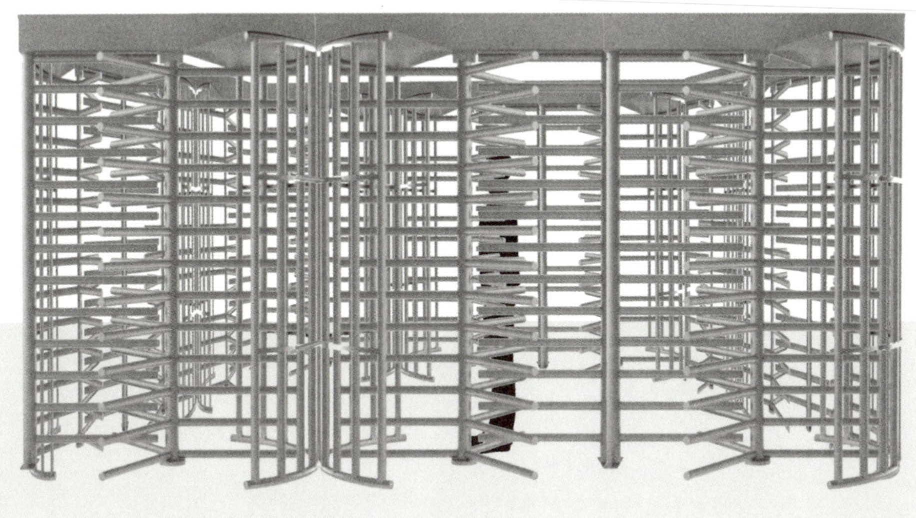

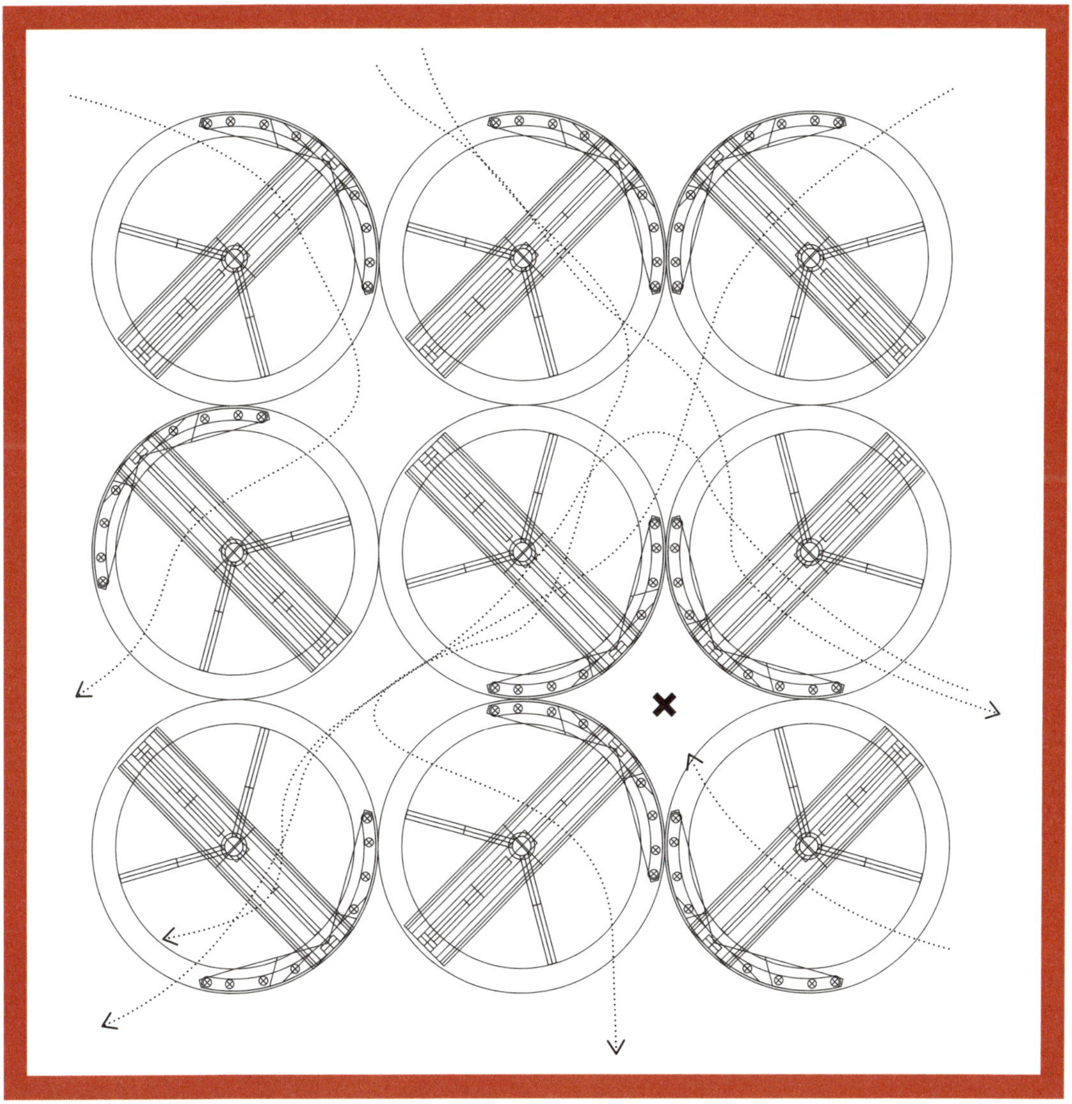

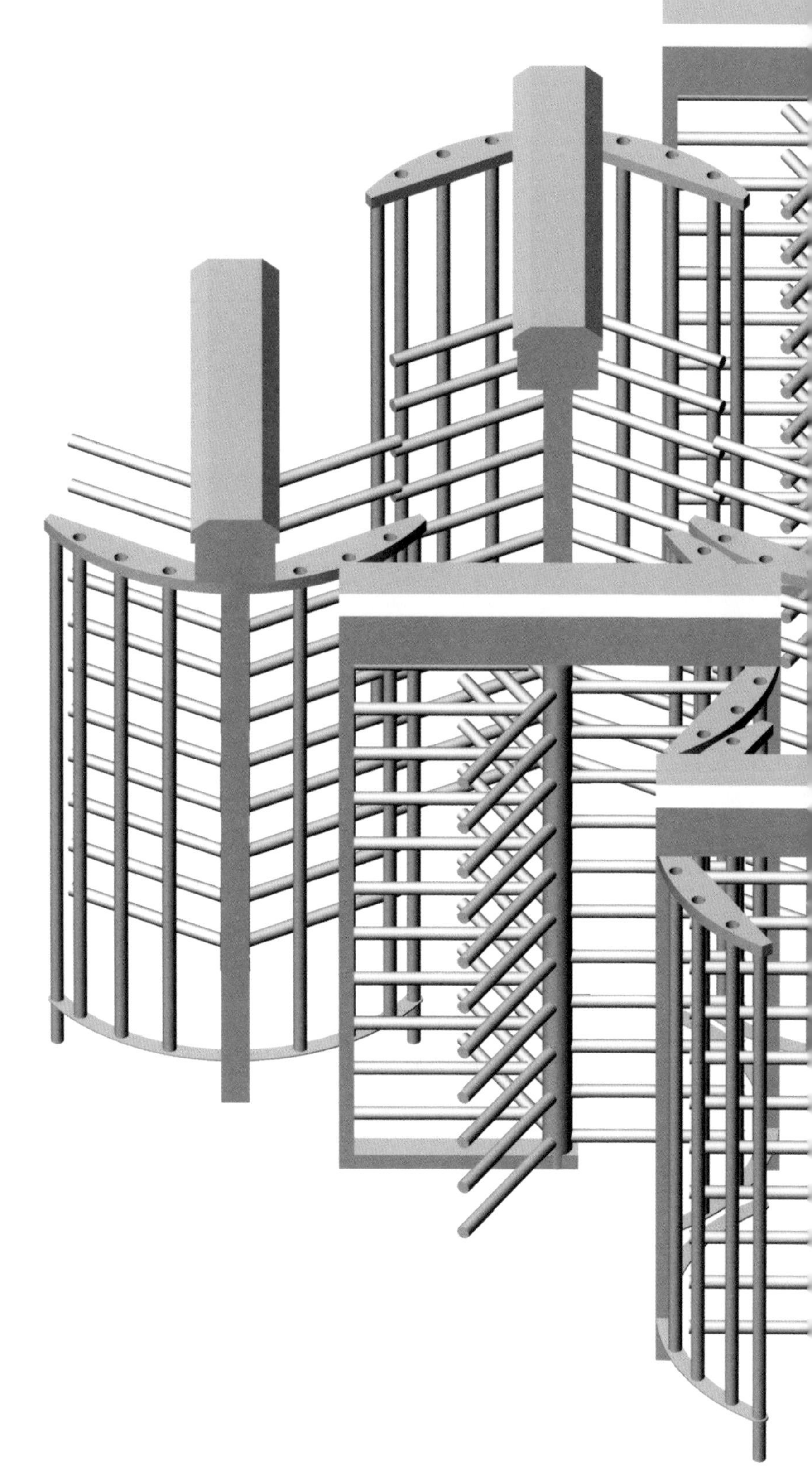

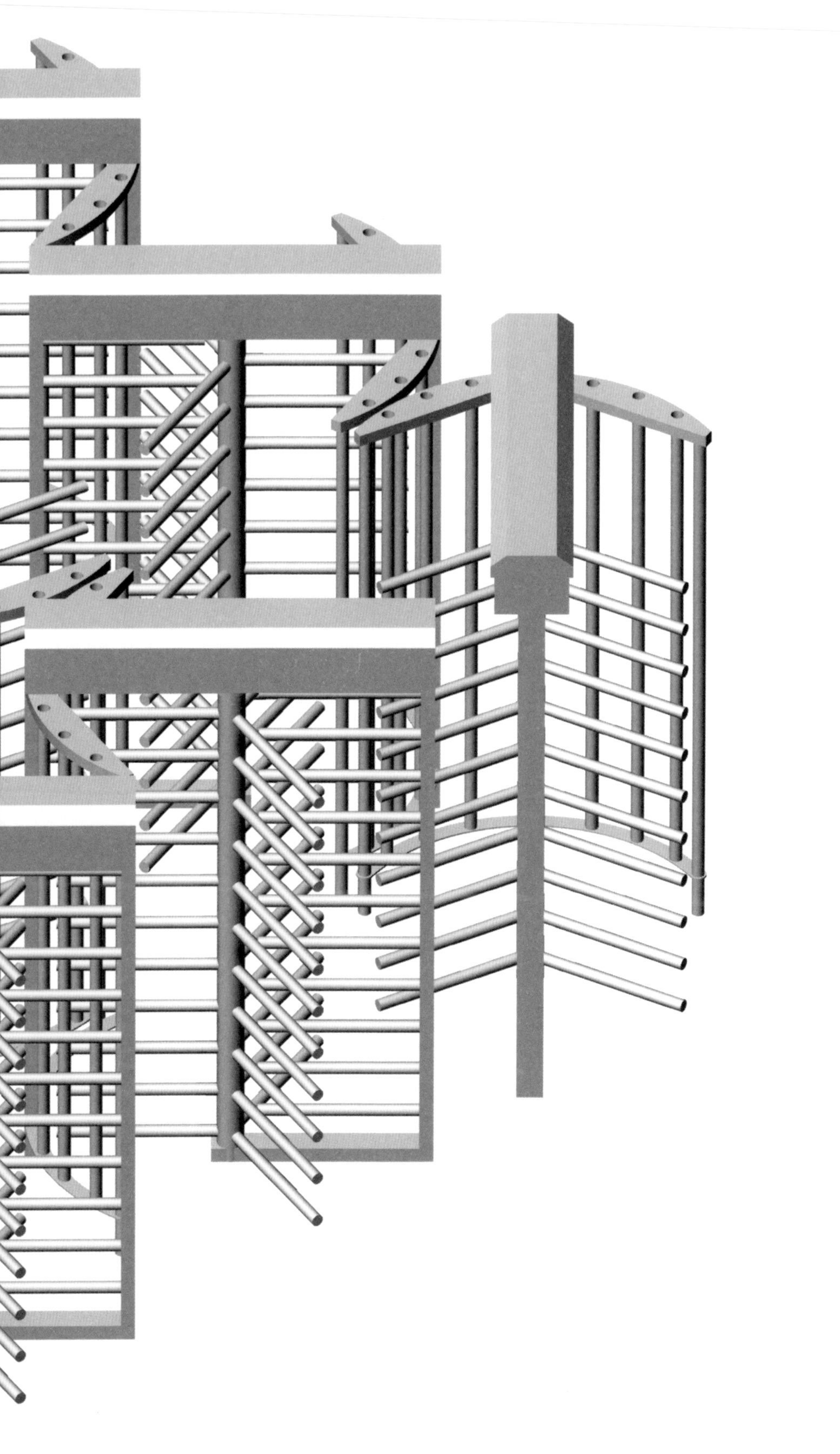

p. 130
Zineb Sedira, collage of press clippings, 2018

p. 131
The Sun, Wednesday, December 18, 2018, front page

pp. 132–39
Farshid Moussavi Architecture, process studies for *Borders / Inclusivity*, 2018, digital renderings

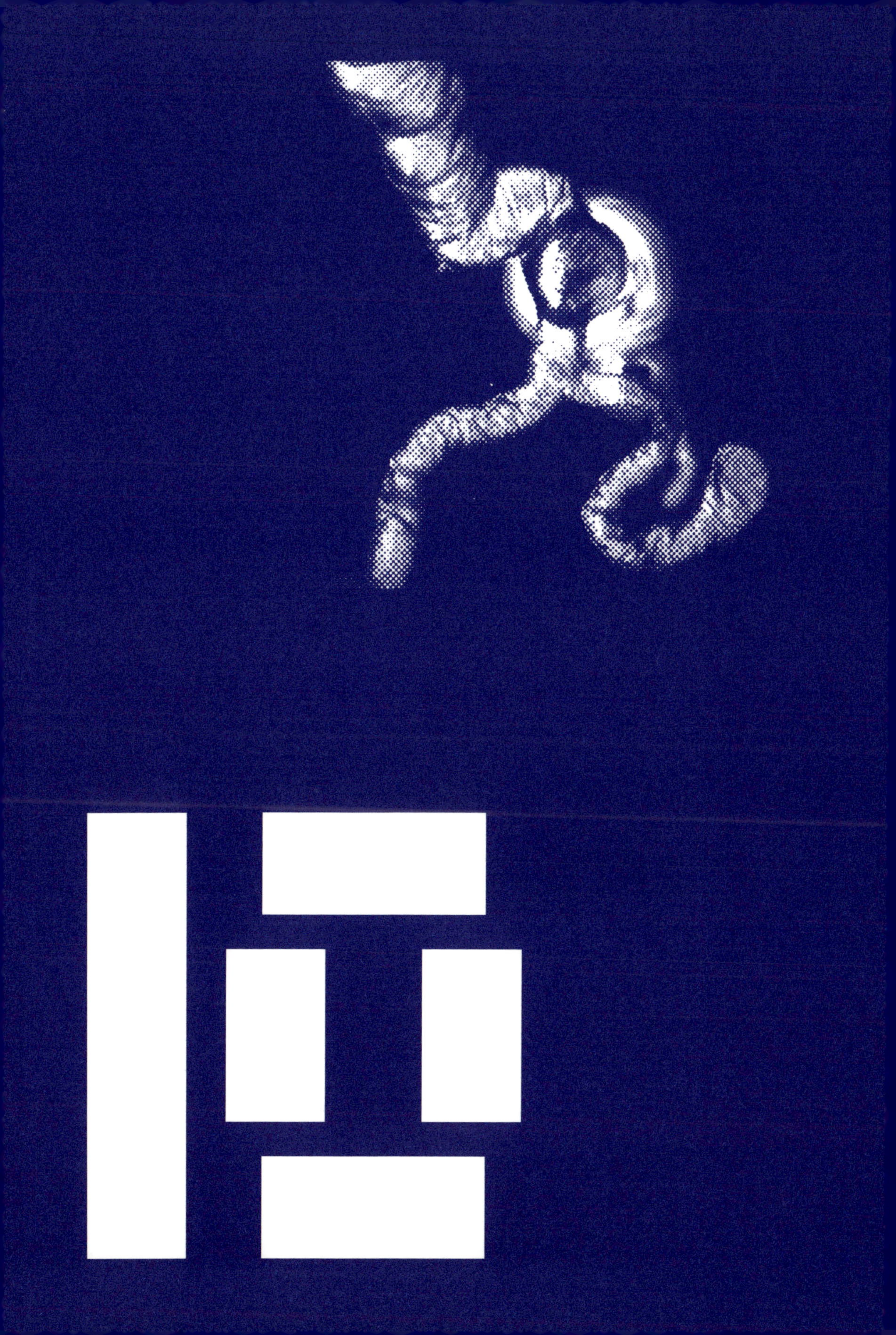

Rachel Armstrong
Cécile B. Evans

PROJECT TEAM

Rachel Armstrong
Cécile B. Evans
Simone Ferracina, *University of Edinburgh*
Ioannis Ieropoulos, *University of the West of England*
Pierangelo Scravaglieri, *Newcastle University*

Living Architecture
Horizon 2020 Research and Innovation
Programme, EU Grant Agreement no. 686585

999 Years, 13 sqm (the future belongs to ghosts)

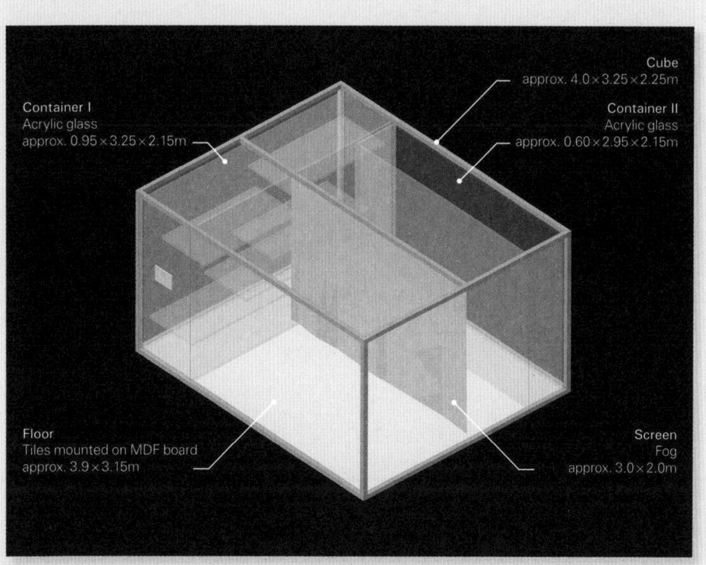

In 2018, a group of flats converted from a seven-storey office block are revealed to be the smallest (official) living spaces in London: 13 sqm. A leading architect denounces them as inhumane in a short, public article but no long-term solution is offered, by anyone.

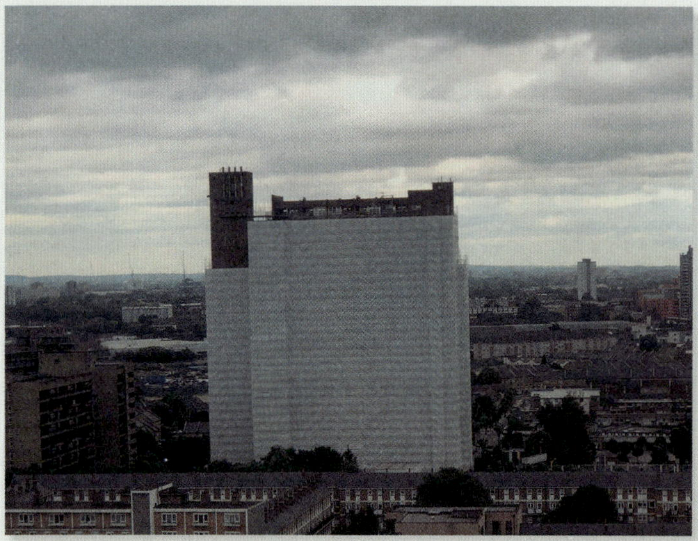

Some time during the Middle Ages, the common law of 'leaseholds' is instituted to reinforce feudal hierarchy: a lord owns the land and the property owner is only a tenant of the land on which their property exists. Leaseholds are still the most frequent agreements made when purchasing property in the UK, the most common duration being 250 years and the longest, 999. At the start of the twenty-first century, large mid-nineteenth-century postwar housing estates designed for a proposed future class, fall prey to units of measurement and are sold to private developers. The tenants are 'decanted' and rehoused, inevitably breaking up communities, individuals and their roots.

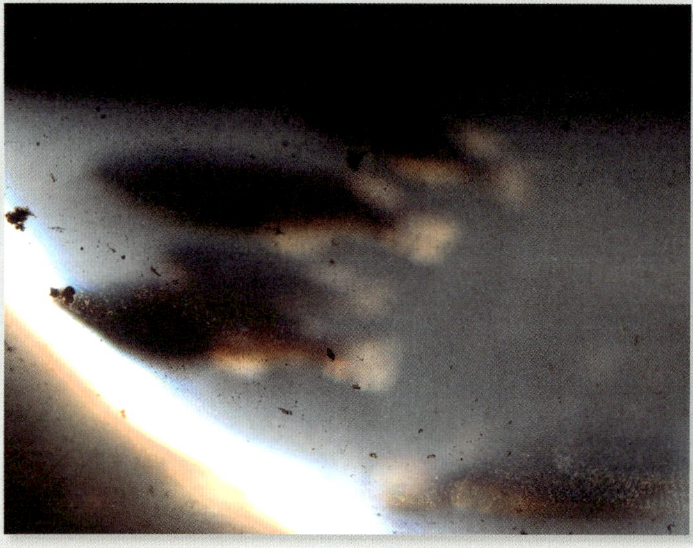

The metrics of space and time are each socio-political constructs that have long been commodified and presented as objective realities for inhabitants. This makes it far less interesting to speculate on any number of possible living futures.

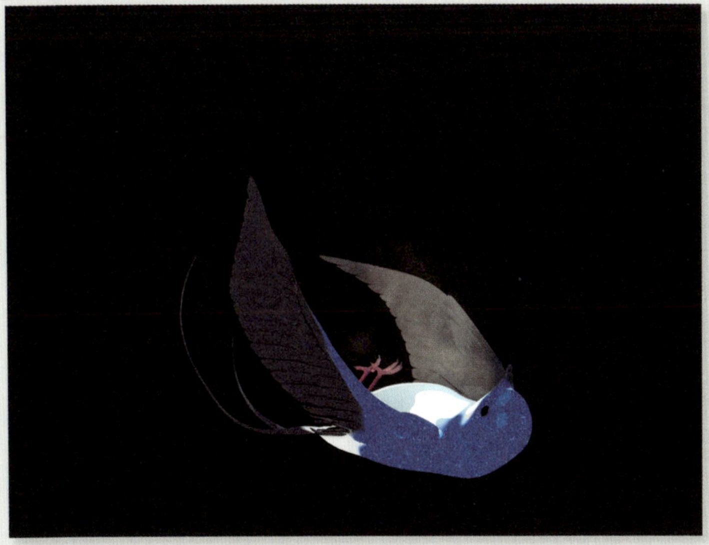

In a programme for *Failed Architecture*, journalist, activist and academic Ash Sarkar describes the very real space that grief occupies in a city, its presence and the sustainable power of memory in the absence or erasure of physical structures – buildings, homes or even bodies.

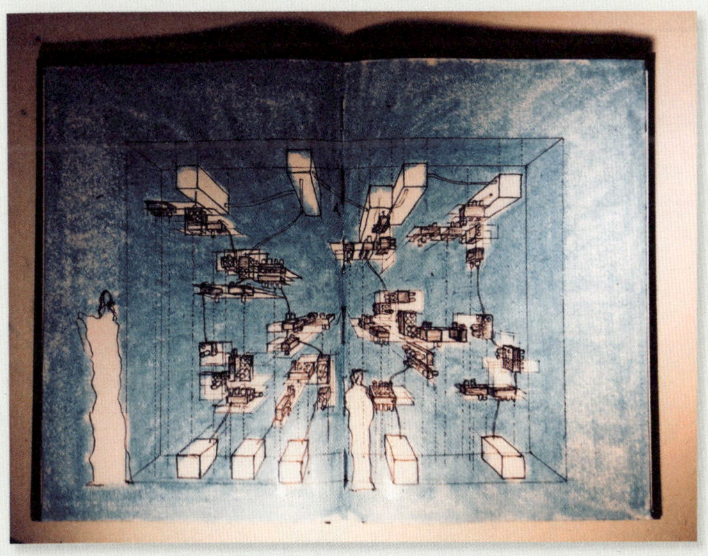

Within her practice, *Living Architecture*, Rachel Armstrong carves out the possibility for new structures formed from self-assembling units, cells or even microbes; recalcitrant formations designed from 'risky particles', a departure from the inevitably fallible models of risk management.

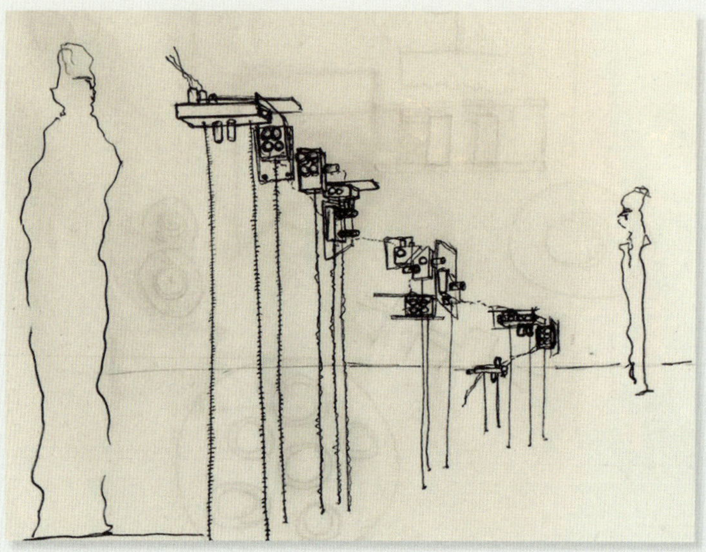

Imagine what these self-assembling units could build in 1,000 years' time (though this would be difficult for any person alive today to envision within the current units of measurement). What could grief, perhaps the most recalcitrant emotion and having the advantage of a historical lead, accomplish in 999 years?

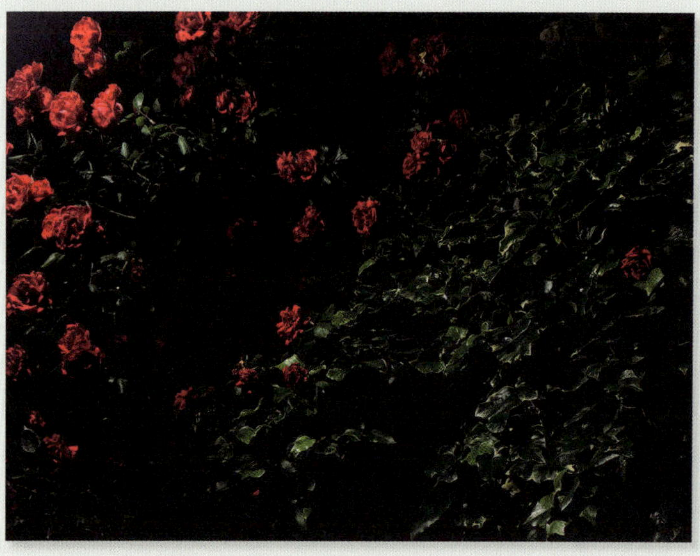

Even in the minimum amount of available space, grief could foreseeably eclipse the units of time, space and capital that aim to contain it. Grief is matter – it matters and takes up space – a restless material that is evidence of life.

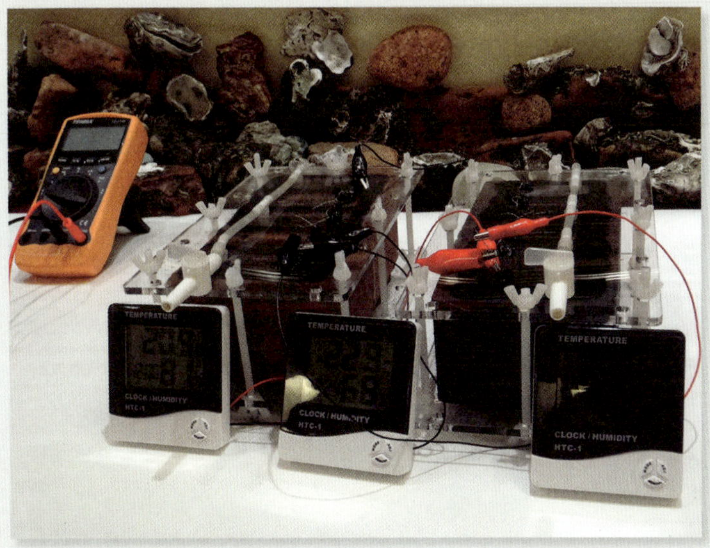

Grief and the microbe are allied; not simply because loss often results in a microbial process, but because they are both generators of energy. They are both markers of life and culture. They thrive in difficult environments, are resilient, diverse, subversive and contagious.

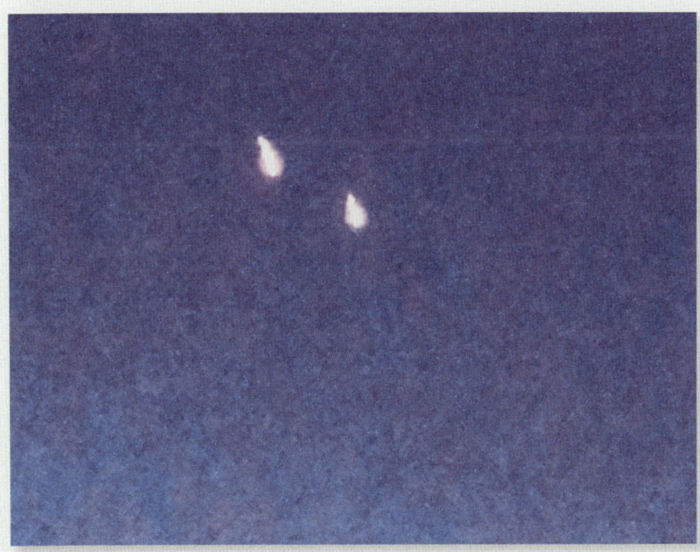

Through metabolic transformation 'lost' matter transitions into alternative states, an act that introduces a complex, vital sense of constant change to the allegory. Lost matter will unavoidably, and maybe even hopefully, shape a very different future and system of values.

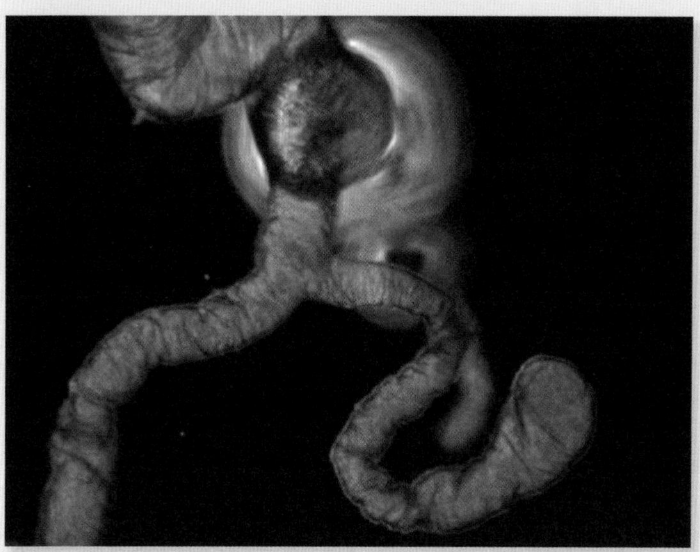

This is suggestive of a microscopic structural system. Times are changing, the weather is changing, microscopic structural systems change all the time. Everything must change.

IMAGES

p. 143
Dominik Arni, project sketch for *999 years, 13sqm (the future belongs to ghosts)*, 2018. Image: Dominik Arni

p. 144
Above: Image: Cécile B. Evans

Below: Rachel Armstrong, *Shadows*, Palais de Tokyo, Paris, photograph, 2018

p. 145
Above: Citation: 'London Undone: Gaika and Ash Sarkar Discuss the City's Past, Present and Future', *Failed Architecture #5*, Podcast, 12 July 2018. Image: Cécile B. Evans

Below: Pierangelo Scravaglieri, study of living wall 1, for 'living bricks' project with Simone Ferracina at Newcastle University and The University of Edinburgh. Image: Pierangelo Scravaglieri

p. 146
Above: Pierangelo Scravaglieri, study of living wall 2, for 'living bricks' project with Simone Ferracina at Newcastle University and The University of Edinburgh. Image: Pierangelo Scravaglieri

Below: Image: Cécile B. Evans

p. 147
Above: 'Living Bricks' prototype developed for the *Living Architecture* project by Ioannis Ieropoulos at The University of the West of England, Bristol. Image: Rachel Armstrong

Below: Image: Cécile B. Evans

p. 148
10 × magnification of protocell forms, University of Southern Denmark, Odense, film still. Image: Rachel Armstrong

6a architects, established in 2001, London, UK, by Tom Emerson (b. 1970, France) and Stephanie McDonald (b. 1966, UK) combines a culture of making and innovation with humanity and playfulness in its contemporary art galleries, educational buildings, artists' studios and residential projects. Recent projects include the new MK Gallery, Milton Keynes, and the South London Gallery Fire Station; Cowan Court, a sixty-eight-room hall of residence at Churchill College, Cambridge; and new photography studios for Juergen Teller, shortlisted for the Stirling Prize in 2017. The practice is currently completing projects in Melbourne, New York and Hamburg. Tom Emerson is professor of architecture at ETH Zurich and in 2018 was awarded the Conrad Ferdinand Meyer Prize. Stephanie Macdonald was nominated for Women in Architecture Award 2018.

Adjaye Associates, established in 2000 by Sir David Adjaye OBE (b. 1966, Tanzania), with offices in London, UK; New York, US, and Accra, Ghana, is a practice influenced by contemporary art, music, science, African art forms and the civic life of cities, and is characterised by a sense of curiosity and a research-based methodology. Current projects include a new home for The Studio Museum in Harlem, New York, as well as a new landmark for London – the UK Holocaust Memorial and Learning Centre. Recently completed projects include the Smithsonian Institution National Museum of African American History and Culture, National Mall, Washington DC, 2016; the design of the 56th Venice Biennale with curator Okwui Enwezor, 2015; and Sugar Hill museum and housing development in Harlem, New York, 2015. Other prominent projects include the Idea Store in Tower Hamlets, London, 2004–5. An exhibition of Sir David Adjaye's work was held at Whitechapel Gallery in 2006.

Andrés Jaque / Office for Political Innovation, established in 2003, Madrid, Spain and New York, US, by Andrés Jaque (b. 1971, Spain) works at the intersection of architecture, research and activism. Its work connects through inquiries and subversions of bodily and geopolitical realities. Projects include art spaces, such as *CA2M*; experimental residential buildings, like *Plasencia Clergy House*, *TUPPER HOMES*, *IKEA Disobedients* or *House in Never Never Land*; temporary installations, such as *PHANTOM. Mies as Rendered Society*; performances such as Superpowers of Ten; and public artifacts, including *Escaravox* and *COSMO PS1*. The practice has been awarded the Frederick Kiesler Prize and the Silver Lion at the 14th Venice Architecture Biennale, 2014. Andrés Jaque, Phd Architect (ETSAM), is the Director of the Advanced Architectural Design Program at Columbia University Graduate School of Architecture, Planning and Preservation, Alfred Toepfer Stiftung's Tessenow Stipendiat (Hamburg) and Graham Foundation Grantee.

APPARATA, established in 2015 in London, UK, is a studio for architecture, design and research founded by Astrid Smitham (b. 1983, UK), Nicholas Lobo Brennan (b. 1983, UK) and Theo Thysiades (b. 1977, Greece). They design and construct buildings, furniture and books. Current projects include *A House for Artists,* a new artists' co-housing block with public events hall in Barking, London. Completed projects include the *Friday Sermon* structure at the Bahrain pavilion at the 16th Venice Architecture Biennale, 2018; exhibition design for *The University Is Now on Air*, CCA Montreal, 2017; and for *Seth Siegelaub: Beyond Conceptual Art*, Stedelijk, Amsterdam, 2015; *The White House*, Dagenham, London, 2016; and the restructuring of a vacated Carnegie Library in Manor Park, London, 2015. Lobo Brennan was a winner of the 2012 Swiss Art Awards for Architecture and co-founded the collective Gruppe in Zurich in 2011. They have lectured and taught across Europe at Sandberg Institute, Royal College of Art, The Cass and hold an associate professorship at Kingston School of Art.

Rachel Armstrong (b. 1966, UK) is Professor of Experimental Architecture at Newcastle University. Her work focuses on establishing the conditions for a 'living' architecture that couples the computational properties of the natural world with building structures and infrastructures. She is Director and founder of the Experimental Architecture Group (EAG) whose work has been published, exhibited and performed at international biennales, and Coordinator for the *Living Architecture* project, which is an ongoing collaboration of experts from universities in the UK, Spain, Italy and Austria. She has written a number of academic books including *Soft Living Architecture: An Alternative View of Bio-informed Practice,* 2018; *Star Ark: A Living, Self-Sustaining Spaceship,* 2016; *Vibrant Architecture: Matter as a Co-Designer of Living Structures*, 2015; and the forthcoming *Experimental Architecture: Prototyping the unknown through design-led research,* 2019; and *Liquid Life: On Non-Linear Materiality,* 2019. Her fiction books include *Invisible Ecologies*, 2019 and *Origamy,* 2018.

Rana Begum (b. 1977, Bangladesh; lives in London, UK) blurs the boundaries between sculpture, painting and architecture. Her visual language draws from the urban landscape as well as geometric patterns from traditional Islamic art and architecture. Light is fundamental to her process. Her works absorb and reflect varied densities of light to produce an experience for the viewer that is both temporal and sensorial. Recent solo exhibitions include *Space, Light, Colour,* Djanogly

Gallery, Nottingham, 2018; *A Conversation with Light and Form*, Tate St Ives, 2018; *The Space Between*, Parasol Unit, London, 2016; and *Rana Begum*, Delfina Foundation, London, 2010. Recent group exhibitions include *Frieze Sculpture Park*, London, 2018; *Actions. The image of the world can be different (part 1)*, Kettle's Yard, Cambridge, 2018; *Tribute to Sol Lewitt*, Gemeente Museum Den Haag, 2016, as well as the 11th Gwangju Biennale, 2016. She was awarded the 2017 Abraaj Group Art Prize and Jack Goldhill Award for Sculpture in 2012.

Cao Fei (b. 1978, China; lives in Beijing) mixes social commentary, popular aesthetics, references to Surrealism and documentary conventions in her films and installations. Her works reflect on the rapid and chaotic changes that are occurring in Chinese society today.Recent solo exhibitions include *Cao Fei*, K21 Kunstsammlung Nordrhein-Westfalen, Dusseldorf, 2018; *A hollow in a world too full*, Tai Kwun Contemporary, Hong Kong, 2018; *Cao Fei*, MoMA PS1, New York, 2016; *Cao Fei*, The Center for Contemporary Art, Tel Aviv, 2016; *Cao Fei: Splendid River*, Secession, Vienna, 2015; and *Haze and Fog*, Tate Modern, Starr Auditorium, London, 2013. Recent group exhibitions include *Art in China after 1989: Theater of the World*, San Francisco Museum of Modern Art, San Francisco, 2018; *Art in the Age of the Internet 1989 to Today*, ICA Boston, 2018 as well as 10th Istanbul Biennale, 5th Shanghai Biennale, 50th, 52nd & 56th Venice Biennales. She received the Chinese Contemporary Art Award (CCAA) Best Artist Award in 2016 and Best Young Artist Award in 2006.

David Kohn Architects, established in 2007, London, UK by David Kohn (b. 1972, South Africa) is a London-based practice working internationally on arts, education and residential projects. Current projects include the refurbishment of the ICA, London, a new campus for New College, Oxford, an architecture faculty in Flanders and an apartment building in Berlin. Past projects include the Photography Centre at the V&A, London, 2018; Thomas Dane Gallery, London, 2013; The White Building, Hackney Wick, London, 2012; *A Room for London* in collaboration with artist Fiona Banner, London, 2011; and an award-winning restaurant at the Royal Academy of Arts, London, 2008.

Mariana Castillo Deball (b.1975, Mexico; lives in Berlin, Germany) takes a kaleidoscopic approach to her practice, mediating between science, archaeology and the visual arts and exploring the way in which these disciplines describe the world. Recent solo exhibitions include *To-Day, February 20th*, Savannah College of Art and Design (SCAD) Museum of Art, Savannah, 2018; *Pleasures of association, and poissons, such as love*, Galerie Wedding – Raum für zeitgenössische Kunst, Berlin, 2017; *¿Quién medirá el espacio, quién me dirá el momento?*, MACO Museo de Arte Contemporáneo de Oaxaca, 2015 and '*What we caught we threw away, what we didn't catch we kept*', CCA: Centre for Contemporary Arts, Glasgow, 2013. Recent group exhibitions include *Statues Also Die: Contemporary reflections on heritage and conflict in the Middle-East*, Fondazione Sandretto Re Rebaudengo, Turin, 2018; *Alors que j'écoutais moi aussi David, Eleanor, Mariana, etc.*, La Criée centre d'art contemporain, Rennes, 2017; *El Orden Natural de las Cosas*, Museo Jumex, Mexico City, 2016; and *Storylines: Contemporary Art at the Guggenheim Museum*, Guggenheim Museum, New York, 2014.

Cécile B. Evans (b. 1983, US; lives in London, UK) works in sculpture, video and video installations, internet platforms, and performances. Starting with the relationship between human beings and machines, Evans focuses on the value of emotions in contemporary society, exploring today's forms of human subjectivity, the representation of social roles and the idea itself of the body and mortality. Recent solo exhibitions include *AMOS' WORLD: Episode One*, mumok, Vienna, 2018; *Cécile B. Evans*, Castello di Rivoli, Turin, 2017; *Cécile B. Evans*, Museum Leuven, 2017; and *Cécile B. Evans*, Tate Liverpool, 2016.Recent group exhibitions include *Blind Faith: Between the Visceral and the Cognitive in Contemporary Art*, Haus der Kunst, Munich, 2018; *Being There*, Louisiana Museum of Modern Art, Humlebaek, 2017–18; and *Äppärät*, Ballroom Marfa, Texas, 2015–16.

Farshid Moussavi Architecture, established 2011, London, UK by Farshid Moussavi OBE RA (b. 1965, Iran) is a practice focused on design intelligence and creative possibilities through the use of new material and construction technologies. Moussavi is Professor in Practice of Architecture at the Harvard University Graduate School of Design, Massachusetts, and was co-founder of the London-based Foreign Office Architects (FOA). Current projects include residential complexes in the La Défense district of Paris and in Montpellier, and an office complex in the City of London. Recent projects include Architecture Room, Royal Academy Summer Exhibition, London, 2017; Victoria Beckham Flagship Store, London, 2014; Museum of Contemporary Art in Cleveland, 2012; and *Architecture and its Affects*, installation at 13th Venice Architecture Biennale, 2012.

Simon Fujiwara (b. 1982, UK; lives in Berlin, Germany) works across performance, painting, video, sculpture and installation. In his work, people, technology, images and objects are tools used to paint a compelling and fragmented portrait of the 21st century. Recent solo exhibitions include *Hope House*, Kunsthaus Bregenz, 2018; *Joanne*, The Photographers' Gallery, London, 2017; *The Humanizer*, Irish Museum of Modern Art, Dublin, 2016; *Grand Tour*, Kunstverein Braunschweig, 2013; and *Simon Fujiwara: since 1982*, Tate St Ives, 2012. Recent group exhibitions include *Storylines: Contemporary Art at the*

Guggenheim, Solomon R. Guggenheim Museum, New York, 2015; *Un Nouveau Festival*, Centre Pompidou, Paris, 2014; as well as the Sharjah Biennial 11, 2013; 9th Shanghai Biennale, 2012; and 53rd Venice Biennale, 2009.

Kapwani Kiwanga (b. 1978, Canada; lives in Paris, France) creates installations, sound, video and performance, intentionally intertwining truth and fiction in order to unsettle hegemonic narratives and create spaces in which marginal discourses can flourish. As a trained anthropologist and social scientist, Kiwanga occupies the role of a researcher in her projects. Recent solo exhibitions include *Kapwani Kiwanga*, MIT List Visual Arts Center, Massachusetts, 2019; *Soft Measures*, Tramway, Glasgow International, 2018; *A wall is just a wall*, Power Plant, Toronto, 2017; *Kijeketile Suite*, South London Gallery, London, 2015; and *Maji Maji*, Jeu de Paume, Paris, 2014. Recent group exhibitions include *Stories for Almost Everyone*, Hammer Museum, Los Angeles, 2018; and *Nouveau parcours et nouvelle présentation des collections contemporaines*, Centre Pompidou, Paris, 2017. She was the recipient of the Sobey Art Award, 2018, Frieze Artist Award, 2018 and twice nominated for a BAFTA.

Marina Tabassum Architects, established 2005, Dhaka, Bangladesh by Marina Tabassum (b. 1969, Bangladesh) prioritises climate, materials, site, culture and local history in order to counteract what she finds impersonal and confused in architecture globally. Tabassum is Academic Director of the Bengal Institute for Architecture, Landscapes and Settlements and won the Jameel Prize in 2018. She was previously a partner in URBANA, which she founded in 1995. Recent projects include *Wisdom of the Land*, 16th Venice Architecture Biennale, 2018; Independence Monument and Liberation War Museum, Dhaka, 2013; Bait Ur Rouf Mosque, Dhaka, 2012; and A5 Architects Residence, Dhaka, 2002. She was awarded the Aga Khan Award for Architecture, 2016.

mono office, established in 2017, Beijing, China by Zhao Liqun (b. 1982, China), Miguel Esteban Alonso (b. 1992, Spain) and Pablo Alfonso Resa Abad (b. 1991, Spain) is an experimental design practice that operates at the intersection of architecture, urbanism and product design. The practice aims to incorporate both ethnographical approaches to aesthetics – emphasising the relationship between local communities, cultural development and craftsmanship – and techniques from scientific research. In doing so, they employ technologies of production from disciplines outside their own. Despite its recent formation, mono office's current projects include local-culture-based hotel prototypes, South China, 2018 and the transformation of an industrial textile warehouse complex into a cultural condenser for the city of Beijing in collaboration with Cano Lasso Arquitectos, 2018. Previous projects include Culture Complex, textile warehouse renovation competition, 1st prize, Beijing, 2018 and Floating Bookstore, Langyuan Vintage, CBD, Beijing, 2018.

Hardeep Pandhal (b. 1985 UK, lives in Glasgow) uses film, animation, sound, textiles, drawing and sculpture to satirise racial and cultural stereotypes. He often works in collaboration, with friends, family and those with experience of different disciplines. Recent solo exhibitions include *Self-Loathing Flashmob*, Kelvin Hall, Glasgow International, Director's Programme, 2018; *Liar Hydrant*, Cubitt, London, 2018; *Konfessions of a Klabautermann*, Berwick Film and Media Arts Festival, Berwick-upon-Tweed, 2018; and *Nightmare on BAME Street*, Eastside Projects, Birmingham, 2017. Recent group exhibnitions include *Knock Knock: Humour in Contemporary Art*, South London Gallery, 2018; *The House of Fame*, Nottingham Contemporary, 2018; *2018 Triennial: Songs for Sabotage*, New Museum, New York, 2018; and *Nothing Happens, Twice: Artists Explore Absurdity*, Harris Museum, Preston, 2016. He was shortlisted for Film London Jarman Award, 2018.

Amalia Pica (b. 1978, Argentina; lives in London, UK) uses sculpture, installation, photography, live performance and drawing to explore the nuances of communication and the various forms that verbal or non-verbal exchange may take. Recent solo exhibitions include *please open hurry*, Perth Institute of Contemporary Art, 2018; *(un)heard*, Cc Foundation, Shanghai, 2018; *ears to speak of*, The Power Plant, Toronto, 2017; *A un brazo de distancia*, NC Arte, Bogotá, 2017; *Asamble (performance)*, Solomon R. Guggenheim Museum, New York, 2017; and *A ∩ B ∩ C (line)*, Van Abbemuseum, Eindhoven, 2014. Recent group exhibitions include *Darbyshire, Gander, Pica, Starling*, Hayward Gallery, London, 2018; *Double Edge*, Folkestone Triennial, 2017; *Un Nouveau festival / Expanding the Field of Play*, Centre Pompidou, Paris, 2015; *Adventures of the Black Square*, Whitechapel Gallery, London, 2015 as well as the 12th Shanghai Biennial, 2018; *Manifesta 11*, Zurich, 2016; and 11th Gwangju Biennale, 2016.

Jacolby Satterwhite (b. 1986, US) is a multi-disciplinary artist who uses video, performance, 3D animation, drawing and printmaking to explore themes of memory, desire and personal and public mythology. Recent solo exhibitions include Lundgren Gallery, Palma de Mallorca, 2018; *Blessed Avenue*, Gavin Brown's Enterprise, New York, 2018; *En Plein Air: Music of Objective Romance*, Performance in Progress, San Francisco Museum of Modern Art, 2017 and How *Lovely Is Me Being As I Am*, OHWOW Gallery, Los Angeles, 2014. Recent group exhibitions include *The Legacy of Architectonic Futurism*, BANK, Shanghai, 2018; *Electronic Superhighway*, Whitechapel Gallery,

2016; *Under the Clouds*, Serralves Museum, Porto, 2015 and *Whitney Biennial 2014*, Whitney Museum of American Art, New York, 2014.

Zineb Sedira (b. 1963, France; lives in London, UK) uses photography and video installation to frame questions about language, transmission, memory and mobility informed by her own experience as a French-born Algerian living in England. Recent solo exhibitions include *Of Words and Stones*, Beirut Art Center (BAC), 2018; *Air Affairs and Maritime NonSense…*, Sharjah Art Foundation Art Spaces, 2018; *Collecting Lines*, Art on the Underground commission, London, 2016; and *Gardiennes d'images*, Palais de Tokyo, Paris, 2010. Recent group exhibitions include *Persona Grata, Hostilité / Hospitalité*, Musée de l'histoire de l'immigration, Paris, 2018; *Sticky Business – The Temptation of Sugar in Art*, Stedelijk Museum Schiedam, 2017; *Après Babel, traduire*, MuCEM, Marseille, 2016; and *Barjeel Art Foundation Collection: Imperfect Chronology – Mapping the Contemporary II*, Whitechapel Gallery, London, 2017.

Tatiana Bilbao Estudio, established in 2004, Mexico City, Mexico and Basel, Switzerland by Tatiana Bilbao (b. Mexico, 1972) is well known internationally for its use of traditional Mexican construction techniques, for creating sculptural effects that merge geometry with nature, and for a collaborative approach towards its clients. Bilbao has been visiting professor at Yale School of Architecture in 2014–15, professor of Design at the Universidad Iberoamericana (UIA) in 2005 and Visiting Professor at the Universidad Andrés Bello, in Santiago, Chile in 2008. She was advisor for Urban Projects at the Urban Housing and Development Department of Mexico City in 1998–99. Current projects include a mixed-use building for the University of Monterrey, Mexico. Past projects include a project for the Botanical Garden Culiacán, Sinaloa, Mexico, 2004–16, a sustainable housing study for Mexico, 2015, and the Rufino Tamayo Museum Pavilion, Mexico City, 2013.

AUTHORS

Iwona Blazwick is Director of Whitechapel Gallery, London, and is a curator, critic and lecturer. Recent exhibitions she has curated at Whitechapel Gallery include *Mark Dion: Theatre of the Natural World*, 2018; *Thomas Ruff: Photographs 1979–2017*, 2017; *William Kentridge: Thick Time*, 2016; *Adventures of the Black Square: Abstract Art and Society: 1915–2015*, 2015. In 2018 she curated *Carlos Bunga: The Architecture of Life*, at MAAT, Lisbon. Blazwick is series editor of *Documents of Contemporary Art*, published by Whitechapel Gallery / MIT, and has written on many contemporary artists, publishing extensively on themes and movements in modern and contemporary art, exhibition histories and art institutions.

Pedro Gadanho is an architect, a curator and a writer. He is the Director of MAAT, the new Museum of Art, Architecture and Technology, in Lisbon, where he curated exhibitions such as *Eco-Visionaries: Art and Architecture after the Anthropocene*, 2018 and *Utopia / Dystopia: A Paradigm Shift*, 2017. Previously he was curator of contemporary architecture at the Museum of Modern Art, New York, where his exhibitions included *A Japanese Constellation: Toyo Ito, SANAA, and Beyond*, 2016; *Uneven Growth: Tactical Urbanisms for Expanding Megacities*, 2014; and *9+1 Ways of Being Political: 50 Years of Political Stances in Architecture and Urban Design*, 2012. He has edited the 'bookazine' *BEYOND: Short Stories on the Post-Contemporary*, the *ShrapnelContemporary* blog and contributes regularly to international publications. Gadanho holds an MA in art and architecture, and a PhD in architecture and mass media. He wrote *Arquitetura em Público*, 2011, recipient of the FAD Prize for Thought and Criticism in 2012.

Lydia Yee has been Chief Curator at Whitechapel Gallery since 2015 and most recently curated *Ulla von Brandenburg: Sweet Feast*, 2018, *Leonor Antunes: the frisson of the togetherness*, 2017, and *Mary Heilmann: Looking at Pictures*, 2016. Before that, Yee was curator at the Barbican Art Gallery, where her exhibitions included *Magnificent Obsessions: The Artist as Collector*, 2015; *Bauhaus: Art as Life*, 2013; and *Laurie Anderson, Trisha Brown, Gordon Matta-Clark: Pioneers of the Downtown Scene*, 2011. Yee was formerly a senior curator at the Bronx Museum of the Arts in New York. She is co-curator of Frieze Talks and also co-curated *British Art Show 8*, 2015–16.

Co-commissioned with 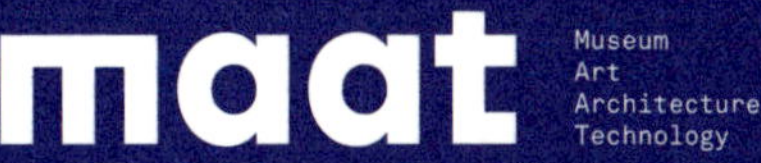

THIS EXHIBITION HAS BEEN GENEROUSLY SUPPORTED BY

Whitechapel Gallery Commissioning Council:
Erin Bell, Leili Huth, Irene Panagopoulos,
Catherine Petitgas, Mariela Pissioti, Alex Sainsbury

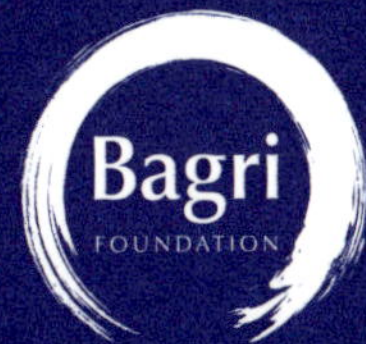

Graham Foundation

The Embassy of the Argentine Republic in the United Kingdom

The High Commission of Canada to the United Kingdom

The Embassy of Mexico in the United Kingdom

The Embassy of Spain in the United Kingdom

Shelley Fox Aarons and Philip Aarons

Collezione Nunzia & Vittorio Gaddi

Living Architecture

Nobuhiro Nishitakatsuji

Personal Improvement Ltd

Walmer Yard

Artwork Insurance Partner: Hiscox

Special Thanks

Sol Aramendi, Malena Bach, Stephanie Black Leon, Chantelle Burndam, Patrick Charpenel, Franka Eberlein, Teo Furtado, Gonzalo Herrero Delicado, Ana Luisa Dias Leite, Pedro Gadanho, Catherine Ince, Crispin Kelly, Julie Kim, Zak Kyes, Marcelo Leyria, Living Architecture (Horizon 2020 Research and Innovation Programme, EU Grant Agreement no. 686585), Yi Luo, Laura Mark, Fredy Massad, Clay Miller, AIA, Duro Olowu, Omar Paris, Alice Rawsthorn, Facundo Santiago, Shirley Surya, Ellis Woodman, Julian Zugazagoitia

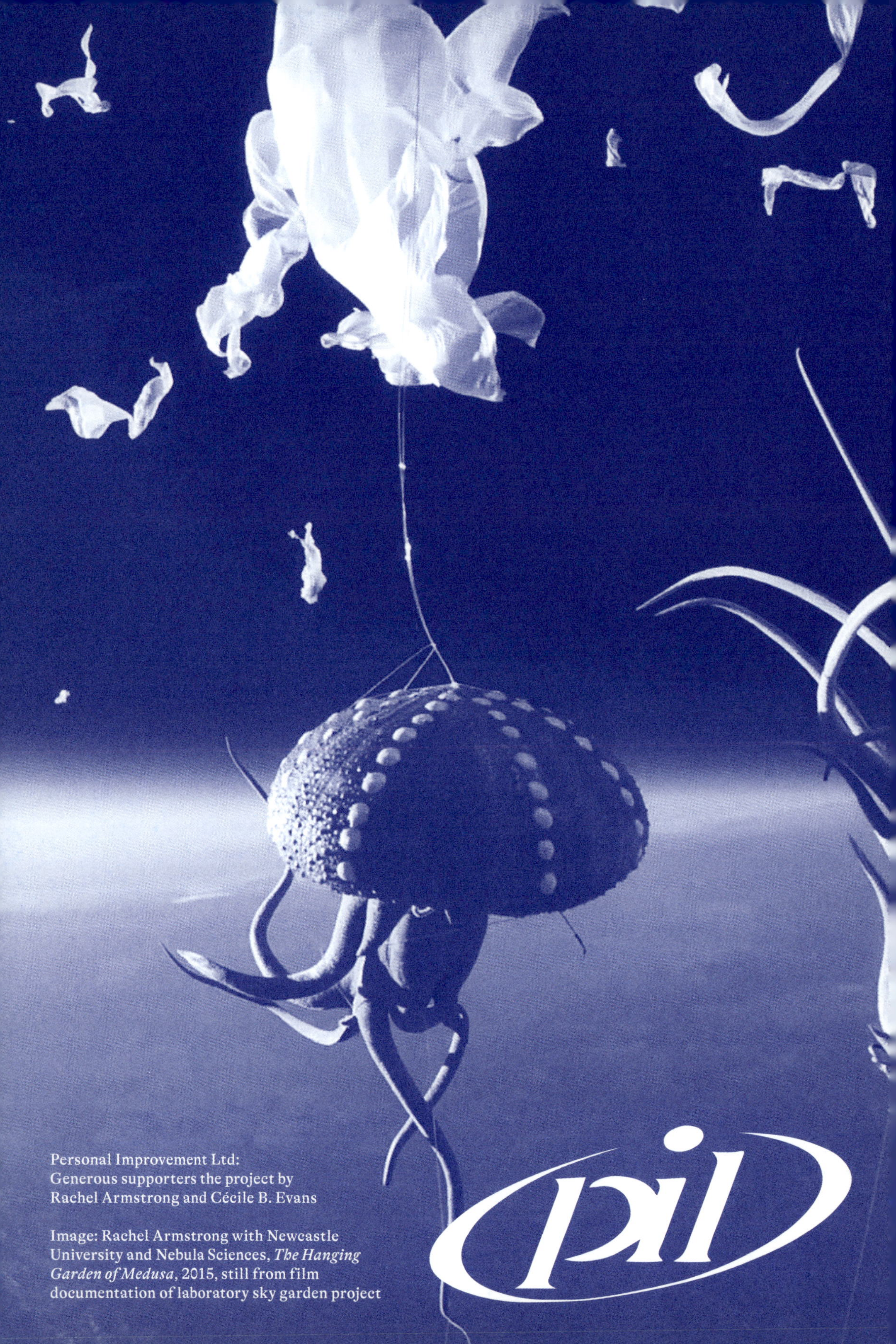

Personal Improvement Ltd:
Generous supporters the project by
Rachel Armstrong and Cécile B. Evans

Image: Rachel Armstrong with Newcastle University and Nebula Sciences, *The Hanging Garden of Medusa*, 2015, still from film documentation of laboratory sky garden project

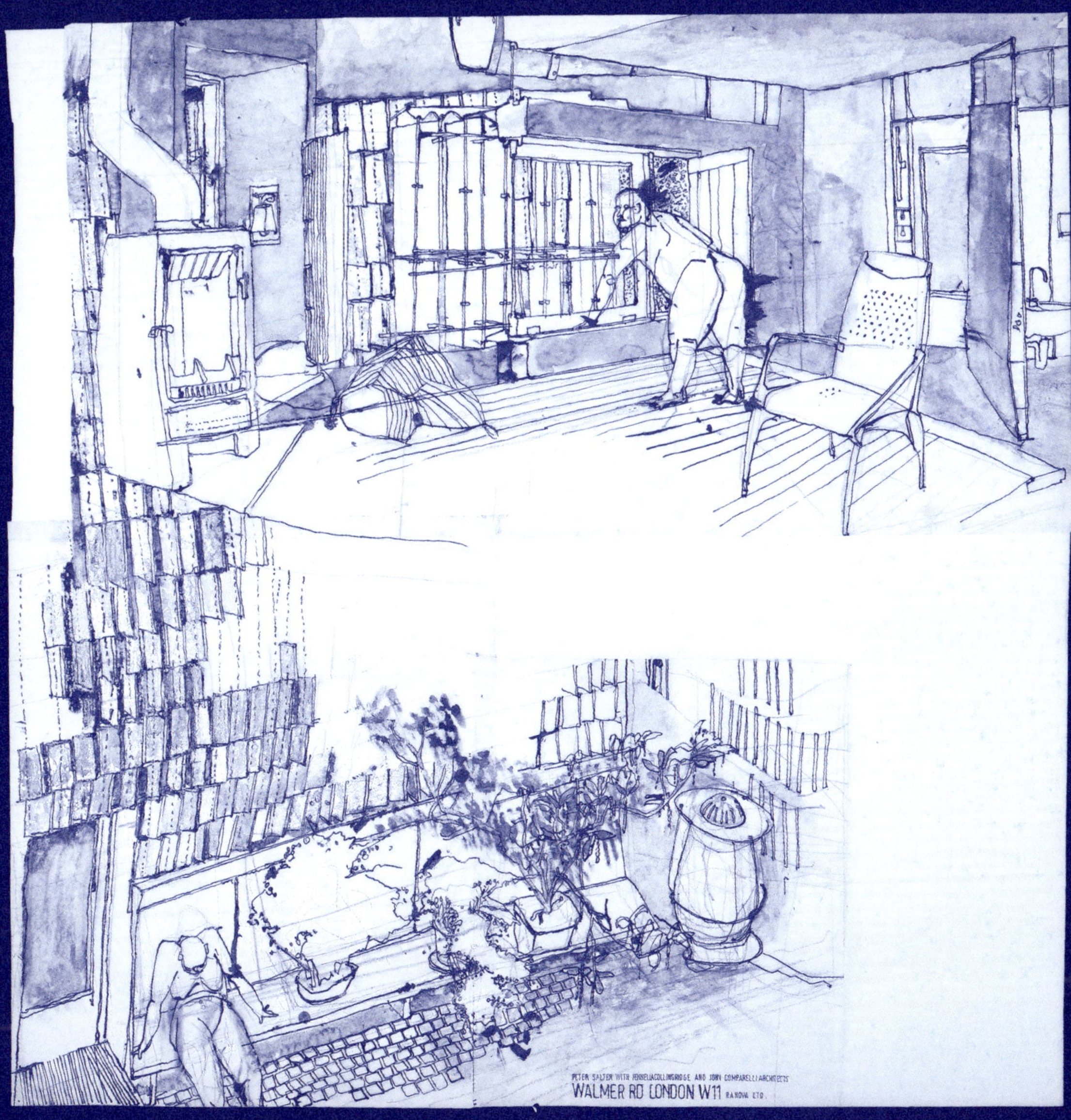

Image: Peter Salter, sketch showing the relationship between living room of House 3 and the courtyard, Walmer Yard, London, 2018

walmer yard

The Whitechapel Gallery would like to thank its supporters, whose generosity enables the Gallery to realise its pioneering programmes

EXHIBITIONS PROGRAMME

Shelley Fox Aarons and Philip Aarons
ADIAF
Air de Paris, Paris
Institut für Auslandsbeziehungen e. V. Stuttgart
Ravi Chidambaram and Yana Frey
Cockayne Grants for the Arts
Beth and Michele Colocci
Aud and Paolo Cuniberti
Danish Arts Foundation
Massimo de Carlo, Milan/London / Hong Kong
Mimi Dusselier and Bernard Soens
Füsun and Faruk Eczacibaşi
Maryam and Edward Eisler
Estonian Contemporary Art Development Center
FACT
Fluxus Art Projects
The Embassy of the Federal Republic of Germany
Greene Naftali
Marian Goodman Gallery
Dr Alex Hooi and Keir McGuinness
Italian Council Directorate-General for Contemporary Art and Architecture and Urban Peripheries
König Galerie
Henry Moore Foundation
London Community Foundation
Collezione Maramotti
Max Mara
Victoria Miro, London / Venice
NEON
New Carlsberg Foundation
Office for Contemporary Art Norway
Paul Mellon Centre for Studies in British Art
Galerie Perrotin
Catherine Petitgas
Phillips
Ministry of Culture and National Heritage of the Republic of Poland and Culture.pl
Polish Cultural Institute in London
The Pollock-Krasner Foundation
The Royal Norwegian Embassy in London
Andrew Simpkin
Maria and Malek Sukkar
Tanya Bonakdar Gallery
Evgeny Tugolukov and Natalya Pavchinskaya
V-A-C Foundation
Galleri Nicolai Wallner
Michael Werner Gallery
Whitechapel Gallery Commissioning Council
and those who wish to remain anonymous

PUBLIC EVENTS PROGRAMME

Goethe-Institut in London
Stanley Picker Trust
The Pictet Group
Office for Contemporary Art Norway
The Royal Norwegian Embassy in London

EDUCATION PROGRAMME

Artworkers Retirement Society
The Barjeel Art Foundation
The Bawden Fund
Capital Group
Paul Hedge and Paul Maslin, Hales Gallery
The Estate of Howard Hodgkin
Luigi Maramotti
Swarovski Foundation
The Embassy of Sweden in London
The London Borough of Tower Hamlets

CAPITAL RENEWAL PROGRAMME

The Wolfson Foundation

ARTWORK INSURANCE PARTNER

Hiscox

FRAMING PARTNER

FRAME London

SIGNAGE PARTNER

Omni Colour

WHITECHAPEL GALLERY
CORPORATE PATRONS

Bloomberg Philathropies
Frasers Property UK
Gazelli Art House
Phillips
South Street Asset Management
SPLIT Music
David Zwirner

WHITECHAPEL GALLERY
CORPORATE PARTNERS

Brick Lane Regeneration Partnership
Broadgate
Crossrail
Derwent London
FRAME London
Hiscox
Konditor & Cook
Kvadrat
Max Mara
Collezione Maramotti
Noirmontartproduction
Omni Colour
Personal Improvement Ltd
Phillips
Swarovski
Whitechapel Bell Foundry

FUTURE FUND FOUNDING
PARTNERS

Mahera and Mohammad Abu Ghazaleh
Sirine and Ahmad Abu Ghazaleh
Swantje Conrad
Dimitris Daskalopoulos
NEON
Maryam and Edward Eisler
V-A-C Foundation
Sir Siegmund Warburg's Voluntary Settlement
Arts Council England Catalyst Endowment Fund

FUTURE FUND SUPPORTERS

John Smith and Vicky Hughes
Dominic Palfreyman

WHITECHAPEL GALLERY
COMMISSIONING COUNCIL

Erin Bell
Leili Huth
Irene Panagopoulos
Catherine Petitgas
Mariela Pissioti
Alex Sainsbury

WHITECHAPEL GALLERY
DIRECTOR'S CIRCLE

Erin Bell and Michael Cohen
D. Daskalopoulos Collection Greece
Peter and Maria Kellner
Yana and Stephen Peel
and those who wish to remain anonymous

WHITECHAPEL GALLERY
CURATOR'S CIRCLE

Rob and Lesley Briggs
Marcelle Joseph
Chris Kneale
Adrian and Jennifer O'Carroll
Dasha Shenkman
Audrey Wallrock
and those who wish to remain anonymous

WHITECHAPEL GALLERY
PATRONS

Beverley Buckingham
Matt Carey-Williams and Donnie Roark
Sadie Coles HQ
Beth and Michele Colocci
Swantje Conrad
Alastair Cookson
Elizabeth Corley
Loraine da Costa
Aud and Paolo Cuniberti
Dunnett Craven Ltd
Sarah Elson
Nicoletta Fiorucci
James Freedman
Theresa Froehlich
Belinda de Gaudemar
Alan and Joanna Gemes
Richard and Judith Greer
Sarah Griffin
Deborah Gundle
Jill Hackel
Mark Harris
Robert Hiscox
Rami Kim
Frank Krikhaar
Yisi Li
Xi Liu and Yi Luo
Maria Meijer
Jon and Amanda Moore
Heike Moras
Farshid Moussavi
Bozena and William Nelhams
Angela Nikolakopoulou
Maureen Paley
Jasmin Pelham
Darryl de Prez and Victoria Thomas
Alice Rawsthorn
Frances Reynolds
Alex Sainsbury and Elinor Jansz
Cherrill and Ian Scheer
Matthew Slotover and Emily King
Karen and Mark Smith
Louise Spence
Bina and Philippe von Stauffenberg
Mr and Mrs Christoph Trestler
Victoria Miro Gallery
Yusi Xiong
Lian Zhang
Sharon Zhu
and those who wish to remain anonymous

WHITECHAPEL GALLERY
FIRST FUTURES

Cedric Bardawil
Irene Barontini
Crane Kalman Gallery
Isabel Elson
Siena Erbe
Jude Hull
Olimpia Isidori
Zoe Karafylakis Sperling
Ezra Konvitz
Marie Krauss
Dominika Kulczyk
Petra Kwan
Celia Lloyd Davidson
Di Luo
Supriya Menon
Victoria Mikhelson
Reine Okuliar
Indi Oliver
Olga Peftieva
Maria-Cruz Rashidan
Eugenio Re Rebaudengo
Henrietta Shields
Tammy Smulders
Joe Start
Aisha Stoby
Louisa Strahl
Nayrouz Tatanaki
Elisabeth von Schwarzkopf
and those who wish to remain anonymous

We remain grateful for the ongoing support of Whitechapel Gallery Members.

Whitechapel Gallery is proud to be a National Portfolio Organisation of Arts Council England.

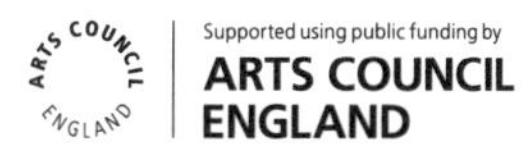

Published on the occasion
of the exhibition

Is This Tomorrow?

Whitechapel Gallery,
London
13 February–12 May 2019

MAAT, Lisbon
Summer 2020

EXHIBITION

Chief Curator
Lydia Yee

Assistant Curators
Trinidad Fombella
and Cameron Foote

Curatorial Advisor
Pedro Gadhanho

Exhibition Assistant
Inês Costa

Head of Exhibition Design and Production
Christopher Aldgate

Gallery Manager
Ryszard Lewandowski

Installation Coordinator
Christopher Spear

PUBLICATION

Editors
Lydia Yee with
Cameron Foote and
Trinidad Fombella

Publications Manager
Francesca Vinter

Copy Editor
Melissa Larner

Designed by Zak Group

Printed by
Printmanagement Plitt
GmbH, Oberhausen

ISBN 978-0-85488-270-0

First published 2019 by
Whitechapel Gallery,
London

A catalogue record for this book is available from the British Library.

Whitechapel Gallery
77–82 Whitechapel High Street
London, E1 7QX
whitechapelgallery.org

Distributed outside the
United States and Canada by
Thames & Hudson
181a High Holborn
London, WC1V 7QX
Tel: +44 (0) 20 7845 5000
sales@thameshudson.co.uk

Distributed in the United
States and Canada by
ARTBOOK | D.A.P.
75 Broad Street, Suite 630
New York, N.Y. 10004
Tel: (212) 627-1999

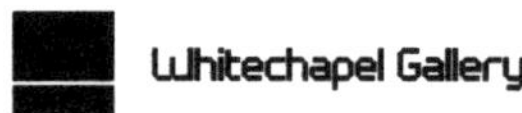